POCKET **ROUGH GUIDE**
NEWCASTLE &
NORTHUMBRIA

written and researched by
DANIEL STABLES

CONTENTS

A note to readers

At Rough Guides, we always strive to bring you the most up-to-date information. This book was produced during a period of continuing uncertainty caused by the Covid-19 pandemic, so please note that content is more subject to change than usual. We recommend checking the latest restrictions and official guidance.

NEWCASTLE AND NORTHUMBRIA

The Northeast of England is large and contains multitudes. 'Northumbria' is not an official term but a historic one, which in the tenth century referred to a kingdom which stretched across northern England and southern Scotland, from the River Mersey to the Firth of Forth. In modern parlance, it refers more often to the Northeast of England – Northumberland, Durham, Teesside and Tyne & Wear – and that is the definition worked along within this book. In Newcastle upon Tyne the region finds its cultural capital, a vibrant and forward-thinking city which is nonetheless firmly rooted in its long and colourful past; more historic still is Durham, which ranks among England's prettiest cities. Beyond the urban conurbations, the countryside is characterised by wild, wide-open spaces, littered with evidence of a turbulent past – lush in places, barren in others, and often beautiful.

Bamburgh beach and castle

Londoners, Scousers and Mancunians all fly the flag proudly for their home city, but it's hard to imagine anywhere in England which engenders such a sense of local pride as Newcastle. "Geordies" are a gregarious bunch, and they will happily hold forth to visitors on subjects as varied as Roman history, the correct serving size for Newcastle Brown Ale, and the tribulations (and latent triumphs) of Newcastle United Football Club. That fierce pride and local identity extends beyond Newcastle and to the wider Northeast, notwithstanding a great many local rivalries – a particularly lively example being that which continues to simmer between Newcastle and Sunderland. For all their quibbles, though, the towns and cities of this region are united by a salt-of-the-earth sense of humour and a grit formed in the furnaces of industry. Coal mining put this area at the forefront of the Industrial Revolution, and in the twentieth century Britain's major shipbuilding yards grew up along the Tyne and Wear rivers; the region endured a difficult period of industrial decline during the 1970s and '80s, but has since undergone a rejuvenation powered by an emphasis on historical preservation and cutting-edge culture. Even in its former industrial heart, though, the Northeast harbours grace and prettiness: the Victorian and Georgian architecture of Newcastle's Grainger Town, for example, is among the most attractive in the country. Today, visitors to Newcastle will be struck by the city's

Monument Metro station in Newcastle

concentration of museums and art galleries, many of which are cropping up alongside voguish restaurants, bars and cafés in former industrial warehouses and shipbuilding yards.

The Northeast's geographical location has made it one of the most significant regions in Britain's history. It has variously found itself at the frontier of the Roman Empire; as a violent borderland between the auld enemies of England and Scotland; and as the port of entry for a varied cast of invaders from the Vikings to the Normans. Relics of this long and colourful history are everywhere in the countryside's bleak northern hills – the last flourish of the Pennines before they cross the borders into

What's new

Newcastle's industrial roots and vibrant modern arts and culture scenes are nowhere better represented than the Ouseburn Valley. Here, former warehouses and factories are being repurposed for use as voguish venues, restaurants and bars like Arch2, The Cluny, and Wylam Brewery; there's also a city farm. Another area reborn is Gateshead, where trendy restaurants like Riverbeat are springing up on the banks of the Tyne – perfect for dinner after a day exploring world-class cultural institutions like Sage Gateshead or the BALTIC modern art gallery

When to go

Like the rest of England, Newcastle and Northumbria have a generally temperate, maritime climate, which means largely moderate temperatures and a decent chance of at least some rain whenever you visit. That said, Newcastle's sheltered position behind the North Pennines means it's one of the UK's driest cities, while its northerly latitude – on a par with Copenhagen – and exposed setting facing the North Sea mean it can feel very chilly. If you're attempting to balance the clemency of the weather against the density of the crowds, even given regional variations and microclimates the best months to come to England are April, May, September and October.

Scotland. This was a grim posting for Roman soldiers stationed along Hadrian's Wall, but it appealed to the Christians, who chose lonely Lindisfarne on the wild, sandy Northumbrian shore as a bastion and exemplar of the early church. Incursions came from the Vikings, who left their language in such local dialect names as stell (sheepfold) and beck (stream): the local "Geordie" dialect is the strongest in England. The Normans came next, ravaging Northumbria in their pitiless "Harrying of the North"; but they were builders, too, and they raised the mighty cathedral at Durham.

The Scottish border was always a volatile place and, for some 300 years until the early 17th century, rustic gangsters called "reivers" ruled the roost. Today, the farming community is finding life as hard as anywhere in Britain. A tourism campaign has dubbed the north Pennines "England's last wilderness" and at Kielder, the country's largest man-made forest has proved a great attraction, as has Kielder Observatory, with its organic yet space-age architecture. The Northumberland Coast, dotted with crumbling castles, is one of the most scenic stretches of coastline in England.

Field of red poppies, near Corbridge

Where to…

Shop

The opportunities for retail therapy are boundless in the Northeast, whether you're after homemade handicrafts or high-street designers. In fact, shopping has such an esteemed history in Newcastle that a couple of establishments are almost tourist attractions in themselves – the department store Fenwick is one of the oldest in the country, dating back to 1882, while the Georgian arches of Grainger Market shelter the charming Penny Bazaar, the smallest outlet in the Marks and Spencer portfolio, which opened in 1895. The city centre has its share of modern shopping centres – Eldon Square has all the high street fashion names, alongside chain restaurants, and was redeveloped in 2016 – but there's much more interesting finds to be had in the many boutiques and artisan producers which can be found in Newcastle and across the region's towns, cities, and countryside. Even the monks of Holy Island tapped into the area's spirit of enterprise, making and selling their own Lindisfarne mead.
OUR FAVOURITES: Fenwick (see page 27), St. Aidan's Winery (see page 78), The Mugwump (see page 104).

Eat

It's hard not to think of seafood when talking about eating in the Northeast, with some of nation's finest fruits de mer being hauled in by the region's hardy fishermen each day. The jewel in a glittering crown is the Craster kipper, the product of the coastal Northumberland village of the same name – this smoked, butterflied herring is a favourite breakfast dish in these parts, and a must-try while you're here. Smoked haddock also often features on menus, as does the catch from Whitby, which is particularly famous for its scampi. It's not all about seafood, though. Other famous Northeast foods include the stottie, a filling and restorative bread with a cake-like, doughy texture; and pease pudding, a traditional savoury pea soup, often served with ham or bacon. Teesside's great contribution to world cuisine, meanwhile, is the parmo: a dish of breaded chicken covered with béchamel sauce and cheddar cheese which is, quite literally, not for the faint of heart.
OUR FAVOURITES: Riley's Fish Shack (see page 68), Blackfriars (see page 33), The Jolly Fisherman (see page 81).

Drink

Say what you like about Geordies, but never let it be said that they don't know how to drink. The notorious 'trebles bars' are packed with locals and students drawn in by the offer of cut-price deals on eye-wateringly strong (or should that be watered-down?) highballs, while the Bigg Market on a Saturday night is worth a visit perhaps only if you have an interest in anthropology. Happily, Newcastle is also full of lovely old riverside pubs, while the Ouseburn Valley in particular is packed with cool bars and music venues housed in repurposed industrial buildings. The smaller towns and cities and the surrounding countryside also boast a high concentration of inns and pubs, which often double as atmospheric places to stay, particularly in rural areas.
OUR FAVOURITES: Old George Inn (see page 34), Arch2 (see page 57), The Redhouse (see page 46).

Duns

Westruther

Greenlaw

Gordon

Kelso

St Boswells

Jedburgh

Lamberton

Berwick-upon-Tweed

Swinton

Cheswick

Coldstream

Duddo

Lowick

Crookham

Kirk Yetholm

Wooler

Chatton

Lindisfarne Castle

Holy Island

Longstone Lighthous

⚓ *Farne Isla*

Grace Darling Museum

Belford

Bamburgh

Bamburgh Castle

High Nev by the Se

Chillingham Wild Cattle

Chillingham Castle

Dunstanburgh Castle

Craster

Northumberland National Park

Alnwick Castle

Alnwick

Warkwor Castle

Warkworth Hermitage

Amb

Byrness

Rothbury

Cragside

Felton

Rochester

Kielder Observatory

◆ Kielder

Otterburn

Elsdon

Kielder Water Bird of Prey Centre

Greenhaugh

Scots Gap

Morpeth

Stannersburn

Bellingham

Kirkharle

Belsay

Blyth

Barrasford

Matfen

Newcastle upon Tyne

Chesters Roman Fort

Chollerford

Housesteads Roman Army Museum

Corbridge

Tyne

Vindolanda

Greenhead

Bardon Mill

Hexham

Riding Mill

Gateshead

Haltwhistle

Langley

Slaley

Gibside Hall

◆ Stanley

Lambley

Allendale

Blanchland

Consett

Chester-le-Stree

Alston

Rookhope

Langley Park

Durha

Nenthead

Frosterley

Crook

Coxho

Langwathby

St John's Chapel

Binchester Roman Fort

Auckland Castle

Bishop Auckland

Newton Aycliffe

Woodland

Locomotion (National Railway Museum Shildon)

Middleton in Teesdale

Appleby-in-Westmorland

Barnard Castle

Darlington

Brough

Bowes

Whorlton

Egglestone Abbey

Melsonby

Kirkby Stephen

NOR

Newcastle and Northumbria at a glance

The Northumberland coast p.71.

Arguably the most beautiful face of the Northeast, the Northumberland Coast sees somnolent fishing villages broken up by cresting bays and the looming remnants of coastal castles. Some of the region's best walking can be had here, along with sumptuous seafood.

Grainger Town p.24.

Any visit to Newcastle begins in its historic core, which encloses some truly gorgeous Georgian and Victorian architecture, centred around Grey Street and Grainger Street. There's also some of the city's best museums, as well as cathedrals of both the religious and sporting varieties.

Quayside and Gateshead p.36.

The heart of Tyneside's modern regeneration lies on each side of the River Tyne in the neighbouring districts of Quayside and Gateshead, connected by Newcastle's seven famous bridges. The other symbols of this region, such as Sage Gateshead and the Angel of the North, are similarly iconic.

Ouseburn and Jesmond p.47.

Fashionable Ouseburn is a vibrant district whose former industrial warehouses have been taken over by creative types and converted into galleries, bars and music venues. Leafy Jesmond, meanwhile, is home both to some of the city's most well-heeled professionals and a buzzing student population.

Tyneside and the coast p.59.

East of Newcastle, the rest of Tyneside includes Wallsend and the pretty coastal towns of Tynemouth and Whitley Bay. This area is rich in history, from the Roman era to the golden age of the British seaside resort.

The Northumberland interior p.84.

By turns barren and windswept, then lush and green, Northumberland's rural interior includes the rugged remnants of Hadrian's Wall and the gorgeous Kielder Forest and Water, presided over by the country's darkest night skies.

Durham and around p.97.

The thriving student city of Durham is famed for its medieval castle and cathedral, which rank among the most beautiful in England. The surrounding county, also called Durham, is home to yet more lovely castles and some gorgeous countryside.

Wingate

Billingham
Redcar
Saltburn by the Sea
Stockton-on-Tees
Middlesbrough
Thornaby
Guisborough
Mickleby
Whitby

15 Things not to miss

It's not possible to see everything that Newcastle and Northumbria has to offer in one trip – and we don't suggest you try. What follows is a selective taste of the area's highlights, from Roman ruins to modern art galleries.

< **Jesmond Dene**
See page 52
Right in the heart of Jesmond is this forested valley, flanked by woodland and with ivy-strewn bridges and tumbling waterfalls along the Ouseburn River.

∨ **The Literary and Philosophical Society**
See page 25
Newcastle's 'Lit & Phil' is much loved by those in the know, but this gorgeous old library remains off the radar of many tourists.

⌄ BALTIC
See page 37
One of the country's finest modern art museums sits right on the River Tyne in Gateshead, and has become a symbol of Newcastle's regeneration since reopening in 2002.

‹ Hadrian's Wall
See page 85
Once the northern frontier of the Roman Empire, the once-mighty Wall is now a much-loved walking trail home to some of the country's best ancient ruins.

∧ Chillingham Castle
See page 91
You can spend the night at "Britain's most haunted castle", or pay a visit to one of the world's last remaining herds of wild cattle.

‹ Bamburgh Castle
See page 75
The most eye-catching of the castles on the Northumberland Coast stands silent guard over the pleasant village of Bamburgh.

∧ Holy Island
See page 75
Separated from the world periodically by the shifting tides, Holy Island is ethereal and beautiful and echoes with spirituality.

∨ Beamish Museum
See page 100
One of England's finest open-air museums brings to life the way things were in this part of the country in the early 20th century.

∧ **Durham Cathedral**
See page 97
Said to be the finest Norman building in Europe, this awe-inspiring cathedral soars above the River Wear.

< **Ouseburn Valley**
See page 47
Industrial warehouses are reborn as hip bars, clubs and venues in this pulsating Newcastle neighbourhood – there's also a city farm with a petting zoo.

< **Kielder Water**
See page 89
England's largest reservoir is surrounded by hundreds of acres of pine forest, home to ospreys, otters, badgers and red squirrels.

∨ **Alnwick Castle**
See page 71
Grand 11th-century castle and manor house whose grounds include a garden of poisonous plants. Its enchanting appearance led to it starring in the *Harry Potter* films.

THINGS NOT TO MISS

Day One in Newcastle

The Literary and Philosophical Society. See page 25. Tour Newcastle's 'secret library', housed in a gorgeous nineteenth-century building, and browse for hidden jewels among the 160,000 books.

Centre for Life. See page 25. Kids of all ages love the educational exhibits at this science museum, which focus on the brain, the cosmos, and life on Earth.

St James' Park. See page 28. Stop in for a stadium tour at the home of Newcastle United Football Club, one-time home of such luminaries as Alan Shearer, Peter Beardsley and Jackie Milburn.

St James' Park

Lunch. See page 33. Enjoy some tapas or tuck into some paella at the popular Spanish restaurant *El Coto*, a short walk from the stadium.

Great North Museum: Hancock. See page 28. Explore the magnificent collections of Newcastle's finest museum, dedicated to world culture and natural history with exhibits on fossils, ancient Egypt, and more.

Laing Art Gallery. See page 29. Next, check out the city's finest art gallery, home to works by some of the country's best artists from the seventeenth century to today, from the Pre-Raphaelites to Henry Moore.

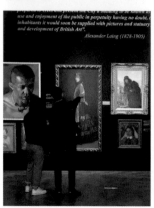

Laing Art Gallery

Grainger Market. See page 30. Finish your walking tour close to where it started, beneath the grand Georgian arches of Grainger Market, where you can browse historic market stalls and food traders.

Dinner. See page 34. Be sure to visit *Nan Bei* for some great-value deals on delicious Chinese dumplings and buns, enjoyed in the historic surrounds of Grainger Market.

Grainger Market

Day Two in Newcastle

The Biscuit Factory. See page 47. Begin your day by drinking in Ouseburn's creative spirit at this large art gallery, which showcases the work of the Northeast's finest artists.

Ouseburn Farm. See page 49. Meet adorable goats, pigs, cows and even tortoises and terrapins at this inner-city farm and petting zoo, which does great work in the local community.

Seven Stories. See page 48. Jump into the magical world of children's literature at this enchanting museum, with exhibits donated by Philip Pullman, Quentin Blake, and other luminaries.

Seven Stories

Lunch. See page 56. Do as the cool kids do and pop into *Ernest* for classic brunch dishes, Moroccan stews and flatbreads, and hearty hash bowls in a hip environment.

Victoria Tunnel. See page 51. After lunch head underground into the atmospheric Victoria Tunnel, built to carry coal from the River Tyne and later serving as a war-time air raid shelter.

Jesmond Dene. See page 52. Take a walk through leafy Jesmond Dene, a forested river valley on the grounds of the former estate of the industrialist Lord Armstrong, spotting squirrels and kingfishers.

Victoria Tunnel

People's Theatre. See page 52. Catch a show this evening at what is one of the country's finest amateur theatrical companies, with a history going back more than a century.

Dinner. See page 55. Indulge in an exquisite British dinner at *Branches*, one of the city's best restaurants, where fresh seasonal ingredients form country and coast are harnessed to delicious effect.

Jesmond Dene

Hadrian's Wall

One of Britain's great hiking adventures is the coast-to-coast walk along what was once the mighty Hadrian's Wall, taking in what remains of the Wall and the Roman forts which lay along it.

Wallsend to Heddon-on-the-Wall

From Newcastle, the trail begins at the end – Wallsend, that is, the wall's eastern terminus – and takes you past the fort of Segedunum and out of the city along the Tyne.

Heddon-on-the-Wall to Chollerford

Pass the remains of turrets and earthworks, and spot a Roman altar inside a Christian church, as you follow the path of an old military road on today's walk.

Mosaic at Segedunum Roman Fort, Walsend

Chollerford to Steel Rigg

Roam the atmospheric ruins of Housesteads and photograph a famous tree between two hills at Sycamore Gap, along the best-preserved section of the Wall.

Steel Rigg to Walton

Northumberland's desolate beauty gives way to the sloping hills of lush, green Cumbria on today's stretch, which takes in more Roman forts at Vindolanda and Birdoswald.

Walltown Crags

Walton to Carlisle

The visible Wall finally fades into grassy ditches on the penultimate day's walk, where the lovely scenery includes the wooded valley of Cam Beck.

Carlisle to Bowness-on-Solway

The final stretch is dotted with quiet churches built from Wall stones. Dip your feet in the water at Bowness and reflect on your magnificent coast-to-coast adventure.

Chesters Roman Fort

Budget Trip

Exploring Newcastle and Northumbria doesn't have to break the bank, with a number of free and low-cost attractions perfect for those on a budget.

Begin in the genteel suburb of Jesmond with a walk through the forest valley of Jesmond Dene (see page 52), home to stone bridges, tumbling waterfalls, and an atmospheric old water wheel.

Walking towards the city centre, pop into the Great North Museum: Hancock (see page 28) for world class displays on world culture and natural history.

Next, walk just a couple of minutes north to the Town Moor and Exhibition Park (see page 52), where a fine bandstand is evidence of an esteemed Victorian heritage.

Great North Museum: Hancock

For lunch, stay in Exhibition Park and head to the Wylam Brewery (see page 58), where some superb burgers are on offer alongside a range of home-brewed beers.

Suitably refreshed, walk south to Grainger Town, where the stately architecture of Grey Street and Grainger Street (see page 24) are free for all to admire.

Pop into Newcastle Cathedral (see page 24), where video displays in the old stone arches tell the story of the church's past as a place of worship and a wartime air raid shelter.

Wylam Brewery

More free culture can be enjoyed at the Discovery Museum (see page 25), where exhibits and displays tell of the long and proud maritime history which shaped Newcastle and the surrounding area over centuries.

Stop in for an early dinner at Grainger Market (see page 34), where *SnackWallah* is among the food stalls which are great for those on a budget.

Grainger Town

PLACES

Hadrian's Wall at Caw Gap

Grainger Town

The heart of Newcastle is known as Grainger Town, one of the best-looking city centres in Britain. Thrown up in a few short mid-nineteenth-century years by businessmen-builders and architects such as Richard Grainger, Thomas Oliver and John Dobson, the area is known for its classical stone facades lining splendid, wide streets. Particularly famous is Grey Street, named for the second Earl Grey (he of the tea), prime minister from 1830 to 1834. The street's Georgian architecture, and that of the surrounding Grainger Town area, deserves as much acclaim as its more celebrated equivalents in Edinburgh and Bath.

Newcastle Castle

MAP P. 26
Castle Garth, NE1. Ⓜ Central.
Ⓦ newcastlecastle.co.uk. Mon, Thurs–Sun 10am–5pm; charge.

The tautologously titled Newcastle Castle is the fortification which gave Newcastle its name. A fortress was first built on this site in medieval times, with the purpose of guarding a bridge over the River Tyne. A Norman castle followed in the 11th century (built by William

Swing Bridge and Newcastle Castle

the Conqueror's son, Robert Curthose), before the current building began to be erected during the reign of Henry II in 1172. A visit to the castle offers a glimpse into what life would've been like for people who made their home here in centuries past. The Great Hall is bedecked with medieval pennants and includes one of the oldest known surviving fireplaces in Britain, while kids love the interactive elements – they can sit on a throne, handle some replica medieval weaponry, and take a photo while locked in the stocks.

Newcastle Cathedral

MAP P. 26
St Nicholas Square, NE1. Ⓜ Central.
Ⓦ newcstlecathedral.org.uk. Mon–Fri 8am–6pm, Sat & Sun 8am–5pm; free.

The seat of the Bishop of Newcastle and the city's foremost Anglican place of worship, Newcastle Cathedral has a history dating back almost 1000 years. A Norman church was built on this site in 1091, but was destroyed by fire in 1216; the English Gothic building which stands today was built in 1350. It is recognisable by its distinctive lantern spire, which can be seen for miles around – even now, it's the ninth tallest building in Newcastle – and was long a landmark for ships travelling along the River Tyne. The lantern's corners bear gilded statues of the biblical figures Adam and Eve; Aaron, the brother of Moses; and King David. Within, the church harbours an impressive wooden choir and some lovely stained glass, most of it replaced in the 18th century after the original windows were destroyed in the chaos of the Civil War. Innovative video displays within the rough-hewn wall arches tell the story of the cathedral's long history of invasion, destruction, and renewal. Movement-sensitive lighting illuminates the ledger stones like a light-up dancefloor, which is some unexpected fun.

The Literary and Philosophical Society

MAP P. 26

Bolbec Hall, 23 Westgate Rd, NE1. Ⓜ Central. Ⓦ litandphil.org.uk. Mon, Wed, Thurs 9.30am–7pm, Tues 9.30am–8pm, Fri 9.30am–5pm, Sat 9.30am–1pm; free.
Known as the Lit and Phil, this temple-like public library and learned society occupies one of the city's finest Georgian buildings: the domed roof, stucco ceilings and wrought-iron galleries are well worth a look. Established in 1825, it now runs a programme of recitals, jazz concerts, talks and exhibitions. It's worth a visit at any time, though, to take in its beautiful architecture and enjoy a tea or coffee, perhaps while leafing through one of its 160,000 books. The Lit and Phil describes itself as "Newcastle's exquisite secret library", and it's hard to disagree.

St Mary's Cathedral

MAP P. 26

Clayton St W, NE1. Ⓜ Central. Ⓦ stmaryscathedral.org.uk. Mon–Sat 10am–3pm, Sun 10am–2pm; free.
Immediately behind Newcastle Central Station sits the Cathedral Church of St Mary, the city's most important Catholic church. Built between 1842 and 1844 in the Gothic Revival style, it is notable for its tall spire, gorgeous vaulted nave, and lovely pastel walls. The *Cloister Café and Restaurant* here does a good line in cakes, teas and coffees, and heartier dishes like corned beef pies. Outside the church is a statue of Cardinal Basil Hume, a proud Geordie, passionate Newcastle United fan, and former Archbishop of Westminster. Hume's popularity transcended the boundaries of the Catholic community, and he was regularly voted Britain's most popular religious figure before his death in 1999.

Centre for Life

MAP P. 26

Times Square, NE1. Ⓜ Central. Ⓦ life.org. uk. Daily 10am–5pm; charge.
A five-minute walk west of Central Station, the sleek buildings of the Centre for Life reach around the sweeping expanse of Times Square. This ambitious "science village" project combines bioscience and genetics research with a science visitor centre that aims to convey the secrets of life using the latest entertainment technology. Children find the whole thing enormously rewarding – from the sparkling Planetarium to the motion simulator – so if you're travelling as a family, expect to spend a good three hours here, if not more. The Centre hosts touring exhibitions like, at the time of writing, Luke Jerram's *Gaia* (a seven-metre, highly detailed sculpture of the Earth) and, in the winter months, hosts an open-air ice rink and winter lights exhibition.

Discovery Museum

MAP P. 26

Blandford Square, NE1. Ⓜ Central. Ⓦ discoverymuseum.org.uk. Mon–Fri 10am–4pm, Sat & Sun 11am–4pm; free.
The Discovery Museum concentrates on the maritime history of Newcastle and Tyneside, and their role in Britain's scientific and technological developments. Highlights include the *Turbinia* – the first ship to be powered by a steam turbine – which

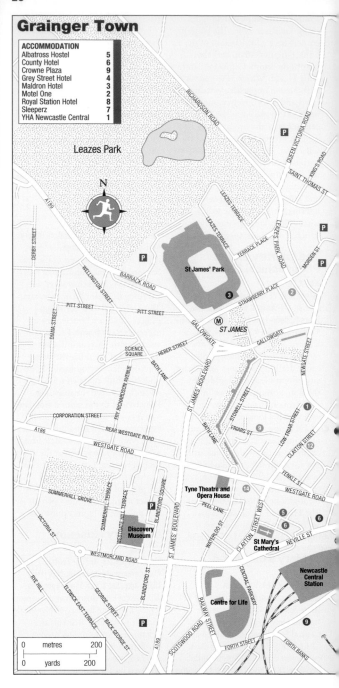

Grainger Town

ACCOMMODATION	
Albatross Hostel	5
County Hotel	6
Crowne Plaza	9
Grey Street Hotel	4
Maldron Hotel	3
Motel One	2
Royal Station Hotel	8
Sleeperz	7
YHA Newcastle Central	1

Leazes Park

N

St James' Park

ST JAMES

Leazes Terrace

Leazes Terrace

Terrace Place

Leazes Park Road

Morden St

Strawberry Place

RICHARDSON ROAD

QUEEN VICTORIA ROAD

KING'S ROAD

SAINT THOMAS ST

A189

DERBY STREET

DIANA STREET

WELLINGTON STREET

BARRACK ROAD

PITT STREET

PITT STREET

SCIENCE SQUARE

HEBER STREET

BATH LANE

GALLOWGATE

GALLOWGATE

Newgate Street

ST JAMES' BOULEVARD

FDK RICHARDSON AVENUE

CORPORATION STREET

REAR WESTGATE ROAD

WESTGATE ROAD

A186

STOWELL STREET

FRIARS ST

BATH LANE

LOW FRIAR STREET

CLAYTON STREET

FENKLE ST

WESTGATE ROAD

SUMMERHILL GROVE

SUMMERHILL TERRACE

WESTGATE HILL TERRACE

BLANDFORD SQUARE

Discovery Museum

Tyne Theatre and Opera House

PEEL LANE

WATERLOO ST

CLAYTON STREET WEST

St Mary's Cathedral

NEVILLE ST

ST JAMES' BOULEVARD

VICTORIA ST

WESTMORLAND ROAD

RYE HILL

ELSWICK EAST TERRACE

GEORGE STREET

BACK GEORGE ST

BLANDFORD ST

A189

SCOTSWOOD STREET

Centre for Life

RAILWAY STREET

CENTRAL PARKWAY

Newcastle Central Station

FORTH STREET

FORTH BANKS

| 0 | metres | 200 |
| 0 | yards | 200 |

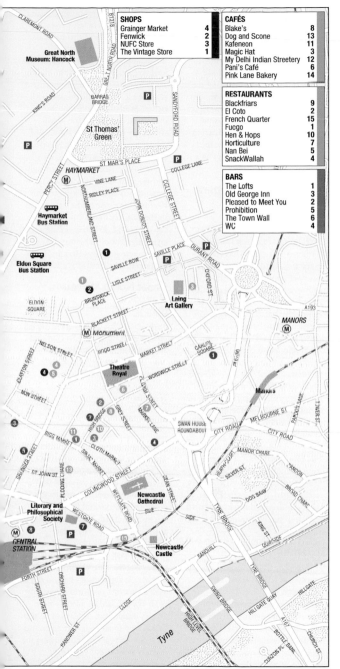

SHOPS

Grainger Market	4
Fenwick	2
NUFC Store	3
The Vintage Store	1

CAFÉS

Blake's	8
Dog and Scone	13
Kafeneon	11
Magic Hat	3
My Delhi Indian Streetery	12
Pani's Café	6
Pink Lane Bakery	14

RESTAURANTS

Blackfriars	9
El Coto	2
French Quarter	15
Fuego	1
Hen & Hops	10
Horticulture	7
Nan Bei	5
SnackWallah	4

BARS

The Lofts	1
Old George Inn	3
Pleased to Meet You	2
Prohibition	5
The Town Wall	6
WC	4

dominates the museum entrance, and the Newcastle Story, a walk through the city's past with tales from animatronic characters along the way. Other exhibitions include Charge! The Story of England's Northern Cavalry, showcasing the important role northern regiments played in battles like Waterloo and modern conflicts in Bosnia and Afghanistan, and Destination Tyneside, which illuminates the area's long and proud history as a home for migrants.

Tyne Theatre and Opera House

MAP P. 26

109–113 Westgate Rd, NE1. Ⓜ Central. Ⓦ tynetheatreandoperahouse.uk; charge.
Another world-class jewel in Newcastle's cultural crown is the city's opera house, which sits in a handsome Grade I-listed building dating back to 1867. The original theatre only lasted 50 years before the encroaching behemoth of cinema swallowed up the theatre market and led to the building's conversion into a picture house. A 1919 screening of *Tarzan of the Apes* kicked off what was a successful half-century's life as a cinema, before the tides turned again and audiences dwindled in the 1960s thanks to the surging popularity of television. A brief and desperate stint as an adult film theatre failed to save the theatre, which fell into disrepair and finally reopened, in more or less its present form, in the early 1980s. Today, comedy and music make up as much of the programme as theatre and opera.

St James' Park

MAP P. 26

Barrack Rd, NE1. Ⓜ St James. Ⓦ nufc. co.uk; charge.
Unlike Manchester and Liverpool, Newcastle is a city united, rather than divided, by football. The travails of Newcastle United – particularly the period between 2007–2021, when the club was owned by billionaire businessman Mike Ashley – were felt personally by the inhabitants of this football-mad city, the vast majority of whom support their local team. The long-awaited takeover of the club in 2021 by a Saudi-backed investment fund made Newcastle one of the richest football clubs in the world overnight; success on the pitch will surely follow in the fullness of time, but controversy remains over the ownership's connections to a regime associated with human rights abuses. That aside, if you have the opportunity to attend a game, this has long been one of the best places in the country to do it – with a capacity of 52,305, this is England's eight largest football ground, and the atmosphere is always electric. Tours of the stadium are also available.

Great North Museum: Hancock

MAP P. 26

Barras Bridge, NE2. Ⓜ Haymarket. Ⓦ great northmuseum.org.uk. Mon–Fri 10am–5pm, Sat 10am–4pm, Sun 11am–4pm; free.
Newcastle's museum of natural history and world civilisation houses a magnificent collection of artefacts which span the entire world over thousands of years of history. The museum has its origins with the private collection of the majestically named Marmaduke Tunstall in the late 1700s; his early ornithological collections have since expanded to include over 450,000 objects, including Ancient Egyptian sarcophagi, Greek and Etruscan sculpture, full-size T-Rex skeletons, and much more. A particular highlight is the gallery dedicated to Hadrian's Wall, containing models and interactive exhibits on the motivation and logistics behind the Wall's construction. Most interesting of all, though, are the pieces which give an insight into the lives of Roman Britons: personal items like coins and weapons, and carvings concerning the mystery religion of Mithraism.

The Geordie Nation

Tyneside and Newcastle's native inhabitants are known as Geordies, the word possibly derived from a diminutive of the name "George". There are various explanations of who George was (King George II, railwayman George Stephenson), all plausible, none now verifiable; one leading theory suggests the nickname derived from local miners' use of the Geordie lamp, itself named after George Stephenson. Geordies speak a highly distinctive dialect and accent, heavily derived from Old English. Phrases you may come across include: howay man! (come on!), scran (food), a'reet (hello) and radgie (lairy or violent) – and you can also expect to be widely addressed as "pet".

Laing Art Gallery

MAP P. 26

New Bridge St, NE1. Ⓜ Monument, Manors. Ⓦ laingartgallery.org.uk. Mon–Sat 10am–4.30pm; free.

The Laing Art Gallery, in the east of the city, is home to the northeast's premier art collection: the permanent display is a sweep through British art from the seventeenth century to today, featuring sculpture from Henry Moore and a large collection of John Martin's fiery landscapes, along with a smattering of Pre-Raphaelites, a group much admired by the English industrial barons. Another permanent display highlights a superb collection of Newcastle silver dating from the seventeenth century and some colourful 1930s glassware by George Davidson. The Northern Spirit exhibition is dedicated to works on the theme of northeast art and industry, while Chris Killip's The Last Ships is an evocative and poignant collection of photography documenting the last years of the shipbuilding trade.

Theatre Royal

MAP P. 26

100 Grey St, NE1. Ⓜ Monument. Ⓦ theatreroyal.co.uk; charge.

One of the crowning achievements of Grey Street's Victorian architecture, this historic theatre was built in 1837 by local father-and-son architects John and Benjamin Green. Its Neoclassical, colonnaded façade is one of the finest of its type in the country, and it is no less spectacular inside; the original auditorium burned down in 1899 and was replaced in 1901 by the legendary theatre architect Frank Matcham, who also designed many of London's most famous theatres. The first show here, in 1837, was a performance of The Merchant of Venice; Shakespeare continues to occupy a prominent role in the fixture list every autumn, when the Royal Shakespeare Company visit for their annual season. Modern plays are also staged here, while international touring comedy, dance, and musical shows also stop by

Statue of Sir Bobby Robson, St James' Park

Grainger Market

Shops

Fenwick

MAP P.26

39 Northumberland St, NE1. Ⓜ **St James.**
Ⓦ **fenwick.co.uk.**

Newcastle's most famous department store opened in 1882 (making London's Selfridges, est. 1909, look a mere spring chicken) as a textiles emporium by JJ Fenwick. In 1890, JJ's son Fred travelled to Paris and was so inspired by visiting *Le Bon Marché* that he decided to replicate the format, and Fenwick became a department store. Today it remains one of the city's best places to shop, with extensive fashion, beauty, home, children's and technology departments.

Grainger Market

MAP P.26

Grainger St, NE1. Ⓜ **Monument.**
Ⓦ **ourgraingermarket.co.uk.**

This centrally located Georgian market is one of the city's oldest and best shopping experiences. Painted in pastel colours and crowned by a glass roof buttressed by red cast-iron trusses, the current building opened in 1835, but a market has stood on this site for far longer. It was Europe's largest covered market when built in the 1830s, and is today home to the smallest branch of Marks & Spencer, known as the Original Penny Bazaar.

NUFC Store

MAP P.26

St James' Park, NE1. Ⓜ **Monument.**
Ⓦ **shop.nufc.co.uk.**

Whether you're a football fan or not, this is an interesting time to be in the vicinity of Newcastle United, and a shirt from the earliest vintage of the club's new era (they became one of the richest football clubs in the world after being taken over by a Saudi-led consortium in 2021) may prove to be a savvy investment. The shop also sells scarves, mugs, loungewear, and assorted other miscellany.

The Vintage Store

MAP P.26

60–62 Northumberland St, NE1.
Ⓜ **Haymarket.** Ⓦ **facebook.com/ thevintagestoreonline.**

Dedicated followers of fashions past flock to this vast vintage clothing store, which has an ever-changing stock of classic items from voguish brands like Ralph Lauren, Champion, Barbour, and many more, as well as classic band tour T-shirts and other rare finds. Vintage fashion's sustainable ethos is giving it a renewed lease of life, and this is one of the best places in Newcastle to find stylish secondhand items.

Cafés

Blake's

MAP P.26

53 Grey St NE1. Ⓜ Central. Ⓦ blakescafes. co.uk.

Something of an institution along photogenic Grey Street, *Blake's* has long been caffeinating a steady stream of shoppers, tourists and locals alike. The Italian-style coffee is good, and the food menu is classic café fare: hearty full English breakfasts sit alongside eggs of the royale, Florentine and Benedict varieties, while the toasted sandwiches are perfect for a quick lunch. Soups and salads are also available if you're looking for something lighter. ££

Dog and Scone

MAP P.26

22 Pudding Chare NE1. Ⓜ Central. Ⓦ dogandscone.com.

Geordies, as we know, are very particular on pronunciation, but even they can't agree on how to pronounce "scone". It's worth chancing your arm for the butter and fruit scones at this café, however, which you can enjoy with a cup of tea in the company of the resident dogs – longhaired miniature dachshund Noodle is particularly charming. The toasties and wraps are also delicious, and good value, although there is also an entry fee. Book ahead online at the weekend. £

Kafeneon

MAP P.26

8 Bigg Market NE1. Ⓜ Central. Ⓦ kafeneon. co.uk.

Looking for all the world like a Greek island *taverna*, right down to the arches in the rough-hewn adobe walls, the Greek flag adornments and the blue-and-white colour scheme, this is a fixture on Newcastle's historic Bigg Market. The menu includes classic offerings like chicken souvlaki, moussaka, and meze platters, and the portions are huge – particularly in the case of the aptly named "big fat gyros". A wide range of wines and beers is served alongside, with the option of retsina if you're feeling brave. ££

Magic Hat

MAP P.26

3–5 Higham House, Higham Pl NE1. Ⓜ Manors. Ⓦ themagichatcafe.co.uk.

This brilliant café near Laing Art Gallery combines delicious food with a worthy cause: eliminating food waste. Run as a not-for-profit, the café rescues surplus food from supermarkets which would otherwise be destined for landfill, and repurposes it into delicious,

Grainger Street shoppers

healthy dishes. The menu changes daily according to what ingredients are available, but might include pumpkin on toast, steak and spicy wedges, salmon and *pak choi*, and pretty much anything else. **£**

My Delhi Indian Streetery

MAP P.26
87a Clayton St NE1. Ⓜ Central.
Ⓦ mydelhistreetfood.com.
Having garnered multiple curry awards in recent years, this laidback, vibrant restaurant celebrates Delhi's street eats. There's crispy battered Amritsari fish bites, fiery chilli chicken, tandoori lollipops, and a selection of more substantial curries and biryanis, alongside less traditionally Indian offerings like fish or chicken nuggets with chips. A sense of fun pervades, with colourful cartoon wall art and some fiery cocktails to choose from. **££–£££**

Pani's Café

MAP P.26
61–65 High Bridge NE1. Ⓜ Monument.
Ⓦ paniscafe.co.uk.
On a side street below the Theatre Royal and easily accessible from

Grainger Market, this lively Sardinian café has won a loyal clientele for its good-value sandwiches, pasta and salads. Back in 1995, when *Pani's* opened, a Sardinian café in central Newcastle was an exotic thing – that's no longer the case, but the quality of the food and friendliness of the service remain. The house ravioli, a chef's special, is particularly good. **££**

Pink Lane Bakery

MAP P.26
40 Pink Ln NE1. Ⓜ Central.
Ⓦ pinklanebakery.com.
The city's best-loved bakery (with another outlet in Gosforth) is impossible to miss, with its coral-pink exterior catching the eye and its window display bursting with plump sourdough bloomers, stacks of giant cookies, buttery croissants, *pain au chocolat, pastéis de nata*… I could go on. Savoury options, like sausage rolls and beef, caramelised onion and stilton pies, are also available, while the offerings change according to the season. Can get very busy at weekends. Takeaway only. **£–££**

Blackfriars

Restaurants

Blackfriars

MAP P.26

Friars St, NE1. ⓦ St Jamoc.
ⓦ blackfriarsrestaurant.co.uk.

Housed in a beautiful stone
building dating to 1239, Blackfriars
offers superb traditional British
dishes made with local ingredients.
Mains could include pork loin
with a bacon and cheese floddie
(potato cakes, originating from
Gateshead, and traditionally eaten
for breakfast) or a Doddington
cheese and onion Wellington with
chive cream sauce. For afters, dig
into sticky toffee pudding with
green grape ice cream and Brown
Ale caramel. Book ahead. **£££**

El Coto

MAP P.26

21 Leazes Park Rd NE1. ⓦ St James.
ⓦ elcoto.co.uk.

Cute and cosy, this lovely tapas place
is a great option if you get peckish
after visiting St James' Park. It boasts
an extensive, good-value menu
featuring all the classic tapas dishes,
such as patatas bravas and marinated
sardines, with a choice of taster-style
'selection menus' also available along
with big, hearty sharing paellas. A
wide range of Spanish beers and
wines are on hand to accompany
your food. **££–£££**

French Quarter

MAP P.26

Arch 6 Westgate Rd NE1. ⓦ Central.
ⓦ frenchquarternewcastle.co.uk.

One third each deli, wine bar and
French restaurant, this cosy spot
showcases the best things about
French cuisine – flavour and
quality of cooking and ingredients
– in a down-to-earth way (a rare
combination in Britain). The lunch
menus in particular are superb
value; dishes change regularly but
may include buttered sea bream,
smoked duck breast salad, and
crème brulée. The main small plates

Pink Lane Bakery on Pink Lane

menu includes such delights as
skewered monkfish with chorizo
and gratin dauphinois. **££–£££**

Fuego

MAP P.26

39 Northumberland St, NE1. ⓦ St James.
ⓦ fenwick.co.uk.

One of the highlights of the
ground-floor food hall at historic
department store Fenwick (see
above), this Mediterranean
restaurant serves a wide-ranging
menu which includes Basque pork
belly pinxos, Neapolitan pizzas, and
Spanish tortillas. The northeast's
famous seafood is harnessed to
delicious effect too, with roast
hake, tuna crostini, and crab
croquettes. For something smaller,
the charcuterie boards – including
jamón iberico and *prosciutto di
parma* – are very tempting. **££**

Hen & Hops

MAP P.26

12 High Bridge NE1. ⓦ Central.
ⓦ horticultureuk.co.uk.

There's a lot to love about this
modish restaurant, built on the
sturdy twin pillars of chicken wings
and beer. Both are offered in vast

array – there are no fewer than 20 chicken wing flavours to choose from, each taking you to a different corner of the world and bearing names like Got My Big Boy Pants On! and Thai Me Down. Come on Wednesday for cut-price wings. Hot sauce afficionados can also buy bottles to take away. ££

Horticulture

MAP P.26

1 Market Ln NE1. ⓂCentral. Ⓦhorticultureuk.co.uk.

The brainchild of Newcastle-born owner-chef Peter Breckon, *Horticulture* does a great line in brunch dishes, with the soy-soaked mushrooms on toast and shakshuka both being great dishes. The main menu has a global reach – that can be off-putting, but here it's all done superbly, from the octopus tagine to the Korean pork belly. The interior, dimly lit with exposed brick, wall-mounted flowerbeds and shiny parquet floors, is as lovely as the food. ££

Nan Bei

MAP P.26

Grainger Market NE1. ⓂCentral.

SnackWallah

Ⓦfacebook.com/Nan-Bei-Dumpling-Tea-Bar-958159467533020.

If it's cheap eats in Grainger Market you're after, there's nowhere better than this lovely hole in the wall, which serves magnificent Chinese dumplings, buns, and a wide range of teas. Savoury options include chilli beef, roast pork, and scrambled egg and mushroom; wontons and noodle soups are also available. For something sweet, try lotus bean, custard, or smashed bean buns. A world-class way to have lunch. £

SnackWallah

MAP P.26

Grainger Market NE1. ⓂCentral. Ⓦsnackwallah.uk.

Giving Nan Bei a run for its money as Grainger Market's best eatery is this Indian place, which serves a superb array of classic dishes for great value. The curry of the day, with daal, rice and naan, is a snip; pani puri, samosa chaat, and dahi toast (with yoghurt and chili) are among the side dishes you might find hard to resist. Drink options include masala chai and ever-changing lassi of the day. £

Bars

The Lofts

MAP P.26

Newgate St NE1. ⓂCentral. Ⓦtheloftsne1.co.uk.

One of the newest additions to Newcastle's nightlife scene, this club opened to great fanfare in 2021, with a performance by legendary DJ Pete Tong. The club's sound and audio-visual systems are spectacular, and the soundtrack is provided by a succession of international touring electronic acts who play in one of three rooms, sometimes accompanied by other performers like fire dancers. £££

Old George Inn

MAP P.26

Old George Yard NE1. ⓂCentral, Manors. Ⓦfacebook.com/TheOldGeorgeInn.

The oldest pub in Newcastle, the *Old George* dates back to 1582, and it looks great for it, wearing its heritage well with its cobbled courtyard, ceiling beams and dark wood bar. No less a personage than King Charles I is said to have enjoyed a pint or two here, when he was held as an 'open prisoner' on nearby Grey Street during the Civil War – the chair on which he supposedly sat can still be seen here, and his ghost is said to stalk the corridors. **££**

Pleased to Meet You

MAP P.26
41–45 High Bridge NE1. Ⓜ Monument. Ⓦ ptmy-newcastle.co.uk.

The gin pandemic has made it to Newcastle, and it reaches its apotheosis at this self-described 'gin palace', where mother's ruin finds expression in dozens of spirits and many more cocktails, including creative offerings like the Bonfire Negroni, made with jenever and sherry. If gin's not your thing, there's a long wine list, too, while the food menu includes hearty Sunday roasts and British seafood like oysters, Shetland mussels, and fish pie. **£££**

Prohibition

MAP P.26
25–27 Pink Lane NE1. Ⓜ Central. Ⓦ prohibitionbar.co.uk.

Evoking the lost glamour of 1920s America, this bar on lively Pink Lane has something going on most nights of the week, from cabaret performers to live blues and jazz, with comedy and quiz nights also being a regular fixture. The decor and dimly-lit vibe evoke the Jazz Age, as does the cocktail menu, which includes classics like Old Fashioneds and martinis. **£££**

The Town Wall

MAP P.26
Pink Ln NE1. Ⓜ Central. Ⓦ thetownwall.com.

Named for the ruins of the city's medieval defensive wall which run nearby, this splendid pub is itself a piece of history, sitting within a Grade II-listed townhouse. Atmospherically lit, with dark walls and vintage leather Chesterfield sofas, it's a lovely place to sink away a few hours in the company of a craft beer, with northern English breweries particularly well represented – try the offerings from Northern Monk and Cloudwater. **££**

WC

MAP P.26
Corner of Bigg Market and High Bridge NE1. Ⓜ Central. Ⓦ wcnewcastle.co.uk.

A former public toilet may not be the obvious choice for a trendy cocktail bar, but the subterranean setting adds a certain cosiness, compounded by the compact size – booking a table is a good idea, especially on weekends. There's a wide-ranging menu of wines from France, Spain, California and beyond, and some beautifully considered cocktails like spiced orange espresso martinis and hibiscus margaritas. The prices are reasonable, too. **££–£££**

Old George Inn

Quayside and Gateshead

From between the castle and the cathedral a road known simply as the Side – formerly the main road out of the city, and home to the excellent Side Gallery (see below) – descends to Newcastle's Quayside. The river is spanned by seven bridges in close proximity, the most prominent being the looming Tyne Bridge of 1928, symbol of the city. Facing Quayside across the Tyne is the town of Gateshead. Something of a hinterland for much of the twentieth century, its postwar profile was dominated by Brutalist architecture and mediocrity – but the arrival of some of the area's most iconic attractions, such as Sage Gateshead and the Angel of the North, is changing all that.

Side Gallery

MAP P. 40
5–9 Side, NE1. Ⓜ Central, Manors.
Ⓦ amber-online.com/side-gallery. Hours vary; free.

Hosting a rotating programme of photography exhibitions, on subjects as diverse as British youth culture and women's and indigenous rights in South Asia, Side Gallery is a must-visit for

Millennium Bridge and Sage Gateshead

artistically-minded visitors to Newcastle. Opening in 1977 as a humanist photography gallery and cinema, the remit hasn't changed much in the intervening decades, and it remains the only gallery in the United Kingdom dedicated solely to documentary photography. Hours vary, and exhibitions are often not announced until shortly before they begin, so looking on the website – where you must book free tickets before you visit – is the best idea.

Bessie Surtees House

MAP P. 40
41–44 Sandhill, NE1. Ⓜ Central. ☎ 0191 2691255; free.

This gorgeous five-storey Jacobean building actually takes the form of two conjoined houses, dating back to the 16th and 17th century respectively. The eponymous Bessie was the daughter of one of the house's tenants, who eloped through a first-floor window with one John Scott, the son of a local coal miner who went on to become Lord Chancellor of England. They married in Scotland, and later returned to Newcastle and married again upon the reconciliation of their families. Today the houses remain as gorgeously preserved examples of Jacobean domestic architecture; though some of the building is used as offices, a portion on the first floor is devoted to a free exhibition telling the story of the building's history. It was closed for renovations at the time of writing, but should have reopened by the time you read this.

Tyne Bridge

MAP P. 38

The great symbol of Newcastle is the hulking Tyne Bridge, which spans the River Tyne between Quayside and Gateshead. A handsomely proportioned arch bridge opened in 1928, it was built by the civil engineers Mott, Hay and Anderson and was based in part on the design of Hell Gate Bridge in New York City. It is an icon of modern Newcastle and the Northeast in general, and often plays a role in civic events: vast Olympic rings were hoisted to the bridge's girders when St James' Park hosted Olympic football matches in 2012, while the Great North Run half marathon sees 52,000 runners cross the bridge every September.

Millennium Bridge

MAP P. 40

Connecting the Quayside with the galleries of Gateshead's arts quarter, this bridge is something of a masterpiece in itself. The world's first tilting bridge, it's known locally as the Blinking Eye for the graceful action of its two semi-circular 'lids', which tilt upwards to allow boats to pass beneath – a process which takes around four minutes in total. It's highly energy efficient, and the tilting mechanism has a hidden benefit – it rolls any litter left on the bridge by pedestrians or cyclists into special traps on the edge. As its name suggests, the bridge was built in the dawn of

Quayside and Tyne Bridge

new millennium, opening in 2001; it cost £22m to build, and used enough steel to build 64 double decker buses.

Sage Gateshead

MAP P. 40

St Mary's Square, NE8. Ⓜ Gateshead, Manors. Ⓦ sagegateshead.com, charge. Sitting on the riverbank, the Sage Gateshead is an extraordinary billowing steel, aluminium and glass concert hall complex, best seen at night when it glows with many colours. It's home to the Royal Northern Sinfonia orchestra and Folkworks, an organization promoting British and international traditional music, and there's something on most nights – from music concerts to workshops and lectures, as well as the Gateshead International Jazz Festival every April. The public concourse provides marvellous river and city views, and there are bars, a café and a brasserie.

BALTIC

MAP P. 40

S Shore Rd, NE8. Ⓜ Gateshead. Ⓦ baltic. art. Wed–Sun 10am–6pm; free.

Fashioned from an old brick flourmill, BALTIC sits on the Gateshead riverbank, by the Millennium Bridge. Designed to be a huge visual "art factory", it's second in scale only to London's Tate Modern. There's no permanent collection here – instead there's an ever-changing calendar of exhibitions and local community projects, as well as artists' studios, education workshops, an art performance space and cinema, plus a rooftop restaurant with uninterrupted views of the Newcastle skyline. BALTIC has also pioneered a wide range of community outreach programmes, with artist-led workshops for local disadvantaged children during the school holidays, iftar events during Ramadan, and more.

Shipley Art Gallery

MAP P. 38
Prince Consort Rd, NE8. Ⓜ Gateshead.

Ⓦ shipleyartgallery.org.uk. Tues–Fri 10am–4pm, Sat 10am–5pm; free.
Just north of Saltwell Park lies the Shipley Art Gallery, a modest Neoclassical building housing a fine collection of art which includes works by Dutch and Flemish masters and Victorian British works. The gallery was born in 1917 with the bequest of 504 paintings from the private collection of Joseph Shipley, a rather mysterious figure who worked as a solicitor in the local area and lived in the latter part of his life at nearby Saltwell Towers. The gallery's collections have since expanded to include contemporary British pieces and the Henry Rothschild ceramics collection, which brings together works by major British ceramicists in the second half of the 20th century.

Saltwell Park

MAP P. 38

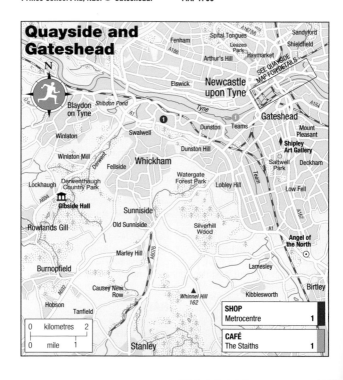

E Park Rd, NE9. Ⓜ Gateshead.
Ⓦ gateshead.gov.uk. Daily 7am–9.30pm;
free.

A masterpiece of Victorian park planning, this lovely collection of lawns, trees, streams and lily ponds was once the private grounds of the majestic Saltwell Towers, a rather eccentric red-brick Gothic mansion with crenellated walls and turrets. It lays claim to a place in the country's ten most popular public parks, and it is a lovely place to spend an afternoon – there's a serene boating lake with pedalos in the shape of dragons, ducks and swans which you can take out for a spin, and a pleasant café serving tea, coffee and sandwiches. There's also a small animal enclosure home to peacocks, parrots, and other birds.

Saltwell Towers

Angel of the North

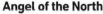
MAP P. 38

Durham Rd, NE9. Ⓑ Durham Rd. Daily
24hr; free.

Since its completion in 1998, the Angel of the North has rapidly come to represent one of the most iconic images of Northeast England. A 75-metre construction in weathering steel, it is the work of acclaimed sculptor Antony Gormley, and, like his installation at Liverpool's Crosby Beach, takes the form of a faceless humanoid figure – this time with the addition of angel's wings. Work on the sculpture began in 1994, and cost £800,000. Overlooking the A1 main road and sitting atop a former mining site, the sculpture is at once elegant and robust, artistic and industrial; in this way it represents the spirit of the Northeast. It countered considerable public outcry and opposition when it was first announced, and even Gormley had his doubts about making a sculpture overlooking a main road – "I don't make motorway art" was his rather haughty initial response. Public opinion has since softened considerably, and it's impossible to imagine the drive towards Newcastle without it.

Gibside Hall

MAP P. 38

Gibside, NE16. Ⓑ Station Rd–The Grove.
Ⓦ nationaltrust.org.uk/gibside. Daily
10am–6pm, chapel Sat–Sun 10am–4pm;
charge.

Five miles west of Gateshead, the National Trust property Gibside Hall is well worth a visit if you want to escape the urban sprawl. Once owned by the aristocratic Bowes-Lyon family, the main house is now an empty, roofless husk, which adds a certain haunting property to it, particularly on a frosty winter's day. Indeed, the ghost of Mary Bowes, an early pioneer of women's rights who was known as the Unhappy Countess, is said to stalk the property. The best-known of the surviving buildings is the chapel (open on weekends), ornately carved and porticoed and dominated by a three-tiered pulpit. The wooded grounds are criss-crossed with walking trails and are lovely and peaceful.

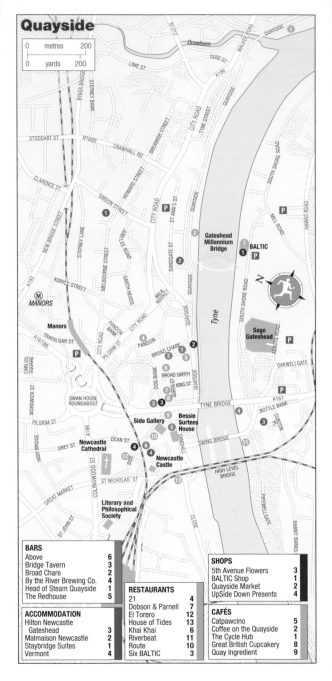

Quayside

BARS

Above	6
Bridge Tavern	3
Broad Chare	2
By the River Brewing Co.	4
Head of Steam Quayside	1
The Redhouse	5

ACCOMMODATION

Hilton Newcastle Gateshead	3
Malmaison Newcastle	2
Staybridge Suites	1
Vermont	4

RESTAURANTS

21	4	Khai Khai	6
Dobson & Parnell	7	Riverbeat	11
El Torero	12	Route	10
House of Tides	13	Six BALTIC	3

SHOPS

5th Avenue Flowers	3
BALTIC Shop	1
Quayside Market	2
UpSide Down Presents	4

CAFÉS

Catpawcino	5
Coffee on the Quayside	2
The Cycle Hub	1
Great British Cupcakery	8
Quay Ingredient	9

Shops

5th Avenue Flowers

MAP P.40
7 Queen St, NE1. Ⓜ Central. ⓦ 5af.com.
The perfect souvenir or gift
for lovers of all things floral
can be found at this Quayside
florist, which has become a local
institution since its opening in
1981 (there's another branch on
the Team Valley trading estate in
Gateshead). Offerings, naturally,
change with the seasons – an
autumnal hedgerow bouquet is
a riot of orange and red, while
fragrant tulips and carnations
usher in the spring – but a range of
tropical options are also available
year-round.

BALTIC Shop

MAP P.40
BALTIC, S Shore Rd, NE1. Ⓜ Manors,
Gateshead. ⓦ baltic.art.
You'd be forgiven for spending
all day in the BALTIC complex,
such is its variety of diversions.
Don't rush for the exit under
the impression that this is your
ordinary museum gift shop –
the range includes gorgeous
prints, jewellery, ceramics and
homeware from artists based in
the Northeast, across the UK, and
beyond. BALTIC also publishes
its own books and magazines,
which usually accompany art or
photography exhibitions being
staged in the gallery.

Metrocentre

MAP P.38
St Michael's Way, NE11. Ⓜ Metrocentre.
ⓦ themetrocentre.co.uk.
Gateshead's Metrocentre is the
most popular shopping attraction
in the Northeast, a large shopping
mall and entertainment complex
home to some 300 shops – ranking
as the second biggest of its kind
in the country behind Westfield
London. You'll find most of the
major high street chains here, from
fashion to tech, and the food hall
has over 60 cafés, restaurants, and
fast-food joints. Try to avoid at
weekends and school holidays,
unless you enjoy feeling like a
sardine in a tin can.

Quayside Market

MAP P.40
Between the Swing Bridge and Millennium
Bridge, NE1. Ⓜ Central, Manors.
This Sunday market dominates
the Quayside between the Swing
Bridge and the Millennium
Bridge, a succession of stalls selling
everything from Greek street food
to vintage fashion, via churros,
refillable organic toiletries, coffee,
toys, and more. A market or fair
has been recorded on this site as
far back as 1736, and it remains a
great place to tap into the rhythm
of the city.

UpSide Down Presents

MAP P.40
61 Side, NE1. Ⓜ Central. ⓦ 61side.co.uk.
Sitting next to the famous Dog Leap
staircase, which winds impressively
up the hill towards the cathedral,
this is the best place to come for
Geordie-themed souvenirs, with

Metrocentre

the quality of the items tending to be higher than in many touristy gift shops. Items range from the kitsch – stromtrooper angels of the north and Tyne Bridge thimbles – to those of some historical interest, like coasters printed with leaflets from iconic Newcastle concerts, like Led Zeppelin at City Hall.

Cafés

Catpawcino

MAP P.40

77 Quayside NE1. Ⓜ Manors. Ⓦ catpawcinocafe.com.

The feline equivalent to *Dog and Scone* (see page 31) is this cat café, home to no fewer than 21 gorgeous animals who are a mixture of rescues and cats raised from kittens by the owner, Sarah Zong. The decor is designed to bring the outdoors in, with wooden floors, astroturf rugs and wicker chairs, and your small entry fee goes towards good causes – a percentage of profits is donated to a cat charity, and free classes are offered to children with autism, who benefit from interaction with animals.

Quayside Market

Toasties, cakes, and lovely Chinese teas are also on offer. **££**

Coffee on the Quayside

MAP P.40

The Quayside, next to Pitcher & Piano. Ⓜ Manors. Ⓦ facebook.com/ coffeeonthequayside.

A few minutes' walk from the BALTIC art gallery is this tiny coffee truck, which has become a Quayside institution in the 15 years since it first parked up here. The Italian-style coffee is superb and very reasonably priced, while a range of breakfast rolls are also available in the morning, though you'll have to be quick – they get snapped up fast. Samosas make the occasional appearance on the menu too. **£**

The Cycle Hub

MAP P.40

Cycle Route 72, Quayside NE6. Ⓜ Manors, Byker. Ⓦ thecyclehub.org.

Right on the riverfront, this bike café and workshop has been welcoming in hungry wayfarers, cyclists and otherwise, since 2012. The menu is small, but everything's done well, and it's great value; the bacon butties are the signature

offering, but the sausage rolls and their vegan equivalents are lovely too. If you're craving something sweeter, the scones, crumpets and waffles go great with a cup of tea. £

Great British Cupcakery

MAP P.40
15 Queen St NE1. Ⓜ Central.
Ⓦ gbcupcakery.co.uk.

The afternoon teas at this saccharine-pink café – hung with blossoms and balloons year-round – are legendary. The sandwiches combine the classic (ham and Dijon mustard; cheddar cheese and caramelised onion) with the exotic (lemon chicken; red pepper hummus) and the cheddar and herb scone, topped with melted cheese and a sprig of candied thyme, is a lovely creation. The real speciality is the sweets, with the mere sight of the chocolate and honeycomb slice enough to make your arteries scream. £££

Quay Ingredient

MAP P.40
4 Queen St NE1. Ⓜ Central.
Ⓦ quayingredient.co.uk.

Nestled beneath the mighty steel limbs of the Tyne Bridge, this is the kind of unpretentious yet quality coffee house which Newcastle does so well. The highlight of the food menu is the grilled Craster kippers – pride of the Northumberland Coast – while the sausage and bacon breakfast sandwiches are also impossible to argue with. Great coffee and a wide tea menu, too. £

The Staiths

MAP P.38
1 Autumn Dr, Quayside NE8. Ⓜ Manors, Byker. Ⓦ thestaithscate.co.uk.

In the historic surrounds of the renovated Dunston Staiths estate, a former coal-loading industrial yard, this community café is laidback, down-to-earth, and staffed by locals. The muffins, scones, cakes and sandwiches are simple and reliable, and more substantial offerings – full English breakfasts, Lebanese kebabs, quinoa salads – are also available. A great place to meet some locals. £

Restaurants

21

MAP P.40
Trinity Gardens, NE1. Ⓜ Manors.
Ⓦ 21newcastle.com.

This Parisian-style bistro has been a fixture on the Quayside since 1988, and has remained so throughout the area's fashionable renaissance. The crisp white tablecloths and leather banquettes are classically French, as are the menu and slick service. Expect dishes like confit duck with Lyonnaise potatoes or smoked haddock with softly poached hen's egg, followed by delicious desserts – the Florentine doughnut with strawberry jam and crème Chantilly is particularly good.

Dobson & Parnell

MAP P.40
21 Queen St, NE1. Ⓜ Manors.
Ⓦ dobsonandparnell.co.uk.

Stylish brasserie, all red-brick walls, hanging lamps and studded olive-green leather booths, in the Georgian surrounds of Queen Street. The food showcases the best of British and European food – opt for a tasting menu for a good overview, featuring gourmet delights in the vein of roasted salsify with Beenleigh blue cheese and steamed halibut with clams and kohlrabi. Wine pairings are also available. £££

El Torero

MAP P.40
Milburn House, Side NE1. Ⓜ Central.
Ⓦ eltorero.co.uk.

The spirit of Andalucía abides at this atmospheric Spanish restaurant, with bullfighting artwork adorning the walls and an authentic menu courtesy of Granada local Toni Almirón. The classic tapas offerings – *jamón serrano, gambas al pil-pil, patatas al infierno* – are all here and all superb, but even better are the grandstand traditional sharing dishes, like paella, oxtail, and suckling pig. A wide range of Spanish wines and beers accompany the food. **££**

House of Tides

MAP P.40

28–30 The Close, NE1. Ⓜ **Central, Manors.** Ⓦ **houseoftides.co.uk.**

One of the classiest places to eat in town, this top-drawer British eatery is Newcastle's only Michelin-starred restaurant. Chef Kenny Atkinson serves up exquisite modern British dishes, using the finest seasonal ingredients to create artful offerings of Norfolk quail, Isle of Mull scallop, and venison with beetroot and elderberries, to name a few. The service is as high-quality as the food, and the wine pairings are perfect. The set menus are good value, particularly at lunch. **£££–££££**

Khai Khai

MAP P.40

29 Queen St NE1. Ⓜ **Central.** Ⓦ **khaikhai.co.uk.**

Indian cuisine is a much more variegated thing than is often presented in Britain, and this brilliant restaurant, with a lovely Victorian dining room, is on a mission to rectify that. The country's diverse culinary traditions are represented in dishes such as Old Delhi butter chicken and Kashmiri lamb rogan josh; the speciality is grilled dishes like Josper lamb chops and grilled sirloin with a Keralan spice rub. **££–£££**

Riverbeat

MAP P.40

Pipewell Gate House NE8. Ⓜ **Central.** Ⓦ **riverbeat.co.uk.**

The craze for small plates shows no sign of abating, and the format continues to be foisted on the unlikeliest of cuisines – although it must be said that the "Asian tapas" at *Riverbeat* is a successful experiment. The oysters three ways (tempura, smoked *nouc cham* and dashi seaweed and ginger) are mouth-watering, while the Mongolian lamb, gochujang and char siu pork, and Japanese tataki beef are tip-top. **££–£££**

Route

MAP P.40

35 Side NE1. Ⓜ **Central.** Ⓦ **routenewcastle. co.uk.**

The decor at this bistro, all whitewashed breeze blocks, wall-mounted pot plants, bare bulbs and exposed pipework, is impossibly modish, but the menu is pared-down and classic, geared towards showcasing the glory of the Northeast's homegrown ingredients. It varies according to the season, but dishes may include chalk-stream trout with wine-soaked beetroot, smoked cod roe with *lavosh* flatbread, and Lindisfarne oysters. **£££**

Six BALTIC

MAP P.40

BALTIC, S Shore Rd, NE1. Ⓜ **Manors, Gateshead.** Ⓦ **sixbaltic.com.**

BALTIC

By The River Brew Co.

Perched prettily on a rooftop terrace in the brilliant BALTIC contemporary art gallery, *Six* is a stylish place for fitting in brunch, lunch or dinner around your gallery wanderings. The unpretentious but beautifully presented food incudes classic brunch dishes like eggs Benedict and smashed avocado on toast, along with burgers, steaks, salads and fish. A local focus pervades – look out for Northumberland goats' cheese and other regional goodies. **££**

Bars

Above

MAP P.40
Vermont Hotel, Lower Dean St NE1. Ⓜ Manors, Gateshead. Ⓦ abovenewcastle. com.
Perched atop the sleek *Vermont Hotel*, this rooftop bar boasts some of the best views in Newcastle, with the cathedral's lantern spire and the crenellated tower of Newcastle Castle both right next door. The view within isn't bad either, with an extremely stylish, neon-lit labyrinthine decor which brings

to mind a temple in the world of *Tron*. Bookings are advisable, as is making an effort – smart casual is *de rigueur*. **£££**

Bridge Tavern

MAP P.40
7 Akenside Hill NE1. Ⓜ Central, Manors. Ⓦ thebridgetavern.com.
Another establishment hiding within the girders of the Tyne Bridge, this place can actually trace its roots back far further than the bridge itself, the construction of which caused the original pub on this site to be demolished in 1925. The building that replaced it retains old-school red-brick walls and now has cosy snugs, lined with books and fitted with leather sofas – the perfect place to enjoy the range of fantastic lagers, IPAs and golden ales brewed on site. **££**

Broad Chare

MAP P.40
25 Broad Chare NE1. Ⓜ Central, Manors. Ⓦ thebroadchare.co.uk.
Amid modern Britain's ever-swelling wave of bistros, "gin palaces" and cocktail bars, sometimes all you want is a

The Redhouse

good, traditional pub. Enter the *Broad Chare*, which does a great line in cask ales, is replete with comfy leather banquettes, and has cosy snugs, shielded by frosted glass, where you can hide away from the North Sea chill for a few hours. The food – including haggis on toast and calf's liver – is similarly old-school and good quality. **££**

By The River Brew Co.

MAP P.40

Hillgate Quays NE8. Ⓜ **Central.** Ⓦ **thebridgetavern.com.**

Riverside locations don't come much better than that enjoyed by this trendy microbrewery, whose setting in repurposed shipping containers draws in hipsters from Westerhope to Wallsend. Craft beers are brewed on-site and served in the taproom, which also has a rotating support cast of brews from around the world; if you're hungry, a street food market takes up residence here every weekend from spring to autumn, while Dot Bagels, contained within the on-site bike shop, serves fantastic New York-style bagels. **££**

Head of Steam Quayside

MAP P.40

11–17 Broad Chare NE1. Ⓜ **Central, Manors.** Ⓦ **theheadofsteam.co.uk.**

If it's variety you're after, you could do a lot worse than this friendly place, which has the feel of a large café but the menu of a beer festival: dozens of Trappist, Belgian, American, and British beers, with plentiful low- and zero-alcohol versions too. There's also a good-value menu of classic cocktails done well. Kebabs, burgers, pizzas and bar platters make up the food offerings. **££**

The Redhouse

MAP P.40

32 Sandhill NE1. Ⓜ **Central.** Ⓕ **facebook. com/redhousencl.**

Housed in a tall, thin, Grade II-listed building with a coral pink paint job, there's an ancient feel to this pub, where dogs loll beside a crackling log fire and there's an ever-changing selection of hand-pulled beers – real ale enthusiasts rejoice. The food menu fits, with a focus on hearty pies handmade by Northumberland's Amble Butchers. A lovely cosy place to pass a chilly afternoon. **££**

Ouseburn and Jesmond

Fashionable Ouseburn has followed a path which is becoming familiar in British cities – a former industrial neighbourhood whose factories and warehouses have been occupied by creative minds and turned into galleries, boutiques, and hipster-magnet bars, restaurants, cafés and nightclubs. Neighbouring Jesmond, by contrast, has long been one of Newcastle's most affluent suburbs, as its abundance of splendid Georgian and Victorian architecture attests. A lively student population, however, keeps things fresh and stops the area getting stuffy, and the bars and restaurants of Osborne Road lend a buzzing energy to Jesmond's villagey feel – not for nothing is this neighbourhood known as the Notting Hill of Newcastle.

The Biscuit Factory

MAP P.50
16 Stoddart St, NE2. Ⓜ Manors.
Ⓦ thebiscuitfactory.com. Daily 10am–5pm; free.

Set over two floors of a Victorian warehouse which in a previous life, as the name suggests, produced biscuits, in its present day incarnation this is the largest independent contemporary art, craft & design gallery in the country. Period elements like the red brick walls and wooden beams have been beautifully preserved, and serve as a picturesque backdrop for exhibitions by predominantly local artists. At the time of research, the main exhibition space on the upper floor was dedicated to the work of Anthony Marshall, whose colourful landscapes and cityscapes portray his native Newcastle and beyond.

Cobalt Studios

MAP P.50
10 Boyd St NE2. Ⓜ Manors, Byker. Hours vary.

A real cradle for innovative local art and artists, this is primarily a complex of studios, used by painters, sculptors, musicians, and creative types of all persuasions, but it also regularly hosts exhibitions and multimedia events. Every Thursday sees performances by local musicians, while Tuesday hosts an evening called Crossings, when refugees, asylum seekers, migrants and anyone else are invited to come and play, sing and listen to each other's music. Life drawing classes are also held

The Biscuit Factory

regularly if you'd like to sharpen an artistic skill, and are often given to the relaxing soundtrack of live jazz. A fantastic, soulful place.

Ouseburn Farm

MAP P.50
Ouseburn Rd, NE1. Ⓜ Byker.
Ⓦ sevenstories.org.uk. Daily 10am–5pm; free, donations appreciated.

For the perfect antidote to the urban hustle and bustle head to this city farm, a riot of green beneath the railway arches in Ouseburn. Beginning life in 1976 as a community project by parents in Byker, who wanted to cultivate a space for their children to connect with nature, grow food and care for animals, the farm has developed into a registered charity. It welcomes some 36,000 visitors each year, and does a lot of work with adults with learning difficulties, helping them to foster a connection to nature, make friends, and learn new skills. Sheep, chickens, pigs and goats roam in large enclosures; feeding time and petting sessions are among the most popular events. The on-site café serves delicious sandwiches, herbal

Ouseburn Farm

teas from the farm's herb garden, and scones with home-made jam.

Jim Edwards Gallery

MAP P.50
57 Lime St NE1. Ⓜ Manors, Byker. Mon–Fri 10am–4pm, Sat 11am–2pm.

One of the many artists to have set up shop in Ouseburn is Jim Edwards, whose work you may well have seen in the other galleries and souvenir shops of Newcastle. It is characterised by cartoonish cityscapes of Newcastle, Edinburgh and London, all bold lines and bright colours. His gallery is open throughout the week except Sunday, and is a great place to come and admire his work and pick up a souvenir, be it a print, an original artwork, or a piece scaled-down in the form of greetings card. Kielder Observatory, the Tyne Bridge, and Grey Street are among the regional attractions depicted.

Seven Stories

MAP P.50
30 Lime St, NE1. Ⓜ Manors, Byker.
Ⓦ sevenstories.org.uk. Daily 10am–5pm; free.

This charming museum, also known as the National Centre for Children's Books, is housed in a restored Victorian mill and dedicated to the magic of children's literature. Highlights include handwritten drafts by Michael Morpurgo, relating to his classic works like *War Horse* and *The Butterfly Lion*; and drafts donated by Philip Pullman which reveal much about the creative mind behind *His Dark Materials* – doodles of cats smoking cigars sit alongside thoughts on optimal stationery and the workings of the writing process. Other exhibits include vintage pens and typewriters, many used in the creation of classic children's stories. Much of the material exhibited in the museum has been donated by the authors themselves, and the patrons

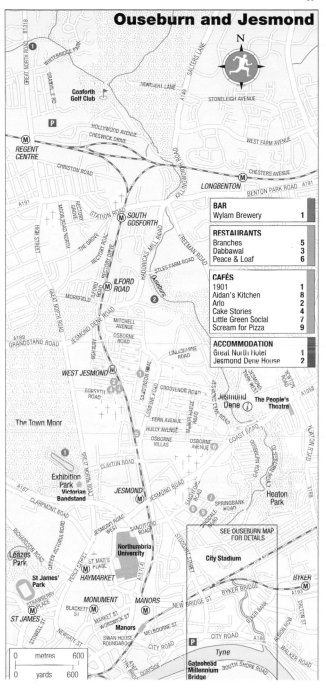

Ouseburn and Jesmond

BAR	
Wylam Brewery	1

RESTAURANTS	
Branches	5
Dabbawal	3
Peace & Loaf	6

CAFÉS	
1901	1
Aidan's Kitchen	8
Arlo	2
Cake Stories	4
Little Green Social	7
Scream for Pizza	9

ACCOMMODATION	
Great North Hotel	1
Jesmond Dene House	2

SEE OUSEBURN MAP FOR DETAILS

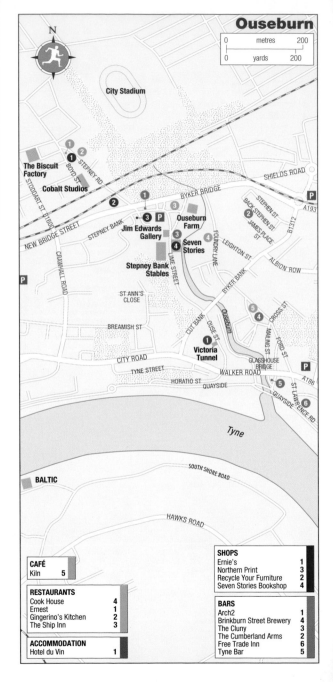

Ouseburn

City Stadium

The Biscuit Factory

Cobalt Studios

Jim Edwards Gallery

Ouseburn Farm

Seven Stories

Stepney Bank Stables

Victoria Tunnel

BALTIC

Tyne

CAFÉ

Kiln	5

RESTAURANTS

Cook House	4
Ernest	1
Gingerino's Kitchen	2
The Ship Inn	3

ACCOMMODATION

Hotel du Vin	1

SHOPS

Ernie's	1
Northern Print	3
Recycle Your Furniture	2
Seven Stories Bookshop	4

BARS

Arch2	1
Brinkburn Street Brewery	4
The Cluny	3
The Cumberland Arms	2
Free Trade Inn	6
Tyne Bar	5

include some of the country's foremost authors and illustrators including Jacqueline Wilson and Quentin Blake.

Stepney Bank Stables

MAP P.50

Stepney Bank, NE1. Ⓜ Manors, Byker. Ⓦ stepneybank.co.uk. Mon–Fri 9am–8pm, Sat & Sun 8.30am–4.30pm; book online.

Would-be horse riders and seasoned equestrians alike can hop on the saddle at this stables and riding school, a pillar of the community in Byker for two decades. With a mission statement to "enhance lives through horses", the centre does a lot of community work with young people in the local area, helping them to learn new skills, network, and maximise their potential; anybody is welcome, though, to book a class, with options for total beginners and more experienced riders and lessons taking place both indoor and outdoor. There's also a modest café selling coffee, tea and light bites, and a gift shop where you can pick up some equestrian miscellanea.

Victoria Tunnel

MAP P.50

Ouse Street, NE1. Ⓜ Byker. Ⓦ ouseburntrust.org.uk. Daily 10am–4 or 5pm; book online; charge.

Carved out in the mid-19th century to ferry coal between Spital Tongues Colliery and the River Tyne, the Victoria Tunnel stretches all the way from the Town Moor to the riverbank and was used for its original purpose from 1842 to the 1860s. Abandoned for decades, it then renewed its usefulness during the Second World War, being converted into a huge air raid shelter in 1939, capable of sheltering thousands of the city's citizens. Guided tours through the tunnel bring to life its long and often harrowing history – in 1852, worker William Coulson was crushed to death when a load of debris was released into the tunnel in error; rather disconcertingly, he himself was giving a tour of the tunnel at the time, to prospective buyers. Sound effects recreate the air raid sirens and passing bombers of the war years, the wooden beds and benches which people slept

OUSEBURN AND JESMOND

Horse on Stepney Bank

on during air raids have been recreated, and there is a poignant crucifix and roll of honour to those lost in the war.

Exhibition Park

MAP P.49

Claremont Rd, NE2. Ⓜ Jesmond. Daily 9am–3.30pm; free.

Occupying the southeastern corner of the Town Moor, Exhibition Park is a splendid Victorian garden complete with manicured lawns, a boating lake and a bandstand, together with the more modern additions of a skatepark and the Wylam Brewery, which took up residence in the former Palace of Arts building in 2016. Originally christened Bull Park on its opening in the 1870s, it was renamed Exhibition Park in honour of its hosting the Royal Mining Engineering Jubilee Exhibition in 1887 (though it remained known as Bull Park until 1929). The jubilee attracted a whopping two million visitors; today, its most visible legacy is the bandstand, which was built especially for the fair. It has remained a venue for festivities, with Northern Pride

Old stone bridge in Jesmond Dene

held here yearly and the Newcastle Mela, every August bank holiday weekend, celebrating South Asian food, music, and culture.

Jesmond Dene

MAP P.49

Jesmond Dene Rd, NE7. Ⓜ Jesmond. Daily 24hr; free.

Following the River Ouseburn from Jesmond Vale to Gosforth, Jesmond Dene is a lovely forested corridor home to some iconic British wildlife, including the kingfisher and the red squirrel. At times, it's so photogenic it looks like a film set: the river tumbles down neat waterfalls, and stone bridges span the walkways and the water, sprouting green shoots and looking like they were built in the dawn of time. All in all, it's a lovely place to pass a temperate afternoon. Don't miss Pets Corner (daily 10am–4pm; free), a petting zoo home to goats, alpacas, pot-bellied pigs and rabbits, as well as some technicolour tropical birds.

The People's Theatre

MAP P.49

Stephenson Road, NE6. Ⓜ Jesmond, Chillingham Rd. Ⓦ peoplestheatre.co.uk.

Run by local people and home to one of the country's oldest and largest amateur theatrical companies, the People's Theatre was established in 1911. An early associate was George Bernard Shaw, who had dozens of plays performed here in the theatre's early years. In the 500-seater auditorium, and a smaller, newer studio theatre, a range of performances are staged including, at the time of research, *Sleeping Beauty*, Mike Leigh's *Abigail's Party*, and Agatha Christie's *The Hollow*. The company also has a history of esteemed collaborations, the most recent of note being when they played the Mechanicals in a joint production of *A Midsummer Night's Dream* with the Royal Shakespeare Company.

Shops

Ernie's

MAP P.50

1 Boyd St NE1. Ⓜ **Manors, Byker.**
Ⓦ **ernieouseburn.com.**

Inside the Cobalt Studios complex, downstairs from the bar-restaurant *Ernest* and run by the same folks, this shop and deli was dreamt up during coronavirus lockdowns as a means of showcasing local produce: one third of the 1000-plus items come from within 20 miles, and are bought directly from producers and growers in most cases. Pick up some pesto, pickles, herbal remedies, or beers from Northumberland brewery Rigg & Furrow, or get some artisan cheese, bread and charcuterie and put together a countryside picnic.

Northern Print

MAP P.50

Stepney Bank NE1. Ⓜ **Manors, Byker.**
Ⓦ **northernprint.org.uk.**

This shop, gallery and studio is dedicated to the great art of printmaking, and is the leading institution of its kind in the Northeast. The work for sale encompasses a huge range of prints from local and international artists. John Grey's monochrome work depicts Newcastle's foreboding bridges and windswept coastal landscapes, while Janet Dickinson's colourful prints depict animals and plants. Cricket, Earl Grey, the Queen of Hearts – you name it, it's printed here, and you can buy it.

Recycle Your Furniture

MAP P.50

1 Stepney Rd NE1. Ⓜ **Manors, Byker.**
Ⓦ **recycleyourfurniture.co.uk.**

No prizes for guessing what's on the agenda at this secondhand and antique store, which has old wooden chairs hanging from the entranceway, dressers, tables, drawers, shelves, lamps, pianos – indeed, anything you could think of which once furnished a home has been rescued from the scrapheap and exhibited for your perusal. A 'Refunk Your Junk' section sells upcycled mannequins and other junk repurposed into quirky household items.

Seven Stories Bookshop

MAP P.50

Cleaning refills at Ernie's

30 Lime St NE1. Ⓜ Manors, Byker.
Ⓦ sevenstories.org.uk.
It would be remiss of you to visit
this monument to children's
literature and not take home a
slice of the magic yourself in the
form of a book or two. Happily,
there's a wide selection at the on-
site bookshop – one of the largest
independent children's bookshops
in the UK, in fact – from Enid
Blyton to Philip Pullman and
everything in between. With
sections devoted to a wide age
range, from baby books up to
young adult fiction, there will be
something here for you no matter
the age of your kids – or, indeed, if
you're a big kid yourself.

Cafés

1901

MAP P.49
68 St George's Terrace, NE2. Ⓜ West
Jesmond. Ⓦ 1901caffe.co.uk.
Well-heeled brunchers flock to this
extremely homely café, which has
sofas scattered with soft cushions,
rustic wood tables and cosy
armchairs flooded with natural

Cake Stories

light through elegant bay windows.
The menu features classic fare
like full English breakfasts, eggs
royale and Benedict, bacon butties,
burgers and club sandwiches, while
some more adventurous attempts
at fusion cuisine – an 'Italian banh
mi', for example – are generally
successful. ££

Aidan's Kitchen

MAP P.49
11 Starbeck Ave, NE2. Ⓜ Jesmond.
Ⓦ adainskitchen.co.uk.
The breakfast and brunch at this
welcoming café are hard to beat,
with yoghurty Turkish eggs, spicy
shakshuka, hearty steak and eggs
and some zingy offerings like chilli
salmon and jalapeño royale. Boozy
brunch cocktails kick off at 11am,
while regular themed evenings
are held including Drum 'n'
Thigh, which pays homage to the
mighty chook in all its forms – the
chicken sriracha sandwich is justly
celebrated. ££

Arlo

MAP P.49
36–38 Brentwood Ave, NE2. Ⓜ West
Jesmond. Ⓦ arlojesmond.com.
There's a playful feel about this West
Jesmond bistro, decorated with
colourful skulls and toy animals
and with an eclectic menu of dishes
from across the world. This kind of
culinary variety can be something
of a red flag, but not here, where
everything is done well, from Baja
fish tacos to Korean beef. The
breakfasts, with meat and vegetarian
options, are particularly good, but
the highest praise is reserved for the
cakes, with vegan chocolate, Biscoff,
fruit scones, and red velvet cookies
regularly on the agenda. ££

Cake Stories

MAP P.49
12 Brentwood Avenue, NE2. Ⓜ West
Jesmond. Ⓦ cakestories.com.
This charming family business
specializes in cakes of all kinds,
from Biscoff blondies to sea salt

brownies, raspberry slices to carrot cakes and everything in between. If your sweet tooth isn't tingling, or you just can't eat any more cake, there's plenty of savoury options to choose from, with poached eggs on toast, home-made soups, and baked camembert among them. There are lots of dishes for people with specific dietary requirements, too, including coeliac and vegan options. **££**

Kiln

MAP P.50

4 Hume St, NE6. Ⓜ Byker. Ⓦ kiln.cafe.
Started by the ceramicists who work next door at the 1265 Degrees North workshop, *Kiln* serves delicious espresso-style coffee and superb hot chocolates (try the white mint or mince pie versions if visiting in autumn), as well as a wide range of teas. There's also a good line in Mediterranean food, from labneh and hummus to nduja butter cod and slow-roasted lamb shoulder – all served, naturally, on the team's very own crockery, lovingly thrown and fired next door. You can also buy plates and mugs to take away with you. **££**

Little Green Social

MAP P.49

83–89 Goldspink Ln, NE2. Ⓜ Jesmond.
Ⓦ littlegreensocial.co.uk.
"Wholesome" doesn't quite do justice to this cute vegan café-restaurant, where the menu is bursting with goodness in dishes like Thai noodle stir fries, jackfruit pizzas, meze platters, and a wide range of vegan chocolate and cheesecakes. Organic wines are also available to accompany your food, as are a range of health-giving juices. The all-day breakfasts are a great healthy alternative to a traditional full English, and cheaper to boot. **££**

Scream for Pizza

MAP P.49

21–25 Starbeck Ave, NE2. Ⓜ Jesmond.
Ⓦ screamforpizza.com.

Chilling out at Ernest

A worthy contender for the crown of Newcastle's best pizza, this popular joint has a presence at the *Free Trade Inn* in the form of Goliath, its travelling pizza van. The best place to taste it though, is at the trendy mothership restaurant, which draws you in with a bright red neon window sign. Menu highlights include the Brooklyn Bee (fior di latte, spianata salami, chilli honey drizzle) and the Shuffle Truffle (a white pizza with truffle cream and chestnut mushrooms). **££–£££**

Restaurants

Branches

MAP P.49

9 Osborne Rd, NE1. Ⓜ Jesmond, West Jesmond. Ⓦ branchesrestaurant.co.uk.
This Osborne Road stalwart is helmed by former Northeast Chef of the Year Cevat Robert Elat, who uses only the freshest seasonal British ingredients to whip up simple, considered dishes like seafood linguine, butternut squash and wild mushroom risotto, and steamed Shetland mussels with white wine. For dessert, the

Dave Coulson at Peace & Loaf

bourbon sticky toffee pudding and Black Forest gateaux are hard to resist. Long one of Newcastle's best restaurants, *Branches* shows no sign of letting up any time soon. **£££**

Cook House

MAP P.50
Foundry Lane NE6. Ⓜ **Manors, Byker.**
Ⓦ **cookhouse.org.**
Another fashionable offering just off the river in Ouseburn, *Cook House* is the brainchild of Anna Hedworth, a cook and food writer who has a commitment to local, seasonal ingredients. Dishes include nduja fried eggs on toasted sourdough, goat ragù on toast with cheese and pea shoots, smoked chalk stream trout, and more. It's on the pricier side, but it's worth every penny for the quality of the food and the convivial atmosphere in the hipsterish interior, warmed by a wood-burning stove. **£££**

Dabbawal

MAP P.49
1 Brentwood Mews NE2. Ⓜ **West Jesmond.**
Ⓦ **dabbawal.com.**
The trend of pricey, sit-down restaurants claiming to serve

"Indian street food" shows no sign of abating, so you might as well embrace it. Happily, that's easy to do at *Dabbawal*, where sweet potato chaat, chicken chilli fry, and Chettinad chicken madras are among the zingy, aromatic offerings. The early evening set menu (5–6.30pm) is good value for two courses, and a great choice for an early dinner; non-carnivores will be pleased to find plenty of options, including a wide vegan menu. **£££**

Ernest

MAP P.50
1 Boyd St NE1. Ⓜ **Manors, Byker.**
Ⓦ **weareernest.com.**
Just down the road from the Biscuit Factory (see page 47), *Ernest* is one of Ouseburn's best-loved bars, cafés, and cultural spaces. Open every day from the morning 'til late, it offers a varied programme of events from cosmology and tango classes to life drawing and live jazz. Even when nothing's on, though, this is a lovely place to while away a few hours, over a full English breakfast, a dinner of Moroccan lamb, or a beer or glass of wine; the coffee is great, too. **££**

Gingerino's Kitchen

MAP P.50
9 Osborne Rd, NE1. Ⓜ **Manors, Byker.**
Ⓦ **gingerinoskitchen.co.uk.**
No-frills, friendly place serving some of the best pizzas and calzones in Newcastle. Servings are by the slice (or 'mini calzone' – a folded quarter-pizza) and the offerings include *pollo all'aglio* – slow-cooked garlic chicken – and a superb rocket and parmesan. It's a great option for a takeaway or delivery to your hotel room or apartment, but you can also sit in. Good-value deals are on offer involving two slices, a drink, and a cake – the chocolate brownies and carrot cake are particularly good. **££**

Peace & Loaf

MAP P.49

217 Jesmond Rd NE2. Ⓜ Jesmond.
Ⓦ peaceandloaf.co.uk.

Winner of a bevy of awards since
opening in 2013 for its lovingly
crafted tasting menus based on
fresh, seasonal ingredients, *Peace
& Loaf* is the project of chef Dave
Coulson, who trained under the
legendary Michel Roux Jr. The
beautiful creations include teriyaki
ibérico with cabbage and salt plum,
and elderflower cured trout with
wasabi and fennel; the vegetarian
tasting menu includes Jerusalem
artichoke and caramelised apple,
and shiitake, celeriac, parmesan and
wild leeks. It's good value, too, for
the quality. £££

The Ship Inn

MAP P.50

Stepney Bank, NE1. Ⓜ Manors, Byker.
Ⓦ facebook.com/shipouseburn.

One of the oldest pubs in
Ouseburn, *The Ship Inn* has been
refreshing the good people of the
valley since time immemorial.
There's a great selection of cask, keg
and tap beers, and a hearty selection
of alcohol-absorbing bar food, from
piled-high nachos to juicy burgers;
there's also a wide-ranging vegan
menu, with the meat-free Sunday
nut roast and jackfruit shawarma
garnering rave reviews. ££–£££

Bars

Arch2

MAP P.50

Arch 2, Stepney Bank NE1. Ⓜ Manors,
Byker. Ⓦ newcastlebrewingltd.co.uk/arch2.

Housed in truly voguish style
beneath the arches of Byker Road
Bridge, with benches clustered
around a firepit and hung with
fairy lights, *Arch2* is the archetypal
modern micropub. Run by a father
and son duo, they produce a range
of delicious beers from blondes to
porters, and also offer wines and
spirits should you prefer. They
share the space with Indian street
food purveyors *Thali Tray*, who

The Ship Inn

serve fantastic platters designed to
showcase the best of India's regional
street food. ££

Brinkburn Street Brewery

MAP P.50

1a Ford St NE6 Ⓜ Byker
Ⓦ brinkburnbrewery.co.uk

An independent brewery in the
heart of the Ouseburn Valley,
Brinkburn Street Brewery is a
passionately led affair, and it shows.
A small but lovingly curated choice
of beers include Quayside Blonde
Ale, Tyne Titans IPA, and the rich
Homage to Mesopotamia porter,
flavoured with Shiraz grapes.
Brewery experiences are on offer
in the form of tours and tastings,
and burgers, pizzas and charcuterie
boards are served in the tap room
all day too. ££

The Cluny

MAP P.50

36 Lime St NE1 Ⓜ Manors, Byker
Ⓦ thecluny.com

With enough room for 300
revellers, The Cluny is an intimate
venue which ranks as one of
Newcastle's finest. Housed in a
former flax spinning mill, the

bar has transcended all others in the city by ranking regularly in the World's Best Bars list, thanks to its vast collection of local and world beers. The main attraction, though, is the music venue, famous for promoting future stars, among them Arctic Monkeys, who played a famous gig here en route to superstardom; Seasick Steve, the New York Dolls, and Martha Reeves are among the other acts to have graced the stage. ££

The Cumberland Arms

MAP P.50
James Place NE6 Ⓜ Byker
Ⓦ thecumberlandarms.co.uk
The Cumby, as it is known to all and sundry, has been rehydrating thirsty wayfarers since the 1860s. It retains a Victorian look, with its green and white pillared exterior rather recalling the Exhibition Park bandstand, and its stained-glass windows and wall tiles also typical of the period. A log fire warms up the place in winter, while there's a great beer selection with an emphasis on locally brewed real ales. £

Arch2

Free Trade Inn

MAP P.50
12 St Lawrence Rd NE6. Ⓜ Jesmond.
Ⓦ facebook.com/TheFreeTradeInn.
Much beloved of locals, this long-standing pub is unassuming in the extreme, it looks like it hasn't been decorated in decades, and is all the better for it. Real ale heads will find much to enjoy here, while ciders are also available – ask for a cocktail and you may receive some very funny looks indeed. Wednesday is pizza night, when delicious 'za is served on a pop-up basis courtesy of local purveyors *Scream for Pizza* from a van outside. ££

Tyne Bar

MAP P.50
1 Mailing St NE1. Ⓜ Byker. Ⓦ thetyne.com.
A local favourite since the mid-1990s, this down-to-earth pub sits near the Victoria Tunnel and beside a canal bridge whose arches shelter some of the garden's benches – handy in the event of a rain shower. There's live music at least one night a week, and a free jukebox the rest of the time; a great-value menu of pub grub (nachos, burgers, burritos and the like) is joined by a great selection of beers, with dozens to choose from representing the Northeast and beyond. ££

Wylam Brewery

MAP P.49
Exhbition Park NE2. Ⓜ Jesmond.
Ⓦ wylambrewery.co.uk.
Housed in the Grade II-listed Palace of Arts in Jesmond's Exhibition Park, originally built for the 1929 North East Exhibition to showcase the region's arts and crafts, Wylam Brewery is one of the city's best-loved and best-situated breweries. The beers run the gamut from pale ales to inky-black stouts, and they also produce a gin, using wild juniper berries harvested from Hepple Moor. The tap room also has a burger grill, and serves a damn fine roast on Sundays. £££

Tyneside and the coast

The greater area around Newcastle is known as Tyneside, which continues immediately east of the city with Wallsend – the terminus of the Roman-era Hadrian's Wall, an age memorialized at the atmospheric ruins of Segedunum. Beyond there lies gorgeous coastal scenery and fantastic seafood at Tynemouth, classic British seaside fun at Whitley Bay, and more enchanting Roman ruins at Arbeia. Washington is home to the lovely Washington Old Hall, ancestral seat of the first US president, and some wildlife-rich wetlands, while the city of Sunderland, while no match for Newcastle in the architecture stakes, is nevertheless worth a visit for its fantastic museum.

Segedunum Roman Fort

MAP P. 60
Buddle St, Wallsend NE28. Ⓜ **Wallsend.**
Ⓦ **segedunumromanfort.org.uk. June–mid-Oct daily 10am–6pm, mid-Oct–May Mon–Sat 10am–3pm; charge.**

Wallsend was the last outpost of Hadrian's great border defence, and Segedunum, the "strong fort" a couple of minutes' signposted walk from the Metro station, has been admirably developed as one of the prime attractions along the Wall. The grounds contain a fully reconstructed bathhouse, complete with heated pools and colourful frescoes, while the "wall's end" itself is visible at the edge of the site, close to the river and Swan Hunter shipyard. From here, the Hadrian's Wall Path runs 84 miles westwards to Bowness-on-Solway in Cumbria;

The viewing platform at Segedunum

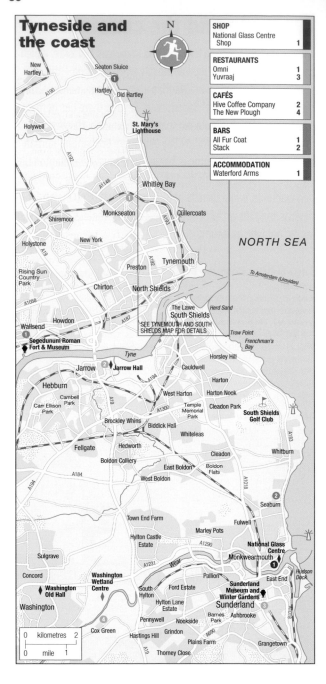

Tyneside and the coast

N

SHOP	
National Glass Centre Shop	**1**

RESTAURANTS	
Omni	**1**
Yuvraaj	**3**

CAFÉS	
Hive Coffee Company	**2**
The New Plough	**4**

BARS	
All Fur Coat	**1**
Stack	**2**

ACCOMMODATION	
Waterford Arms	**1**

New Hartley
Seaton Sluice
Hartley Old Hartley
Holywell
St. Mary's Lighthouse

Whitley Bay
Shiremoor Monkseaton Cullercoats
Holystone New York
Rising Sun Country Park Preston Tynemouth
Chirton North Shields

NORTH SEA

To Amsterdam (IJmuiden)

The Lawe
South Shields Herd Sand
SEE TYNEMOUTH AND SOUTH SHIELDS MAP FOR DETAILS
Trow Point
Frenchman's Bay

Wallsend
Segedunum Roman Fort & Museum
Tyne
Jarrow Jarrow Hall Cauldwell Horsley Hill
Hebburn West Harton Harton
Carr Ellison Park Cambell Park Harton Nook
Brockley Whins Temple Memorial Park Cleadon Park South Shields Golf Club
Fellgate Biddick Hall
Hedworth Whiteleas
Boldon Colliery Cleadon Whitburn
East Boldon Boldon Flats
West Boldon
Seaburn

Town End Farm
Marley Pots
Fulwell
Hylton Castle Estate
National Glass Centre
Sulgrave Monkwearmouth
Hudson Dock
Concord South Hylton Pallion East End
Washington Old Hall Washington Wetland Centre Ford Estate
Hylton Lane Estate Sunderland Museum and Winter Gardens
Washington Pennywell Nookside Sunderland Ashbrooke
Cox Green Barnes Park
Hastings Hill Grindon
Plains Farm Grangetown
Thorney Close

| 0 | kilometres | 2 |
| 0 | mile | 1 |

you can get your walk "passport" stamped inside the museum.

Jarrow Hall

MAP P. 60

Church Bank, Jarrow NE32. Bede ⓦ jarrowhall.com. Mid-Feb–March, Oct–late Dec 10am–4pm, April–Sept until 5pm; charge.

Jarrow Hall sits at the edge of the town of Jarrow – ingrained on the national consciousness since the 1936 Jarrow Crusade, when 201 people marched three hundred miles down to London to protest against the government's refusal to ease unemployment and poverty in the Northeast. The complex is made up of the eighteenth-century Jarrow Hall House; a reconstructed Anglo-Saxon Farm and Village; and the Bede Museum, which explores the life of Venerable Bede (673–735 AD), who lived here as a boy. Bede grew up to become one of Europe's greatest scholars and England's first historian – his History of the English Church and People, describing the struggles of the island's early Christians, was completed at Jarrow in 731.

Arbeia Roman Fort

MAP P. 64

Baring St, South Shields NE33. ⓜ South Shields. ⓦ arbeiaromanfort.org.uk. Mon–Fri 10am–5pm Sat 11am–4pm, Sun 1–4pm; free.

Built in the second century AD to guard the eastern terminus of Hadrian's Wall, Arbeia was once a mighty and bustling Roman fort overlooking the mouth of the River Tyne. This was a cosmopolitan sort of place, and the name Arbeia – "fort of Arab troops" – refers to the presence of Mesopotamian soldiers once garrisoned here. Spanish troops were also stationed here, as is evidenced by the survival of a monument commemorating the life of Victor, a former Moorish slave who died at the age of 20. Another surviving monument is dedicated to a British woman

called Regina, the wife of an Arab merchant from Palmyra. Such poignant snapshots help you imagine Arbeia as a lived-in place, as does the reconstruction of various areas, such as the imposing West Gate and the commanding officers' courtyard, brightly painted in red, white, blue and yellow. This is the most excavated Roman supply centre in the former Empire, and the fascinating finds, from jewellery and coins to furniture, are exhibited at the on-site museum.

Tynemouth Priory and Castle

MAP P. 64

Pier Rd, NE30. ⓜ Tynemouth. ⓦ www. english-heritage.org.uk. Daily 10am–5pm, reduced hours in winter; charge.

Looming mightily on a grassy headland where the River Tyne meets the North Sea, Tynemouth Priory, in keeping with the surrounding area, has a history stretching back at least 2000 years. The remains of wooden houses have been found here dating back to the first century AD, as well as some stones from the Roman era, but more concrete evidence begins to

The Anglo-Saxon Village at Jarrow Hall

emerge from the seventh century, when Oswin, King of Deira, became the first in a succession of rulers to be buried here. The third was Malcolm III of Scotland, later to be featured in William Shakespeare's *Macbeth*. It's known that a priory stood here in 800, when it was destroyed (for the first time of several) by plundering Danes; the atmospheric, crumbling ruins which you see today, however, date from the Norman era. What remains is a gatehouse, keep, and towers, as well as the shell of the old church beside a graveyard, which you are free to wander among; information boards provide some history, but there's not much in the way of exhibits.

Spanish City

MAP P. 64

Spanish City Plaza, Whitley Bay NE26. Ⓜ Whitley Bay. Ⓦ spanishcity.co.uk. Hours vary.

Fans of local heroes Dire Straits will recognize the name Spanish City from the 1981 single 'Tunnel of Love', with its refrain *"Girl, it looks so pretty to me, like it always did // Oh, like the Spanish City to me, when we were kids"*. That couplet captures

the air of nostalgia which hangs over this leisure and entertainment complex, a fixture on Whitley Bay's waterfront since 1910. While the climate is more Burgos than Barcelona (and that at a stretch), and the architecture isn't particularly Spanish at all – the name arose because the original performance venue on this site was painted with scenes representing a Spanish village – it is undeniably lovely, having been completely renovated in 2018. If anything, it exceeds its former glory – a ceiling which once lay across the first floor has been removed, so you can gaze up at the glorious central dome while you enjoy afternoon tea at *The Gallery*. Other highlights of the Spanish City include the *1910 Restaurant* (see page 68), while the spirit of the classic seaside resort is upheld here thanks to regular performances from tribute artists paying homage to everyone from George Michael to Neil Diamond.

St Mary's Lighthouse

MAP P. 60

Pier Rd, Whitley Bay NE26. Ⓜ Whitley Bay, Monkseaton. Ⓦ my.northtyneside.gov. uk. Hours change according to tide, check online; charge.

Connected to the mainland by a causeway, the tidal St Mary's Island would be totally unremarkable were it not for the beautiful Victorian lighthouse which was built there in 1898 to ward passing ships away from the rocky coast. It served in this capacity for almost 100 years, but was rendered redundant by modern navigational techniques in 1984. Happily, the council decided to keep it and open it to the public, along with the lovely former lighthouse keepers' cottages. Climbing the 137 steps to the top of the lighthouse is rewarded by magnificent views over the coastline and the North Sea; if you're unable to make the ascent, the same panoramas are showcased in a video display on the ground floor. The tides create rock pools full of marine life, while the tiny island also

St Mary's Lighthouse

includes grassy clifftops, wetlands, and a beach where you can often spot basking seals.

Washington Old Hall

MAP P. 60
The Avenue, Washington NE38. ⓦ nationaltrust.org.uk. April–Oct Mon, Fri–Sun 10am–5pm, manor house closes 1hr earlier; charge.

Anyone with an interest in American history will find much to divert them at Washington Old Hall, the ancestral seat of George Washington's family. The president's ancestor William de Hertburne took possession of the estate, then known as the Wessyngtonlands, in the late 12th century; it served as a family home for centuries, ending with the last Wessyngton heir, the spectacularly named Dionysia Tempest, after whom the manor was sold to the Bishop of Durham in 1613. Now maintained by the National Trust, Old Hall is beautifully atmospheric, and really does feel very old, with its charmingly wonky stonework and ceilings, beautiful wooden beams and flagstoned floors.

Washington Wetland Centre

MAP P. 60
Barnston Ln, Washington NE38. ⓦ wwt. org.uk. Daily 10am–4.30pm, last entry 1hr before closing; charge.

Taking up one hundred acres of the north bank of the River Wear in Pattinson, the popular Washington Wildfowl and Wetlands Centre is a lush conservation area of meadows, woods and wetlands that acts as a winter habitat for migratory birds, including geese, waders and ducks. In summer, you can watch fluffy ducklings hatch in the Waterfowl Nursery and spot hawthorns and woodpeckers in Hawthorn Wood; come May, the ancient Spring Gill Wood is a riot of bluebells, and the Chilean flamingos have emerged from their winter indoors. Ganderland, meanwhile, is home to some rare waterbirds including Hawaiian and emperor geese, while many visitors find their favourite residents to be the Asian short-clawed otters, who love to frolic in the mud while crowds watch on.

Sunderland Museum & Winter Gardens

MAP P. 60
Burdon Rd, Sunderland SR1. ⓦ Park Lane. ⓦ sunderlandculture.org.uk. Mon–Fri 9.30am–5pm, Wed until 7pm, Sat 10am–4pm; free.

Sunderland is fifteen miles southeast of Newcastle and shares that city's long history, riverside setting and industrial heritage – but cannot match its architectural splendour. However, it's worth a trip to visit the Sunderland Museum, easily accessible by Metro from Newcastle. The museum does a very good job of telling the city's history, relating how Sunderland's ships were once sent around the world, and also has much to say about the city's other major trades, notably its production of lustreware and glass. The Winter Gardens, housed in a steel-and-glass hothouse, invite a treetop walk to view the impressive polished-steel column of a water sculpture.

Winter Gardens

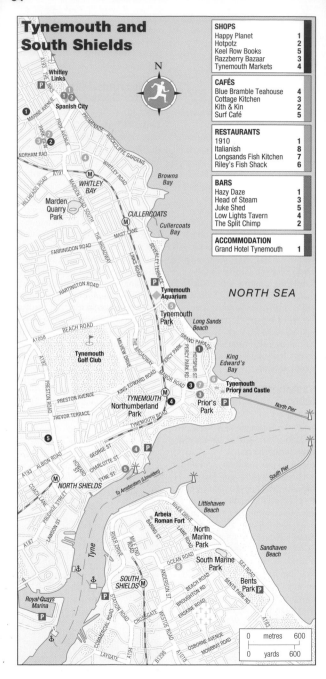

Tynemouth and South Shields

N

SHOPS

Happy Planet	1
Hotpotz	2
Keel Row Books	5
Razzberry Bazaar	3
Tynemouth Markets	4

CAFÉS

Blue Bramble Teahouse	4
Cottage Kitchen	3
Kith & Kin	2
Surf Café	5

RESTAURANTS

1910	1
Italianish	8
Longsands Fish Kitchen	7
Riley's Fish Shack	6

BARS

Hazy Daze	1
Head of Steam	3
Juke Shed	5
Low Lights Tavern	4
The Split Chimp	2

ACCOMMODATION

Grand Hotel Tynemouth	1

Whitley Links

Spanish City

MARINE AVENUE

THE LINKS

PARK AVENUE

PROMENADE

ROCKCLIFFE GARDENS

NORHAM ROAD.

HILLHEADS ROAD

MARDEN ROAD SOUTH

WHITLEY ROAD

WHITLEY BAY

WHITLEY ROAD

Browns Bay

Marden Quarry Park

CULLERCOATS

Cullercoats Bay

FARRINGDON ROAD

MAST LANE

LINKS ROAD

BEVERLEY TERRACE

THE BROADWAY

HARTINGTON ROAD

BEACH ROAD

MILVAIN DRIVE

THE BROADWAY

Tynemouth Aquarium

Tynemouth Park

NORTH SEA

Long Sands Beach

Tynemouth Golf Club

KING EDWARD ROAD

PERCY PARK

GRAND PARADE

PERCY PARK RD

HOTSPUR ST

King Edward's Bay

PRESTON AVENUE

TREVOR TERRACE

MANOR ROAD

TYNEMOUTH
Northumberland
Park

Prior's Park

Tynemouth Priory and Castle

North Pier

TYNEMOUTH ROAD

GEORGE ST

CHARLOTTE ST

TYNE ST

ALBION ROAD

HOWARD ST

South Pier

NORTH SHIELDS

COACH LANE

PRUDHOE STREET

LAWSON ST

To Amsterdam (IJmuiden)

Littlehaven Beach

River Tyne

RIVER DRIVE

Arbeia Roman Fort

BARING ST

MILE END RD

LANE END ST

North Marine Park

Sandhaven Beach

SEA ROAD

OCEAN ROAD

South Marine Park

Bents Park

Royal Quays Marina

SOUTH SHIELDS

STATION ROAD

COMMERCIAL ROAD

ANDERSON ST

BEACH ROAD

BENTS PARK RD

BROUGHTON RD

ERSKINE ROAD

WESTOE ROAD

CROSSGATE

LAYGATE

OSBORNE AVENUE

MOWBRAY RD

0	metres	600
0	yards	600

Shops

Happy Planet

MAP P.64

3d Illfracombe Gardens, Whitley Bay NE26 Ⓜ Monkseaton. Ⓦ happyplanetstudio.co.uk.

Joyous in both name and nature, *Happy Planet* produces and sells all manner of colourful trinkets, from glass frog ornaments to felt flowers, wood-carved miniature totem poles to tinkling wind chimes. It's the perfect place to pick up a cheerful gift or souvenir to remind you of your time in Whitley Bay; many products, including notebooks, wallets and bamboo soap dishes, are Fairtrade, so you know your purchase is doing some good.

Hotpotz

MAP P.64

156 Park View, Whitley Bay NE26. Ⓜ Monkseaton. Ⓦ hotpotz.co.uk.

Another lovely sanctuary of creativity in Whitley Bay is this ceramics studio, where the main attraction is the chance to paint your own bowl, jug, vase, or mug under the caring tutelage of friendly owners Lisa and Louise. It's a popular activity for people travelling with kids, but in truth it's very therapeutic no matter your age. Very reasonably priced, with teas and coffees available too.

Keel Row Books

MAP P.64

11 Fenwick Terrace, North Shields NE29. Ⓜ North Shields. Ⓦ keelrowbooks.com.

While North Shields is not, in general, a world-class shopping destination, this bookshop is an honourable exception. Open since 1981, it stocks a fantastic collection of rare and first edition books, which are constantly changing but always diverse, ranging from the mainstream (*Harry Potter*) to the more obscure (1920s tracts on Zoroastrianism). The staff have decades of experience and will help you find what you're looking for.

National Glass Centre Shop

MAP P. 60

Liberty Way, Sunderland, SR6. Ⓜ St Peters. Ⓦ nationalglasscentre.com.

Housed within Sunderland's National Glass Centre – a museum within the University of Sunderland dedicated to the history of glass-making – this shop is fantastic for picking up a locally made souvenir. Bowls, glasses, marbles, animal sculptures, and vases are among the glass items blown on-site, while mugs, jewellery, and textiles are also on sale here.

Razzberry Bazaar

MAP P. 64

3 Front St, Tynemouth NE30. Ⓜ Tynemouth. Ⓦ razzberrybazaar.co.uk.

Bohemian types will love this emporium, where incense fills the air and the rails are stocked with one-of-a-kind pieces like Nellore jackets in jacquard wool, cushions stitched with colourful mandalas, and woven backpacks and shoulder bags in colourful rainbow fabrics. Incense holders, handmade bracelets, and aromatherapy sets

National Glass Centre

Tynemouth Markets

are among the other blissed-out offerings.

Tynemouth Markets

MAP P.64
Tynemouth Station NE30.
Ⓦ tynemouthmarkets.com.
Opening every Saturday and Sunday, Tynemouth Markets take up residence beneath the Victorian arches of the town's railway station. The markets comprise more than 150 stalls, selling everything from home-made handicrafts to Greek street food. The cupcake stand is always a hit, while those selling ceramics and jewellery are fantastic if you're in the market for a locally made gift or souvenir. *Bennys Toon Macaroons* is a particular must for anyone with a sweet tooth.

Cafés

Blue Bramble Teahouse

MAP P.64
251–253 Whitley Rd, Whitley Bay. Ⓜ
Whitley Bay. Ⓦ blue-bramble-teahouse.business.site.
Tea in china cups, ham and egg salads, and slices of cake as big

as your head are the order of the day at this lovely café, which is as traditional as befits a teahouse in Whitley Bay. In addition to the cakes – which run the gamut from classic red velvets to imaginative offerings like coconut kiwi slices with pear crème patisserie – there are heartier savoury options on offer, including peas, pies, and gravy. **££**

Cottage Kitchen

MAP P.64
1–5 Countess Ave, Whitley Bay.
Ⓜ Monkseaton. Ⓦ facebook.com/ckswhitleybay.
By the reckoning of many locals this is the best value place to eat in Whitley Bay, with a great line in traditional food done well. The full English breakfasts are legendary, as are the Sunday roasts piled high with all the trimmings; huge portions of chili con carne, chicken curry, and spaghetti bolognese round off the menu, with vegetarian equivalents available too. **£**

Hive Coffee Company

MAP P.60

Church Bank, Jarrow NE32. Ⓜ Bede.
Ⓦ hivecoffeecompany.uk.

On the grounds of Jarrow Hall, this lovely café overlooks the forests and lawns of Charlies Park, and the atmospheric St Paul's Monastery beyond. Take a walk around the attached herb garden, which has information boards relating to Anglo-Saxon herbal lotions and potions, and enjoy the menu of brunchy egg dishes and flavour-packed toasted sandwiches. **£**

Kith & Kin

MAP P.64

172 Park View, Whitley Bay. Ⓜ Monkseaton. Ⓦ kithandkinwb.co.uk.

It takes its name from an old English expression for "friends and relatives", and there's a correspondingly convivial, homely feel to this café, which has a relaxed and slightly upmarket feel. The food comprises artfully presented dishes like halloumi, hummus, mushrooms and eggs sprinkled with dukkah, huge Reuben sandwiches, and juicy steak sandwiches, while the coffee is superb. **££**

The New Plough

MAP P.60

Waterside, Cox Green SR4. Ⓦ kithandkinwb.co.uk.

If you're exploring Washington Wetlands or Washington Old Hall, there's nowhere better to escape for a warming cup of tea or coffee than this trailer overlooking the River Wear, housed in an old horsebox. There are benches to sit on and take in the view in the warmer months, and a heated indoor hut to shelter beneath during the winter. Fruit scones and cakes are also on the menu. **£**

Surf Café

MAP P.64

2 Palace Buildings, Tynemouth NE30. Ⓜ Tynemouth. Ⓦ surfcafetynemouth.co.uk.

Salty seadogs and landlubbers alike flock to this buzzy café overlooking Longsands Beach, where the wooden walls are bedecked with surfboards, T-shirts and other memorabilia and the menu features cockle-warming classics like full English breakfasts, buffalo chicken burgers, and an always-hearty soup of the day. There are also regular live performances from musicians. **£–££**

TYNESIDE AND THE COAST

Spanish City in Whitley Bay

Restaurants

1910

MAP P.64

Spanish City Plaza, Whitley Bay NE26. Ⓜ Whitley Bay. Ⓦ spanishcity.co.uk.
Named for the year in which Spanish City first opened to much fanfare, *1910* has an appropriately traditional menu with a focus on fresh seafood. Begin with Lindisfarne oysters, served with thermidor, mignonette, garlic sauce or Bloody Mary sauce, before enjoying such delights as grilled scallops, beetroot-cured salmon, halibut or grilled lobster; venison and pigeon are among the non-seafood options. £££–££££

Italianish

MAP P.64

118 Ocean Road, South Shields NE33. Ⓜ South Shields. Ⓦ facebook.com/ItalianishSouthShields.
Amid the glut of Indian restaurants for which Ocean Road is famous lies this nice surprise: an Italian-Spanish fusion restaurant presided over by the irrepressibly friendly Giovanni and Eleanora. Try the

Riley's Fish Shack

'wild forest' chicken with onions, mushrooms and truffle, or the breaded rice balls filled with cheesy pork and beef ragù. ££–£££

Longsands Fish Kitchen

MAP P.64

27 Front St, Tynemouth NE30. Ⓜ Tynemouth. Ⓦ longsandsfishkitchen.com.
No British seaside escape would be complete without fish and chips, a tradition elevated to a fine art at this Tynemouth restaurant. Cod and haddock fillet are joined on the menu by jumbo scampi from Whitby, tiger prawns with chilli jam, salmon, or, for non-fish eaters, the Longsands banger (sausage). All are served with chips, but don't miss the other sides, including mushy peas, curry sauce, pickled eggs and onions, and the mighty stottie, a cake-like bread native to the North East. £–££

Omni

MAP P.60

12 Front St, Whitley Bay NE25. Ⓜ Monkseaton. Ⓦ omnicafe.co.uk.
Hung with fairy lights and hanging baskets, and with pot plants occupying every spare inch of shelf space, there's something very wholesome about this café-restaurant. Run by a local couple who were inspired by their travels through Southeast Asia, the place is a homage to the cuisines of that region, with a menu particularly focused on Vietnamese food – superb pho, monkfish curry, and caramelized belly pork are all well worth a try. £–££

Riley's Fish Shack

MAP P.64

King Edward's Bay, Tynemouth NE30. Ⓜ Tynemouth. Ⓦ rileysfishshack.com.
Tynemouth's best dining experience can be found in this humble beach shack on King Edward's Bay, where the menu varies with the catch but often includes Lindisfarne oysters, Craster kippers, chargrilled lobster, squid on a stick, and monkfish, served with lovely sides of garlic

potatoes, aioli, chilli relish, and woodfired bread. Fire pits and electric heaters will keep you warm on a cold night, as will the selection of locally produced beers. Always worth the pilgrimage to the coast. **£££**

Yuvraaj

MAP P.60

6–7 Douro Ter, Sunderland SR2. Ⓜ Park Lane. Ⓦ yuvraajrestaurant.co.uk.

Sunderland's finest South Asian restaurant strives to combine Indian, Bangladeshi and British cooking, resulting in a richer and more varied menu than the classic British curry house. Example dishes include liver tikka, crab piri puri, mango king prawns, and duck with tamarind and honey; the signature Bengali lamb chops are a particularly mouthwatering prospect. **££**

Bars

All Fur Coat

MAP P.60

20 High St E, Wallsend NE28. Ⓜ Wallsend. Ⓦ facebook.com/allfurcoatbarlounge.

Perfect for a drink and a bite to eat after exploring the Roman ruins of Segedunum, this sleek bar-restaurant serves lovely cans of craft beer, a good selection of wines, and classic cocktails like Old Fashioneds, mojitos and margaritas. The food offerings include antipasti boards and cheeseboards, with coffee and pastry deals available at breakfast and tea and toast also on offer. **££**

Hazy Daze

MAP P.64

Spanish City Plaza, Whitley Bay NE26. Ⓜ Whitley Bay. Ⓦ hazydaze.uk.

You'd be forgiven for thinking you've stepped back to 1910 when you're wandering through Spanish City, but that illusion is shattered at this superb bottle shop, which houses a thoroughly modern collection of IPAs, pilsners, blondes, stouts, and indeed any other beer you'd care to think of from a range

Enjoying a drink outside in Tynemouth

of producers including local small-batches. Perfect place to pick up a couple of bottles and cans for a seaside stroll or picnic. **££**

Head of Steam

MAP P.64

3 Front St, Tynemouth NE30. Ⓜ Tynemouth. Ⓦ theheadofsteam.co.uk.

The perfect place to stop in for a pint after exploring Tynemouth Priory or going for a walk on the beach, this pub (which also has branches elsewhere in Northern England) specializes in a wide range of world beers, from local porters to Belgian blondes There are also superb pies courtesy of the long-time favourite, Pieminister, a stalwart at pubs and music festivals across the country. **££**

Juke Shed

MAP P.64

15 Union Quay, North Shields NE30. Ⓜ North Shields. Ⓦ juke-shed-bar-bar. business.site.

There's live music every Friday and Saturday night at this local favourite, an unassuming bar which, if you didn't know better, resembles a barber or nail bar from its anonymous exterior beneath a terrace flat. There's much more character within, with rough stone and brick walls and a wood-pallet ceiling, and a good range of wines and beers; the Sunday roasts, meanwhile, are legendary. £

Low Lights Tavern

MAP P.64

Brewhouse Bank, North Shields NE30. Ⓜ North Shields. Ⓦ facebook.com/thelowlightstavern.

Sitting on North Shields' historic Fish Quay, this is the oldest pub in town and it wears it well, with a roaring log fire, rugged stone walls, and wooden pews. Acoustic guitars hanging on the wall hint at the revelry which descends on the place at weekends, when local musicians take to the stage; throughout the week, it's a lovely place to come for a pint of ale and a pie or fish and chips. ££

The Split Chimp

MAP P.64

Spanish City Plaza, Whitley Bay NE26. Ⓜ Whitley Bay. Ⓦ splitchimp.pub.

Owned by a former paramedic (so you know you're in safe hands), *The Split Chimp* specializes in hand-pulled real ales, with a selection that rotates weekly and showcases the best of the Northeast's producers, both small and larger. A range of ciders is also available, along with a menu of bar snacks; as with the company's two other properties (one in Newcastle and another in Seaton Delaval), the main draw is the friendly welcome and homely, living-room type atmosphere. ££

STACK Seaburn

MAP P.60

Whitburn Rd, Sunderland SR6. Ⓜ Seaburn. Ⓦ stackseaburn.co.uk.

With another outlet in central Newcastle, STACK is the Northeast's answer to the shipping container complex craze which has taken London and other major cities by storm. Here, the corrugated metal boxes are repurposed to house restaurants serving baos, tacos, pizzas and burgers – there's even a whole outlet, *Holy Duck*, dedicated to the glory of all things anatine, serving crispy duck and hoisin wraps, spring rolls, loaded fries, and more. There are bars, too, and a soundtrack provided until late by DJs. ££

STACK Seaburn

The Northumberland coast

Stretching 64 miles north of Newcastle up to the Scottish border, the low-lying Northumberland coast is the region's shining star, stunningly beautiful and packed with impressive sights. Here you'll find mighty fortresses at Warkworth, Alnwick and Bamburgh and magnificent Elizabethan ramparts surrounding Berwick-upon-Tweed; in between there are glorious sandy beaches, the site of the Lindisfarne monastery on Holy Island, and the seabird and nature reserve of the Farne Islands, reached by boat from Seahouses. Foodies, too, will want to linger here – the day's catch, hauled in every day from the North Sea, is put to quite magnificent use in the many pubs and restaurants of the coast.

Warkworth Castle and Hermitage

MAP P.72
Castle Terrace, Warkworth NE65. ☎ Alnmouth. ⟨⟩ www.english-heritage.org.uk Hours vary widely; check website; charge.

Ruined but well-preserved, Warkworth Castle has Norman origins, but was constructed using sandstone during the fourteenth and fifteenth centuries. Home to generations of the Percy family, the powerful earls of Northumberland, it appears as a backdrop in several scenes of Shakespeare's Henry IV, Part II. The cross-shaped keep contains a great hall, a chapel, kitchens, storerooms and the Duke's Rooms, which are kitted out in period furniture and furnishings. A path from the churchyard heads along the right bank of the Coquet to the boat that shuttles visitors across to Warkworth Hermitage, a series of simple rooms and a claustrophobic chapel that were hewn out of the cliff above the river sometime in the fourteenth century, but abandoned by 1567. The last resident hermit, one George Lancaster, was charged by the sixth earl of Northumberland to pray for his noble family, for which lonesome duty he received around £15 a year and a barrel of fish every Sunday.

Alnwick Castle and Gardens

MAP P.72
Alnwick NE66. ☎ Alnwick. ⟨⟩ alnwickcastle.com. Castle April–Sept 10am–5.30pm; charge Garden daily 10am–6pm, until 4pm Nov–March.

The Percys – who were raised to the dukedom of Northumberland

The Grand Cascade at Alnwick Gardens

The Northumberland coast

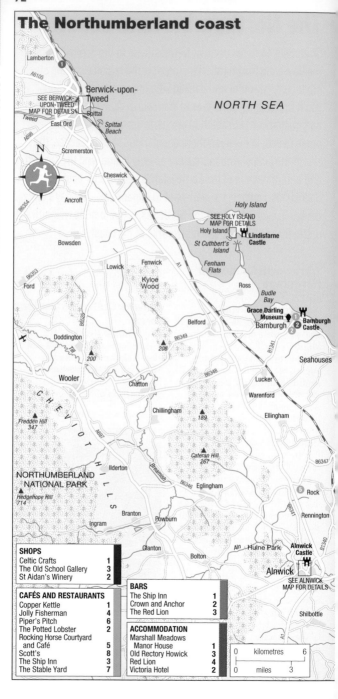

SHOPS

Celtic Crafts	1
The Old School Gallery	3
St Aidan's Winery	2

CAFÉS AND RESTAURANTS

Copper Kettle	1
Jolly Fisherman	4
Piper's Pitch	6
The Potted Lobster	2
Rocking Horse Courtyard and Café	5
Scott's	8
The Ship Inn	3
The Stable Yard	7

BARS

The Ship Inn	1
Crown and Anchor	2
The Red Lion	3

ACCOMMODATION

Marshall Meadows Manor House	1
Old Rectory Howick	3
Red Lion	4
Victoria Hotel	2

0	kilometres	6
0	miles	3

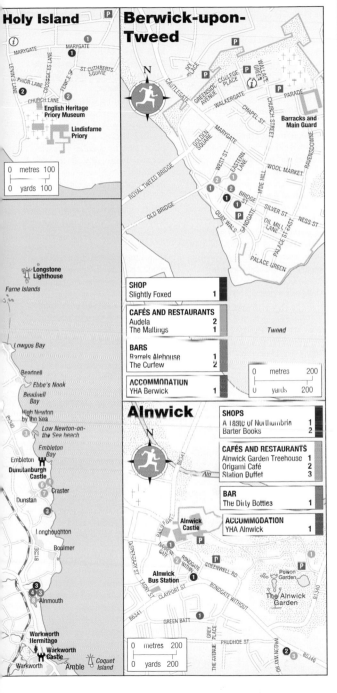

Holy Island

ⓘ

MARYGATE ❶

LEWIN'S LANE

PRIOR LANE

CROSSGATE'S LANE

FENKLE ST

ST CUTHBERT'S SQUARE

MARYGATE ❶

❷ CHURCH LANE

English Heritage
Priory Museum

Lindisfarne
Priory

| 0 | metres | 100 |
| 0 | yards | 100 |

Berwick-upon-Tweed

N

IVY PLACE

CASTLEGATE

GREENSIDE AVENUE

COLLEGE PLACE

WALLACE GREEN

ⓘ

PARADE

WALKERGATE

CHURCH STREET

Barracks and
Main Guard

CHAPEL ST

MARYGATE

RAVENSDOWNE

GOLDEN SQUARE

WEST ST

EASTERN LANE

WOOL MARKET

HYDE HILL

SILVER ST

NESS ST

ROYAL TWEED BRIDGE

OLD BRIDGE

BRIDGE ST

SANDGATE

QUAY WALLS

OIL MILL LANE

PALACE ST EAST

PALACE GREEN

Tweed

SHOP	
Slightly Foxed	1

CAFÉS AND RESTAURANTS	
Audela	2
The Maltings	1

BARS	
Barrels Alehouse	1
The Curfew	2

ACCOMMODATION	
YHA Berwick	1

| 0 | metres | 200 |
| 0 | yards | 200 |

Longstone
Lighthouse

Farne Islands

Lowgos Bay

Beadnell

Ebbe's Nook

Beadnell
Bay

High Newton
by the Sea

Low Newton-on-
the Sea beach

Low Newton-
on-the-Sea

Embleton
Bay

Embleton

Dunstanburgh
Castle

Craster

Dunstan

Longhoughton

Boulmer

Alnmouth

Warkworth
Hermitage

Warkworth
Castle

Warkworth

Amble

Coquet
Island

Alnwick

N

B6341

Aln

BAILIFFGATE

Alnwick
Castle

NARROWGATE

BONDGATE
WITHIN

GREENWELL RD

DISPENSARY ST

Alnwick
Bus Station

CLAYPORT ST

BONDGATE WITHOUT

B6341

GREEN BATT

THE AVENUE

GREY PLACE

PRUDHOE ST

Poison
Garden

The Alnwick
Garden

B1340

WAGON WAY RD

B6346

SHOPS	
A Taste of Northumbria	1
Barter Books	2

CAFÉS AND RESTAURANTS	
Alnwick Garden Treehouse	1
Origami Café	2
Station Buffet	3

BAR	
The Dirty Bottles	1

ACCOMMODATION	
YHA Alnwick	1

| 0 | metres | 200 |
| 0 | yards | 200 |

in 1750 – have owned Alnwick Castle since 1309. In the eighteenth century, the first duke had the interior refurbished by Robert Adam in an extravagant Gothic style, which in turn was supplanted by the gaudy Italianate decoration preferred by the fourth duke in the 1850s. There's plenty to see inside, including remains from Pompeii, though the interior can be crowded at times – not least with families on the Harry Potter trail, since the castle doubled as Hogwarts School in the first two films. The grounds of the castle are taken up by the huge and beautiful Alnwick Garden, designed by an innovative Belgian team and full of quirky features such as a bamboo labyrinth maze, a serpent garden involving topiary snakes, and the popular Poison Garden, filled with the world's deadliest plants. The heart of the garden is the computerized Grand Cascade, which shoots water jets in a regular synchronized display, while to the west is Europe's largest treehouse, which has a restaurant within. The walled Roots and Shoots community veg garden (no ticket required) is a delight.

Craster

Craster and Dunstanburgh Castle

MAP P.72

NE66. Ⓦ www.english-heritage.org.uk. Castle April–Sept daily 10am–6pm; Oct daily 10am–4pm; Nov–March Sat & Sun 10am–4pm; charge.

The tiny fishing village of Craster – known for its kippers – lies six miles northeast of Alnwick, right on the coast. It's a delightful little place, with its circular, barnacle-encrusted harbour walls fronting a cluster of tough, weather-battered little houses and the cheery *Jolly Fisherman* pub (see page 81). Other villages worth visiting round here include Newton-on-Sea and Beadnell, both exuding windswept, salty charm. The coastline between Dunstanburgh and Beadnell is made up of the long sandy beaches that Northumberland is famous for. The most famous attraction in the area, however, is stunning Dunstanburgh Castle, looming in the distance about a thirty-minute walk northwards up the coast from Craster. Built in the fourteenth century, in the wake of civil war, its shattered remains occupy a magnificent promontory, bordered by sheer cliffs and crashing waves.

Seahouses and the Farne Islands

MAP P.72

NE68. Ⓦ nationaltrust.org.uk/farne-islands. Around ten miles north from Craster, beyond the small village of Beadnell, lies the fishing port of Seahouses, the only place on the local coast that could remotely be described as a resort. It's the embarkation point for boat trips out to the wind swept Farne Islands, a rocky archipelago lying a few miles offshore. Owned by the National Trust and maintained as a nature reserve, the Farne Islands are the summer home of hundreds of thousands of migrating seabirds, notably puffins, guillemots, terns, eider ducks and kittiwakes, and home to the only grey seal colony on

the English coastline. A number of
boat trips potter around the islands
– the largest of which is Inner Farne
– offering birdwatching tours, grey
seal-watching tours and the Grace
Darling tour, which takes visitors to
the lighthouse on Longstone Island,
where the famed local heroine lived.

Bamburgh Castle

MAP P.72
Bamburgh NE69. ⓦ bamburghcastle.com.
Daily 10am–4pm, last entry 1hr before
closing; charge.

One-time capital of Northumbria,
the little village of Bamburgh, just
three miles from Seahouses, lies
in the lee of its magnificent castle.
Solid and chunky, it is a spectacular
sight, its elongated battlements
crowning a formidable basalt crag
high above the beach. Its origins
lie in Anglo-Saxon times, but it
suffered a centuries-long decline –
rotted by sea spray and buffeted by
winter storms, the castle was bought
by Lord Armstrong in 1894, who
demolished most of the structure
to replace it with a hybrid castle-
mansion. Inside there's plenty to
explore, including the sturdy keep
that houses an unnerving armoury
packed with vicious-looking pikes,
halberds, helmets and muskets; the
King's Hall, with its marvellous teak
ceiling that was imported from Siam
(Thailand) and carved in Victorian
times; and a medieval kitchen
complete with original jugs, pots
and pans. From behind the castle
it's a brisk, five-minute walk to two
splendid sandy beaches, backed by
rolling, tufted dunes.

Grace Darling Museum

MAP P.72
Radcliffe Rd, Bamburgh NE69.
ⓦ bamburgh.org.uk/visiting-bamburgh/
grace-darling. March–Oct Tues–Fri
10am–5pm, Sun 12–4pm, Nov–Feb Tues–Fri
10am–4pm; free.

The Grace Darling Museum
celebrates the life of famed local
heroine Grace Darling. In September
1838, a gale dashed the steamship

King's Hall, Bamburgh Castle

Forfarshire against the rocks of the
Farne Islands. Nine passengers
struggled onto a reef where they were
subsequently saved by Grace and
her lighthouseman father, William,
who left the safety of the Longstone
lighthouse to row out to them. *The
Times* trumpeted Grace's bravery,
offers of marriage and requests for
locks of her hair streamed into the
Darlings' lighthouse home, and for
the rest of her brief life Grace was
plagued by unwanted visitors – she
died of tuberculosis aged 26 in 1842,
and was buried in Bamburgh, in the
churchyard of the thirteenth-century
St Aidan's.

Holy Island

MAP P.72
Crossing times vary throughout the year;
check online at ⓦ holyislandcrossingtimes.
northumberland.gov.uk.
Lindisfarne Priory Holy Island TD15. ⓦ www.
english-heritage.org.uk. Hours vary widely
throughout the year; check online; charge.

It's a dramatic approach to Holy
Island – only accessible at low
tide – past the barnacle-encrusted
marker poles that line the three-
mile-long causeway. Topped with
a stumpy castle, the island is small

(just 1.5 miles by one), sandy and bare, and in winter it can be bleak, but come summer day-trippers clog the car parks as soon as the causeway is open. Even then, though, Lindisfarne (as the island was once known) has a distinctive and isolated atmosphere. Give the place time and, if you can, stay overnight, when you'll be able to see the historic remains without hundreds of others cluttering the views. The island's surrounding tidal mud flats, salt marshes and dunes have been designated a nature reserve. It was on Lindisfarne that St Aidan of Iona founded a monastery at the invitation of King Oswald of Northumbria in 634. The monks quickly established a reputation for scholarship and artistry, the latter exemplified by the Lindisfarne Gospels, the apotheosis of Celtic religious art, now kept in the British Library. The monastery had sixteen bishops in all, the most celebrated being the reluctant St Cuthbert, who never settled here – within two years, he was back in his hermit's cell on the Farne Islands, where he died in 687. His colleagues rowed the body back to Lindisfarne, which

Lindisfarne Castle

became a place of pilgrimage until 875, when the monks abandoned the island in fear of marauding Vikings, taking Cuthbert's remains with them. The tranquil, pinkish sandstone ruins of Lindisfarne Priory sit just off the modern village green; what you see today dates from the twelfth century. The museum next door displays a collection of incised stones that constitute all that remains of the first monastery.

Lindisfarne Castle

MAP P.72

Holy Island TD15. ⓦ nationaltrust.org.uk/lindisfarne-castle. March–Oct daily except Fri; hours vary according to tides, check website; charge.

Stuck on a small pyramid of rock half a mile away from the village, Lindisfarne Castle was built in the middle of the sixteenth century to protect the island's harbour from the Scots. It was, however, merely a decaying shell when Edward Hudson, the founder of *Country Life* magazine, stumbled across it in 1901. He promptly commissioned Edwin Lutyens (1869–1944) to turn it into an Edwardian country house, and installed a charming walled garden in the castle's former vegetable gardens, to designs by Gertrude Jekyll. The castle reopened in 2018 after extensive restoration work, which lasted two years and buttressed the aged castle against the constant onslaught from the elements: penetrating damp, leaky windows, and deteriorating stonework were among the problems plaguing the castle after centuries of coastal wind and rain.

Berwick-upon-Tweed

MAP P.72

TD15. ⓘ Berwick-upon-Tweed ⓦ visitberwick.com.

Before the union of the English and Scottish crowns in 1603, Berwick-upon-Tweed, twelve miles north of Holy Island, was the quintessential frontier town, changing hands no fewer than fourteen times between 1174 and 1482, when the Scots finally ceded the stronghold to the English. Interminable cross-border warfare ruined Berwick's economy, turning the prosperous Scottish port of the thirteenth century into an impoverished English garrison town. By the late sixteenth century, Berwick's fortifications were in a dreadful state and Elizabeth I, fearing the resurgent alliance between France and Scotland, had the place rebuilt in line with the latest principles of military architecture. Berwick was reborn as an important seaport between 1750 and 1820, and is still peppered with elegant Georgian mansions dating from that period. Look out for panels that mark the Lowry Trail; L.S. Lowry (1887–1976) was a regular visitor to Berwick and his sketches and paintings of local landmarks are dotted about town.

Berwick's walls – one and a half miles long and still in pristine condition – are now the town's major attraction. No more than 20ft high but incredibly thick, the Elizabethan town walls are protected by ditches on three sides and the Tweed on the fourth, and strengthened by immense bastions. It's possible to walk a mile-long circuit (45min) around Berwick, and to take in wonderful views out to sea, across the Tweed and over the orange-tiled rooftops of the town.

Barracks and Main Guard

MAP P.72
Parade, Berwick-upon-Tweed TD15. ⓘ **Berwick-upon-Tweed.** ⓦ **english-heritage. org.uk. April–Sept Mon–Fri 10am–6pm, Oct 10am–4pm; charge.**

The town's finely proportioned Barracks, designed by Nicholas Hawksmoor (1717) functioned as a garrison until 1964, when the King's Own Scottish Borderers regiment decamped. Inside there's the By the Beat of the Drum exhibition, tracing the lives of British infantrymen from the Civil War to World War I, as well as the King's Own Scottish Borderers Museum and the Berwick Museum and Art Gallery, which has a collection of works donated by Sir William Burrell. In 2021, the buildings hosted an art installation by British artist Tim Etchells. At the time of writing, plans were afoot to expand the Barracks into a cultural centre, relocating the Berwick Archives here and providing studio space for local artists.

Berwick-upon-Tweed

Barter Books

Shops

A Taste of Northumbria

MAP P.72

6 Market Pl, Alnwick NE66. Ⓦ facebook.
com/tasteofnorthumbria.

In the likely scenario that you
develop a taste for some local produce
during your time in Northumbria,
this fantastic shop stocks a wide-
ranging selection of items from
Northeast producers. In addition to
traditional Holy Island mead there's
the rather more modish Lindisfarne
pink gin, alongside a choice of beers,
chutneys, honey and more.

Barter Books

MAP P.72

Alnwick Station, NE66. Ⓑ Alnwick.
Ⓦ barterbooks.co.uk.

Housed in the Victorian train
station on Wagonway Road, and
containing visible remnants of the
ticket office, passenger waiting
rooms and the outbound platform,
the enchanting Barter Books is
one of the largest secondhand
bookshops in England. With its
sofas, murals, open fire, coffee and
biscuits – and, best of all, a model

train that runs on top of the stacks
– it is definitely worth a visit.

Celtic Crafts

MAP P.72

Front St, Holy Island TD15. Ⓦ facebook.
com/1celticcrafts.

An eclectic emporium of anything
and everything Celtic, from golden
pendants of St Cuthbert's Cross
to pewter tankards and drinking
horns. Also on sale are tea towels
bearing maps of St Cuthbert's Way,
a long-distance hiking trail between
Melrose in the Scottish borders
and Lindisfarne, which may inspire
budding hikers.

The Old School Gallery

MAP P.72

Foxton Rd, Alnmouth NE66. Ⓣ Alnmouth.
Ⓦ theoldschoolgallery.co.uk.

An unexpected hive of creativity
in the sleepy coastal village of
Alnmouth, this lovely gallery-
café showcases the work of local
and British artists, often with a
preference for those whose work is
inspired by nature. There's a wide
range of artworks, prints, mugs and
homewares to buy, and coffee and
cake are also available.

Slightly Foxed

MAP P.72

31 Bridge St, Berwick-upon-Tweed
TD15. Ⓣ Berwick-upon-Tweed.
Ⓦ slightlyfoxedberwick.co.uk.

This secondhand indie bookshop is
a warren-like place, with the smell
of old books hanging in the air and
the constant sense that you might
be about to discover an obscure
jewel. The proprietors Lisa and
Claire are very knowledgeable and
will talk you through the selection
of books, antique movie posters,
and prints by L.S. Lowry, who
regularly painted Berwick.

St Aidan's Winery

MAP P.72

Holy Island TD15. Ⓦ lindisfarnemead.com.
Despite the name, it's not wine as
you may know it which is produced

at this historic establishment on Holy Island, but rather Lindisfarne mead. This sweet liquor of fermented honey – which can range from 3.5% to upwards of 18% ABV – has been made on Lindisfarne since the first monks arrived in the 7th century, but this company has been producing it, to ancient recipes, since the 1950s.

Cafés

Copper Kettle

MAP P.72
21 Front St, Bambugh NE69. ⓑ Bamburgh. ⓦ copperkettlebamburgh.co.uk.

Sweet little tearoom, with a sunny sitting area out the back, serving tasty cakes, teas and coffees – try the fruit loaf or the tempting carrot cake with icing. Simple meals such as sandwiches, jacket potatoes and pies are also on offer. The owner Annabel is extremely friendly, and the afternoon teas are legendary. **£**

The Maltings

MAP P.72
Eastern Ln, Berwick-upon-Twood. ⓣ Berwick-upon-Tweed.

ⓦ maltingsberwick.co.uk.

Berwick's buzzing arts centre, The Maltings, hosts an ever-changing and eclectic round-up of music, theatre, comedy, film and dance, and this licensed café is the perfect place to come before or after catching a performance. Highlights include crayfish salad and Cullen skink (a hearty Scottish soup), and the river views are some of the best in Berwick. **££**

Origami Café

MAP P.72
5 Narrowgate, Alnwick NE661. ⓑ Alnwick. ⓦ facebook.com/theorigamicafe.

With origami cranes and flowers decorating every spare surface, there's an air of care and calm about this cosy café. Friendly owner Judy serves up a wide range of biscuits, cakes, and sweets, with at least one vegan option every day; there's also some pretty extravagant milkshakes on the menu, including imaginative creations like green tea and strawberry shortcake shakes. **£–££**

Rocking Horse Courtyard and Café

MAP P.72

THE NORTHUMBERLAND COAST

A Taste of Northumbria on Market Place in Alnwick

Farm Rock, Midstead, Alnwick NE66. Ⓑ Alnwick. Ⓦ therocky.co.uk.

Much-loved café and art shop which, with its oak beams, comfy sofas and wooden farmhouse tables and chairs, feels rather like you're stepping into someone's living room. Actually it sits in an old dairy (with some overspill into the farmhouse) and serves lovely breakfast stotties, tea and scones, jacket potatoes, lasagne and more. Homewares and photography are also on sale. **£–£££**

Scott's

MAP P.72
15–16 Northumberland St, Alnmouth NE66. Ⓦ scottsofalnmouth.com.

If you're on the lookout for ingredients for a picnic – perhaps to enjoy on the beach or midway through a coast path walk – look no further than this lovely Alnmouth deli. The coffees, cakes and sausage rolls are all justly famous hereabouts, and the *pasteis de nata* come in for particularly high praise. Bacon butties, pizza and healthier salads are also available. **££–£££**

Station Buffet

MAP P.72

Alnwick Garden Treehouse

Alnwick Station NE66. Ⓑ Alnwick. Ⓦ barterbooks.co.uk.

Set in the old station waiting room at Barter Books, this unique café serves home-made food including cooked breakfasts (from 9–11.30am), hamburgers, sandwiches, salads and cakes. Particularly recommended is the hot roast beef sandwich, served with onion gravy and thrice-cooked chips. A thoroughly British experience, and a lovely place to get stuck into your purchases from the bookshop. **£**

Restaurants

Alnwick Garden Treehouse

MAP P.72
Alnwick Castle, NE66. Ⓦ alnwickgarden.com.

Glorious restaurant in the enormous treehouse in Alnwick Gardens (you don't have to pay the garden entry fee to visit). There's an open fire in the middle of the room and even tree trunks growing through the floor. A set menu is available at lunch and dinner with lots of local produce cooked to perfection (mains include English rack of

lamb or stuffed field mushrooms).
Booking essential. **££–£££**

Audela

MAP P.72
64 Bridge St, Berwick-upon-Tweed. ☎
Berwick-upon Tweed. 🌐 audela.co.uk.
This fancy restaurant is one of
the finest in Berwick, serving
"contemporary British" cuisine
which showcases the bounty of
fresh produce which comes out of
Northumberland and the Scottish
Borders. The menu is small, but
everything is exquisitely presented
and prepared: try wild mushroom
bourguignon with pearl barley,
braised beef shin with pickled
cabbage and horseradish, or
monkfish with potato terrine and a
mussel sauce. **£££–££££**

Jolly Fisherman

MAP P.72
9 Haven Hill Craster, NE66. 🚌 Craster.
🌐 thejollyfishermancraster.co.uk.
Sitting prettily just above the
harbour, this pub has sea views
from its back window and a
lovely summer beer garden. Not
surprisingly for a pub opposite
kipper purveyors L. Robson &
Sons, it serves plenty of fish – crab
sandwiches, kipper pâté and a
famously good crab meat, whisky
and cream soup. The fish board
– with both smoked and cooked
salmon, pickled herring, kippers,
crab sandwiches and more – is justly
legendary, and the best way to get
an introduction to the menu. **£££**

Piper's Pitch

MAP P.72
Craster Quarry Car Park NE66. 🚌 Craster.
🌐 piperspitch.com.
This extremely popular food stall
sits right beside Craster's tourist
information centre and opposite
Dunstanburgh Heughs nature
reserve. Alongside mugs of coffee and
tea and simple but hearty burgers and
bacon sandwiches, it offers traditional
dishes including Craster kippers in a
bun, and the Scottish Auchtermuchty

The Potted Lobster

(haggis, bacon and spicy chutney)
and Lorne sausage, also Scottish,
made of minced meat. **£**

The Potted Lobster

MAP P.72
3 Lucker Rd, Bam,burgh NE69. 🚌
Bamburgh. 🌐 pottedlobster.co.uk.
Among the coast's finest seafood
restaurants, there is nevertheless a
relaxed air about *The Potted Lobster*,
whose wood-panelled exterior is
adorned with nautical trinkets.
Menu highlights include chalk
stream smoked trout, Shetland
mussels, and the potted lobster
of the name, while the sirloin of
Northumbrian beef also comes
highly recommended. **£££**

The Ship Inn

MAP P.72
Low Newton-by-the-Sea, Alnwick NE66. 🚌
Alnwick. 🌐 shipinnnewton.co.uk.
Great country pub in a coastal
hamlet serving dishes using
ingredients from local suppliers –
there's plenty of L. Robson smoked
fish on the menu. Mains are
good value, and ales are supplied
by their own brewery next door.
The stone walls are warmed by a

Alnmouth

crackling log fire, and there's often live folk music; the kind of place rural England does so well, where it's easy to nestle in and slip into a rustic reverie. Dinner reservations essential in the evening. **££**

The Stable Yard

MAP P.72
Craster Tower NE66. Ⓑ Craster.
Ⓦ thestableyardcraster.co.uk.
Housed in the historic Craster Tower (actually an eighteenth-century Georgian mansion home to a modest pele tower), *The Stable Yard* serves classic sandwiches, like ham and mustard, crab, and bacon, brie and caramelized onion chutney; superb home-made soup and sausage rolls; and some lovely cakes and scones to accompany a cup of tea, coffee or hot chocolate. **£**

Bars

Barrels Alehouse

MAP P.72
59–61 Bridge St, Berwick-upon-Tweed.
Ⓣ Berwick-upon-Tweed. Ⓣ 01289 308013.
Atmospheric pub specializing in (frequently changing) cask ales, lagers and stouts, a selection for which it has won awards from the beloved and esteemed organization CAMRA (Campaign for Real Ales). It's also a great music venue, hosting an eclectic mix of jazz, blues, rock and indie bands. **££**

Crown and Anchor

MAP P.72
Market Place, Holy Island TD15.
Ⓦ holyislandcrown.co.uk.
A holy island it may be, but there is no shortage of places to indulge in the demon drink on Lindisfarne. The *Crown and Anchor* sits on the Market Place and offers a range of cask ales, a solid menu of pub food, and a beer garden overlooking the priory. When the weather doesn't quite facilitate a drink in the garden (i.e., most of the time), the interior is lovely, cosy and traditional. **££**

The Curfew

MAP P.72
46A Bridge St, Berwick-upon-Tweed.
Ⓣ Berwick-upon-Tweed. Ⓦ facebook.com/
curfewmicropub.

One of Berwick's best-loved bars, this micropub is a must-visit for beer lovers. Four rotating cask beers are on offer, as well as three ciders and a wide selection of world beers, from light blondes to rich porters. The staff are passionate about beer and very friendly, and will happily advise on the best options. Traditional snacks, like pork pies and scotch eggs, are the perfect accompaniment to your drinks.

The Dirty Bottles

MAP P.72

32 Narrowgate, Alnwick NE661. ⓑ Alnwick. ⓦ thedirtybottles.co.uk.

Far from dirty, this lovely pub actually doubles as a rather fancy four-star hotel. The building is some 400 years old, and a pub has stood here for around half that time – it's still a free house, meaning it's not tied to any brewery, and showcases Northumberland's finest beers. The roof terrace overlooking Alnwick Castle is a particularly special place for a pint. Good pub food – burgers, kebabs, and steaks included – is also on offer. **££–£££**

The Red Lion

MAP P.72

22 Northumberland St, Alnmouth NE66. ⓣ Alnmouth. ⓦ redlionalnmouth.com.

Offering food and board to weary wayfarers since the eighteenth century, this half-timbered black-and-white building originated as a coaching inn, and hasn't changed much in the intervening centuries. A beer garden overlooks the Alnmouth estuary, and is a lovely spot on a warm day; the rest of the time, nestle into the lovely wood-panelled pub, perhaps by the toasty fire, and enjoy a Northumberland ale or a glass of wine. **££**

The Ship Inn

MAP P.72

Marygate, Holy Island TD15. ⓦ theshipinn-holyisland.co.uk.

This pub on Holy Island is friendly and traditional, with open fires and wood-panelled walls. The ales are good, as is the inexpensive pub grub. They have four cosy, en-suite rooms upstairs. Sitting near the harbour at Marygate, the pub is perfectly placed for exploring the castle and priory, and the beer garden has lovely island views (when the weather allows). **££**

THE NORTHUMBERLAND COAST

The Dirty Bottles

The Northumberland interior

The bulk of the Northeast – and, for the purposes of this book, Northumbria – is formed by the remote and beautiful county of Northumberland, an enticing medley of delightful market towns, glorious golden beaches, wooded dells, wild uplands and an unsurpassed collection of historical monuments. Indeed, it's here you'll find Britain's best and most concentrated collection of Roman ruins, including the iconic remains of Hadrian's Wall – which only adds to the frontier, edge-of-the-world atmosphere. It's criminally overlooked by most visitors to the UK and even by Brits themselves, but when it means you have more of this glorious county to yourself, you might be quite glad of that.

Hexham Abbey

MAP P.86
Beaumont St, Hexham NE46. ⓦ hexhamabbey.
org.uk. Daily 10am–4pm; free.

Hexham is the only significant stop between Newcastle and Carlisle, and however keen you are on seeing the Wall, you'd do well to spend a night at this handsome market town – or even make it your base. The focal point is the abbey, whose

Hexham Abbey

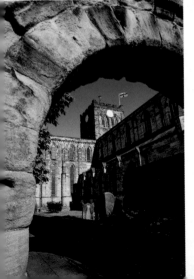

foundations were originally part of a fine Benedictine monastery founded by St Wilfrid in 671. Claimed, according to contemporaneous accounts, to be the finest this side of the Alps, the church – or rather its gold and silver – proved irresistible to the Vikings, who savaged the place in 876. It was rebuilt in the eleventh century as part of an Augustinian priory, and the town grew up in its shadow. The stately exterior of the abbey dominates the west side of the central marketplace. Entry is through the south transept, where there's a bruised but impressive first-century tombstone honouring Flavinus, a standard-bearer in the Roman cavalry, who's shown riding down his bearded enemy. The memorial lies at the foot of the broad, well-worn steps of the canons' night stair, one of the few such staircases – providing access from the monastery to the church – to have survived the Dissolution. The chancel, meanwhile, displays the inconsequential-looking frith-stool, an eighth-century stone chair that was once believed to have been used by St Wilfrid.

Hexham Old Gaol

MAP P.86
Hallgate, Hexham NE46.

museumsnorthumberland.org.uk/
hexham-old-gaol. Feb, March & Oct Tues
& Sat 11am–4.30pm; April–Sept Tues–Sat
11am–4.30pm.

Britain's first purpose-built prison,
Hexham Old Gaol occupies a solid
sandstone building to the east of
the abbey. It was commissioned by
the powerful Archbishop of York
in 1330, and constructed using
stone plundered from the Roman
ruins at Corbridge. Inside there's
an entertaining museum extolling
the virtues and pitfalls of medieval
crime and punishment (it was
no bed of roses, without wishing
to spoil any surprises). Many of
the prison's regular residents were
'border reivers', raiders on the
English-Scottish frontier who
could be of either nationality, and
whose victim profile similarly knew
no borders – if you were unlucky
enough to come across them,
they would steal your cattle, your
belongings, and maybe even you, if
you looked like a valuable prisoner.

Hadrian's Wall

MAP P.86

hadrianswallcountry.co.uk.

Hadrian's Wall was constructed in
122 AD at the behest of the Roman
emperor Hadrian. Keen for peace
and safety within his empire, fearing
attacks from Pictish Scotland,
Hadrian commissioned a long wall
to act as a border, snaking its way
from the Tyne to the Solway Firth.
It was built up to a height of 15ft
in places and was interspersed by
milecastles, which functioned as
gates, depots and mini-barracks. The
Wall far transcends the boundaries
of this book, but its best-preserved
portions are concentrated in
Northumberland, between Chesters
Roman Fort, four miles north
of Hexham, and Haltwhistle,
sixteen miles to the west, which
passes Housesteads Roman Fort,
Vindolanda and the Roman Army
Museum. Most people come to walk
or cycle the length of the Wall, but if
you're only planning to walk a short

Hadrian's Wall at Walltown Crags

stretch, start off at Housesteads
and head west for sweeping views.
There are plenty of interesting places
to stay and eat around and along
the Wall, including the handsome
market town of Hexham.

Chesters Roman Fort

MAP P.86

4 miles north of Hexham NE46. www.
english-heritage.org.uk April–Sept daily
10am–6pm; Oct & Nov daily 10am–5pm;
Nov–April Sat & Sun 10am–4pm; charge.
Beautifully sited next to the
gurgling River Tyne, Chesters
Roman Fort, otherwise known as
Cilurnum, was built to guard the
Roman bridge over the Tyne. With a
history dating back to 123 AD, the
fort is thought to have been built
shortly after the Wall itself. Enough
remains of the original structure to
pick out the design of the fort, but
the highlight is down by the river
where the vestibule, changing room
and steam range of the garrison's
bathhouse are still visible, along
with the furnace and the latrines.

Housesteads

MAP P.86

Around 8 miles west of Chesters NE47.

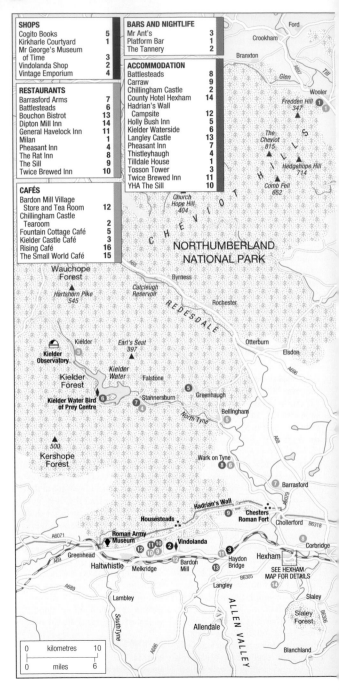

SHOPS

Cogito Books	5
Kirkharle Courtyard	1
Mr George's Museum of Time	3
Vindolanda Shop	2
Vintage Emporium	4

RESTAURANTS

Barrasford Arms	7
Battlesteads	6
Bouchon Bistrot	13
Dipton Mill Inn	14
General Havelock Inn	11
Milan	1
Pheasant Inn	4
The Rat Inn	8
The Sill	9
Twice Brewed Inn	10

CAFÉS

Bardon Mill Village Store and Tea Room	12
Chillingham Castle Tearoom	2
Fountain Cottage Café	5
Kielder Castle Café	3
Rising Café	16
The Small World Café	15

BARS AND NIGHTLIFE

Mr Ant's	3
Platform Bar	1
The Tannery	2

ACCOMMODATION

Battlesteads	8
Carraw	9
Chillingham Castle	2
County Hotel Hexham	14
Hadrian's Wall Campsite	12
Holly Bush Inn	5
Kielder Waterside	6
Langley Castle	13
Pheasant Inn	7
Thistleyhaugh	4
Tilldale House	1
Tosson Tower	3
Twice Brewed Inn	11
YHA The Sill	10

The Northumberland interior

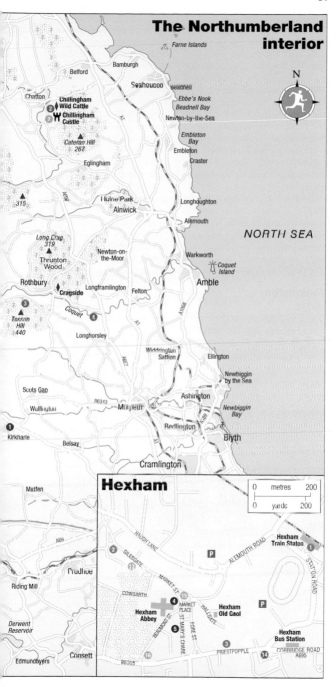

Hexham

Ⓦ www.english-heritage.org.uk. Daily 10am–4pm; charge.

Housesteads Roman Fort is one of the most popular sites on the Wall. The fort is of standard design but for one enforced modification – forts were supposed to straddle the line of the Wall, but here the original stonework follows the edge of the cliff, so Housesteads was built on the steeply sloping ridge to the south. Enter via the tiny museum, and walk across to the south gate; next to this lies the ruins of a garrison of up to one thousand infantrymen. It's not necessary to pay for entrance to the fort if you're simply walking along the Wall west from here; the three-mile hike takes in wonderful views as it meanders past Crag Lough and over to Steel Rigg (which has a car park).

Vindolanda

MAP P.86
13 miles west of Hexham NE47.
Ⓦ vindolanda.com. Daily mid-Feb to late March & Oct 10am–5pm; April–Sept 10am–6pm; Nov & Dec 10am–4pm; charge.

The garrison fort of Vindolanda is believed to have been built and occupied before the construction of the Wall itself. Guarding the important central section of the east–west supply route across Britain, a series of early forts in this location were built of timber, eventually replaced with a stone construction during Hadrian's reign. Preserved beneath the remains of the stone fortress, these early forts are now being excavated – around three to four hundred volunteers take part every day. The museum contains the largest collection of Roman leather items ever discovered on a single site – sandals, purses, an archer's thumb guard – and a fascinating series of writing tablets dating to 90 AD. The earliest written records found in Britain, they feature shopping lists, duty rotas and even a birthday party invitation from one Claudia Severa to Sulpicia Lepidina. The Roman Army Museum (additional charge) aims to illustrate how the Roman soldiers stationed here lived. There's everything from armour and weapons – including javelins, shields and swords – to a full-size chariot and a wagon. It's all very entertaining, and successfully brings to life the ruins you may just have seen at Vindolanda.

Ruins at Vindolanda

Roman Army Museum

MAP P.86

20 miles west of Hexham CA8.
Ⓦ vindolanda.com. Daily mid-Feb to
late March & Oct 10am–5pm; April–Sept
10am–6pm; Nov & Dec 10am–4pm; charge.
The Roman Army Museum aims
to illustrate how the Roman
soldiers stationed here lived. There's
everything from armour and
weapons – including javelins, shields
and swords – to a full-size chariot
and a wagon. As ever, though, the
most affecting pieces are the small,
personal effects: the silver brooches,
archers' thumb guards, and other
day-to-day items. Requiring less use
of the imagination, but good fun
nevertheless, is an immersive 3D film,
'Edge of Empire', which recreates life
for the soldiers stationed along the
Wall. It's all very entertaining, and
successfully brings to life the ruins you
may just have seen at Vindolanda.

Northumberland National Park

MAP P.86

Ⓦ northumberlandnationalpark.org.uk.
Northwest Northumberland,
the great triangular chunk of
land between Hadrian's Wall and
the coastal plain, is dominated
by the wide-skied landscapes of
Northumberland National Park,
whose four hundred windswept
square miles rise to the Cheviot Hills
on the Scottish border. The bulk
of the park is taken up by Kielder
Water and Forest nature reserve, a
superb destination for watersports
and outdoor activities; the small
town of Bellingham on the eastern
edge of the park makes a good base
for the reserve, as do Rothbury and
Wooler, both of which also provide
easy access to some superb walking
in the craggy Cheviots.

Kielder Water and Forest

MAP P.86

Ⓦ visitkielder.com.
Surrounded by 250 acres of dense
pine forest, Kielder Water and
Forest is the largest reservoir in
England; the mass of woodlands
and wetlands means that wildlife
is abundant – you might spot
badgers, deer, otters, ospreys
and red squirrels. The road from
Bellingham follows the North
Tyne River west and skirts the
forested edge of the lake, passing
an assortment of visitor centres,
waterside parks, picnic areas and
anchorages that fringe its southern
shore. Mountain biking, hiking,
horseriding and fishing are some
of the land-based activities on
offer, and of course watersports
(waterskiing, sailing, kayaking and
windsurfing) are hugely popular,
too. The skies here are some of the
darkest in Europe and star-gazing
can be magical; award-winning
Kielder Observatory (see below)
hosts over forty night-time events a
month (booking essential). Kielder
Waterside, on the western flank of
the reservoir, is the best place to
head if you're visiting for the first
time and need to get your bearings.

Kielder Observatory

MAP P.86

Black Fell, Kielder. Ⓦ kielderobservatory.
org.uk. Events only; book online.

Kielder Water

Kielder Observatory

An estimated 85% of the UK population has never gazed into a truly dark night sky, according to the Northumberland International Dark Sky Park. This is the largest protected dark sky park in Europe, and boasts the darkest, most pristine night skies in Britain. The best place to observe them is the gorgeous Kielder Observatory, a marriage of the earthy and the space-age which rises in clean lines of spruce and larch above the fells and forests of the national park. With stargazing and introduction to astronomy nights held every day of the week, this is an unbeatable place to get an introduction to the beauty of Britain's night skies.

Kielder Water Birds of Prey Centre

MAP P.86

Leaplish Waterside Park, Kielder. W kielderbopc.com. April–Oct daily 10.30am–4pm, Nov–March daily 10am–3pm; charge.

Anyone with an interest in things avian will flock to Kielder Water's Birds of Prey Centre, home to one of northern England's largest collections of birds. It includes

some 70 magnificent creatures, with falcons, eagles, hawks and owls among them. The centre's stated aim is to encourage awareness of the importance of conservation through education, particularly of young people – experiences at the centre include courses in bird management for prospective owners, and hawk walks, which see you walk through the countryside as a raptor hovers above and occasionally swoops down to take some food from your fist.

Wallington

MAP P.86

13 miles south of Rothbury NE61. W nationaltrust.org.uk/wallington. Hours vary widely through the year, check online; charge.

South of Rothbury, down the B6342, stands Wallington, an ostentatious mansion rebuilt in the 1740s by Sir Walter Blackett, the coal- and lead-mine owner. The house is known for its Rococo plasterwork and William Bell Scott's Pre-Raphaelite murals of scenes from Northumbrian history. Children will love the collection of doll's houses, one of which has thirty-six rooms and was originally fitted with running water and a working lift. However, it's the magnificent gardens and grounds that are the real delight, with lawns, woods and lakes laced with footpaths. There are events, concerts and activities throughout the year, as well as a café and farm shop on site.

Cragside

MAP P.86

Nr Rothbury NE65. W nationaltrust. org.uk/cragside. House March–Oct daily 11am–4pm, Nov–Feb Sat & Sun 11am–4pm, gardens and woodland March–Oct daily 10am–5pm, Nov–Feb daily 11am–5pm; charge.

Victorian Rothbury was dominated by Sir William, later the first Lord Armstrong, the wealthy nineteenth-century arms manufacturer, shipbuilder and engineer who built his country home at Cragside, a mile to the east of the village. He hired Richard Norman Shaw, one of the period's top architects, who produced a grandiose Tudor-style mansion entirely out of place in the Northumbrian countryside. Armstrong was an avid innovator, and in 1880 Cragside became the first house in the world to be lit by hydroelectric power. The surrounding gardens, complete with the remains of the original pumping system, are beautiful, and there's a pleasant tearoom for a light snack.

Chillingham Castle

MAP P.86

6 miles southeast of Wooler NE66.
ⓦ chillingham-castle.com. Easter–Oct daily 11am–5pm; charge.

Chillingham Castle started life as an eleventh-century tower. The castle was augmented at regular intervals until the nineteenth century, but from 1933 was largely left to the elements for fifty years, until the present owner set about restoring it in his own individualistic way: bedrooms, living rooms and even a grisly torture chamber (designed to "cause maximum shock") are decorated with historical paraphernalia. It describes itself as Britain's most haunted castle, with babbling voices heard in the chapel, a frail figure said to approach people in the old pantry begging for water, and a lady who emerges from her own portrait. Perhaps the most unsettling, though, is the story of the Blue Boy, long said to haunt the Pink Room after being buried alive in its walls – just another myth, everyone thought, until workmen excavating the room found the remains of a boy in the wall in the 1920s.

Chillingham Wild Cattle

MAP P.86

Next door to Chillingham Castle NE66.
ⓦ chillinghamwildcattle.com. Visitor centre daily 9.30am–2pm; book cattle tours online; charge.

In 1220, Chillingham Castle's adjoining 365 acres of parkland were enclosed to protect the local wild cattle for hunting and food. And so the Chillingham wild cattle – a fierce, primeval herd with white coats, black muzzles and black tips to their horns – have remained to this day, cut off from mixing with domesticated breeds. The herd's isolation and inbred nature has had the unusual effect of strengthening, rather than weakening, their genetic resilience, by purging the gene pool of harmful mutations – a kind of hereditary herd immunity. This goes against everything scientists usually observe with inbreeding, and may even be unique in the animal kingdom. It's possible to visit these unique relicts, who number around one hundred, but only in the company of a warden, as the animals are potentially dangerous, and also need to be protected from outside infection. The visit takes about two hours and involves a short country walk before viewing the cattle at a safe distance – the closest you're likely to get to big game viewing in England. Bring strong shoes, or walking boots if it's wet.

Cragside

Shops

Cogito Books

MAP P.86

5 St Mary's Chare, Hexham NE46. ⊙ Hexham. ⓦ cogitobooks.com.

If you run out of reading material while on the road, you could do a lot worse than ducking into this independent bookshop, where an intellectual atmosphere abounds and the shelves are stocked with everything from children's classics to philosophical treatises. You'll also find the ultimate mark of quality: a good range of Rough Guides titles.

Kirkharle Courtyard

MAP P.86

Courtyard, Kirkharle. ⓦ kirkharlecourtyard. co.uk.

Worth a stop off on the way from Newcastle to Kielder, the tiny hamlet of Kirkharle sits around 11 miles east of Bellingham. This 18th-century courtyard has been repurposed into a little craft centre with outlets selling pottery, glassware, handcrafted furniture, and more. There's also cream teas and light bites at a modest café.

Shopping on Market Street in Hexham

Mr George's Museum of Time

MAP P.86

2 Ratcliffe Rd, Haydon Bridge NE47. ⓦ timeforgeorge.com.

A rather unexpected find in the village of Haydon Bridge is this gift shop, workshop and watch museum run by local watch and clock repairer, the aptly named Diana Bell ('Mr George' is also the name of a series of children's books she has written). The museum contains beautiful pieces ranging from elaborate cuckoo clocks to tiny pocket watches, and at the gift shop you can pick up a cuckoo clock, weather house, or just a candle or decorative box.

Vindolanda Shop

MAP P.86

13 miles west of Hexham NE47. ⓦ vindolanda.com.

While you may not be able to literally take a piece of Roman Britain home with you (the Vindolanda Trust might have a thing or two to say about that) you can certainly pick up a memento at the fort's well-stocked shop. Items include a replica brooch of a duck, which in ancient times was a symbol of honesty and simplicity; an umbrella emblazoned with a Roman shield; and, for history buffs, research reports which dig into Vindolanda's history.

Vintage Emporium

MAP P.86

20a Market Place, Hexham NE46. ⊙ Hexham. ⓦ thevintageemporuimhexham. business.site.

All sorts of odds and ends, from vinyl records both classic and obscure to tea sets and carafes, handbags and floral shirts, are on offer at this pleasingly bohemian secondhand shop in Hexham Market Place. The building fits the brief perfectly, all quirky furniture, checkerboard tiling and creaky stairs, which house three floors of miscellany.

Cafés

Bardon Mill Village Store and Tea Room

MAP P.86

Henshaw, Bardon Mill NE47. ⊕ Bardon Mill. ☎ 07756 790108.

This charming red-brick corner building in Bardon Mill, just a mile south of Vindolanda, serves as the village shop but also is a lovely café serving tea, coffee, confectionary and cakes. More substantial offerings, such as toasted sandwiches, are also available, and the welcome is always very friendly and accommodating. **£**

Chillingham Castle Tearoom

MAP P.86

6 miles southeast of Wooler NE66. ⓦ chillingham-castle.com.

Having toured the grisly torture chamber and, perhaps, spent a sleepless night being kept up by the castle's resident ghosts, Chillingham's lovely tearoom is just the place to take the edge off. The stone walls and roaring log fire are authentically medieval, and the

sandwiches, cakes, tea and coffee all good. **£**

Fountain Cottage Café

MAP P.86

Fountain Cottage, Bellingham NE48. ⓦ fountain-cottage.com.

The attractive village of Bellingham is a great place to overnight when you're exploring nearby Kielder Forest and Water. This lovely B&B is one of the best places to stay, but also has a great café, where the 'Full Monty' breakfast ('Half Monty' also available for the less adventurous) goes down well at any time of day, along with paninis, toasties, soups, burgers and jacket potatoes. **£**

Kielder Castle Café

MAP P.86

Kielder Forest Park NE48. ⓦ visitkielder.com.

Housed within the elegant Kielder Castle – formerly a hunting lodge, built for the Duke of Northumberland in 1775 – this café was due to reopen, along with the castle itself, in 2022 after extensive renovations. A lovely place for a cup of tea and a slice of cake overlooking Kielder's Forest Drive – you may even spot a red squirrel. **£**

Chillingham Castle

Rising Café

MAP P.86

Central Chambers, Beaumont St, Hexham NE46. ❶ Hexham. Ⓦ risingcafe.co.uk.
In the shadow of Hexham's mighty monument to Boer War hero Colonel Benson, this is a lovely café focused on a good cause: all profits go towards the Betel Charity, which supports people with drug and alcohol addictions. The café has a trad feel, with fringed lampshades and bunting, and the food varies from cottage pie to Texan barbecue toasties. £

The Small World Café

MAP P.86

27 Market Place, Hexham NE46. ❶ Hexham. Ⓦ thesmallworldcafe.com.
This cosy, wholesome café does indeed feel like a little world of its own, nestled away on Hexham's market place a stone's throw from the abbey. Family run and committed to the use of fresh, seasonal, local ingredients, the café serves all the classics, from all-day breakfasts, pastries and bacon butties to home-made soup, curries, and beans on

General Havelock Inn

toast – just the thing on a chilly Northumbrian afternoon. £

Restaurants

Barrasford Arms

MAP P.86

Barrasford NE48. Ⓦ barrasfordarms.co.uk.
Endearingly local, welcoming and homely, this country pub serves great traditional British food with a French twist; dishes could include pan-roasted lamb rump with creamy mash, wilted spinach, onion gravy and onion rings and for pudding, sticky toffee pudding with butterscotch sauce. Booking advisable. ££–£££

Battlesteads

MAP P.86

Wark NE48. Ⓦ battlesteads.com.
In a charming little village by a trickling stream, this unique hotel (see page 121) is also home to an observatory and a locally renowned restaurant with a lovely beer garden, which uses fresh produce sourced from within a 30-mile radius. Leave room for their famed whisky and marmalade bread-and-butter pudding. Best to book. ££–£££

Bouchon Bistrot

MAP P.86

4–6 Gilesgate Hexham NE46. Ⓦ bouchonbistrot.co.uk.
Very stylish restaurant in a handsome terraced townhouse, serving sophisticated French dishes such as crispy duck confit with gratin potatoes, French onion soup, and crème brûlée. The seafood dishes are particularly good, as tends to be the case in this part of the world – try the sea trout tartare. ££–£££

Dipton Mill Inn

MAP P.86

Dipton Mill Rd, near Hexham NE46. Ⓦ diptonmill.co.uk.
A lovely, traditional country pub, two miles south of Hexham and

smothered in ivy. While the food is excellent — good pub grub like steak and kidney pie and vegetable casserole — it's most famous for the home-brewed ales, made at Hexhamshire Brewery. Try Old Humbug, named after the landlord. **££**

General Havelock Inn

MAP P.86

9 Ratcliffe Rd, Haydon Bridge NE47. Ⓦ facebook.com/TheGeneralHavelock.
Eighteenth-century inn that specializes in tasty Modern British food, from crab cakes and Cumberland sausages to chocolate brûlée and ice-cream sundaes. Great locally brewed ales on offer, too. The pub sits in the village of Haydon Bridge (its black exterior means you can't miss it) and is perfectly placed for Housesteads and Vindolanda. **££**

Milan

MAP P.86

2 High St, Wooler NE71. Ⓣ 01668 283692.
Amid Northumberland's cornucopia of lovely country pubs, sometimes you'll want something a little different. Enter: this good-value Italian restaurant, with exposed brick walls and a jolly ambience, serving large pizzas, pasta dishes, and plenty of meat and fish options. It's just the place to get in a carb-loading meal ahead of a day's hiking, or to put your feet up with a glass of wine after your exertions. It's a very popular place, so book ahead. **££**

Pheasant Inn

MAP P.86

Stannersburn NE48. Ⓦ thepheasantinn.com.
A traditional country pub on the road from Bellingham, the *Pheasant Inn* has very comfortable bedrooms, but the highlight is the food, served downstairs in the cosy, candlelit restaurant; expect game pies, Northumbrian cheeses and plenty of fish. Booking recommended. **££–£££**

The Rat Inn

MAP P.86

Oakwood, Anick NE46. Ⓦ theratinn.com.
In a glorious hillside location overlooking Hexham, this quaint pub has a roaring fire in winter and a pretty summer garden. The food is all locally sourced — try the braised local beef in Allendale beer. Booking is essential for Sunday lunch, and advisable at other peak times. **££**

The Sill

MAP P.86

Once Brewed NE47. Ⓦ thesill.org.uk.
Like the Kielder Observatory (see page 89), *The Sill* is a wholly unexpected, angular and modern building which nevertheless blends into its surroundings thanks to its wooden construction. It houses museum exhibits about the wall and the surrounding landscape, a popular youth hostel (see page 122), and a café serving paninis, soup-and-sandwich deals, and other light bites. **£**

Twice Brewed Inn

MAP P.86

Once Brewed NE47. Ⓦ twicebrewedinn.co.uk.

View from The Sill

Its name a play on the surrounding village of Once Brewed (also known, confusingly, as Twice Brewed, after the inn), this pub is an institution for walkers on the Hadrian's Wall Path. In addition to brewing their own bitters and IPAs, they offer rooms and serve a menu of comforting pub grub, with steak and ale pie and juicy beef burgers figuring prominently. **££**

Bars and nightlife

Mr Ant's

MAP P.86

22 Priestpopple, Hexham NE46. ⊕ Hexham. ⓦ mrants.co.uk.

Northumberland isn't all cosy country pubs, as this friendly Hexham cocktail bar attests. There's live music of a Friday running the gamut from singer-songwriter to rock, and a food menu throughout the day featuring a range of sandwiches, paninis, and other light meals. It's at night, though, that the place really comes alive, with the speciality a wide range of cocktails: try the Moscow Mule or the White Russian. **££**

Platform Bar

MAP P.86

Hexham Railway Station, Hexham NE46. ⊕ Hexham. ⓦ facebook.com/platformbarhexham.

If you're getting the train to Hexham, take advantage of not having to get behind the wheel by having a few drinks at this unique train station bar, housed in the former ladies' waiting room. It's small and cosy, as you might expect, but has the feel of a traditional pub with its wooden benches and comfy bar stools. Local beers and a good selection of wines are available. **££**

The Tannery

MAP P.86

Gilesgate, Hexham NE46. ⊕ Hexham. ⓦ facebook.com/tannery.hexham.

One of the best places in town to catch live music (a not particularly crowded field, admittedly), *The Tannery* describes itself as Hexham's living room, and with its leather Chesterfield sofas, woodburning stove, and plush rugs, it's a fair claim. There's live music every weekend, and often throughout the week; other nights often see a pub quiz. **££**

View of the **Twice Brewed Inn** from the Hadrian's Wall path

Durham and around

The handsome city of Durham is best known for its beautiful Norman cathedral – there's a tremendous view of it as you approach the city by train from the south – and for its flourishing university, founded in 1832. Together, these form a little island of privilege in what's otherwise a moderately sized, working-class city. It's worth visiting for a couple of days – there are plenty of attractions, but it's more the overall atmosphere that captivates, enhanced by the omnipresent golden stone, slender bridges and the glint of the river. The heart of the city is the marketplace, flanked by the Guildhall and St Nicholas Church. The cathedral and church sit on a wooded peninsula to the west, while southwards stretch narrow streets lined with shops and cafés. The surrounding county, also called Durham, has shaken off its grimy reputation in recent years and recast itself as a thriving tourist area. The well-to-do market towns of Bishop Auckland and Barnard Castle make great day-trips from Durham, and there's plenty of excellent walking and cycling in the wilds of the two Pennine valleys, Teesdale and Weardale. You'll find some top class museums in the area, too, including Beamish, Locomotion and The Bowes Museum.

Durham Cathedral

MAP P.101

Station Approach, Durham DH1.
🚉 Durham. 🌐 durhamcathedral.co.uk.
Mon–Sat 10am–4pm, Sun noon–4pm; free except tower.

Durham's history revolves around its cathedral. Completed in just forty years, the cathedral was founded in 1093 to house the shrine of St Cuthbert, arguably the Northeast's most important and venerated saint. Soon after Cuthbert was laid to rest here, the bishops of Durham were granted extensive powers to control the troublesome northern marches of the Kingdom (a rabble of invading Picts from Scotland and revolting Norman earls, ruling as semi-independent Prince Bishops, with their own army, mint and courts of

Durham Cathedral and the River Wear

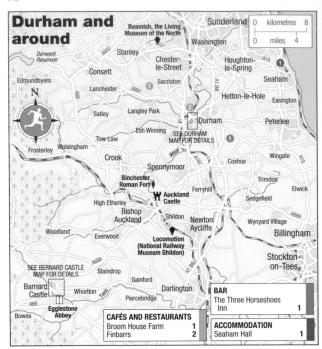

Durham and around

Derwent Reservoir

Edmundbyers

Consett

Stanley

Chester-le-Street

Sunderland

Washington

Beamish, the Living Museum of the North

Houghton-le-Spring

Lanchester

Sacriston

Seaham

Satley

Langley Park

Hetton-le-Hole

Easington

Esh Winning

Durham

SEE DURHAM MAP FOR DETAILS

Peterlee

Tow Law

Frosterley

Wolsingham

Crook

Spennymoor

Coxhoe

Wingate

Binchester Roman Fort

Auckland Castle

Ferryhill

Trimdon

Elwick

High Etherley

Bishop Auckland

Shildon

Sedgefield

Woodland

Everwood

Newton Aycliffe

Wynyard Village

Billingham

Locomotion (National Railway Museum Shildon)

Stockton-on-Tees

SEE BERNARD CASTLE MAP FOR DETAILS

Staindrop

Gainford

Darlington

Barnard Castle

Whorlton

Piercebridge

BAR
The Three Horseshoes Inn   1

Bowes

Egglestone Abbey

CAFÉS AND RESTAURANTS
Broom House Farm   1
Finbarrs   2

ACCOMMODATION
Seaham Hall   1

0   kilometres   8
0   miles   4

law. At the peak of their power in the fourteenth century, the office went into decline, especially in the wake of the Reformation), yet the bishops clung to the vestiges of their authority until 1836, when they ceded them to the Crown. The bishops abandoned Durham Castle for their palace in Bishop Auckland and transferred their old home to the fledgling Durham University, England's third-oldest

seat of learning after Oxford and Cambridge.

A large wooden doorway opposite the cathedral's main entrance leads into the spacious cloisters, which are flanked by the most intact set of medieval monastic buildings in the UK. These now house Open Treasure, a display exploring the history of Christianity in northeast England, which kicks off in the fourteenth-

St Cuthbert

Born in North Northumbria in 653, Cuthbert spent most of his youth in Melrose Abbey in Scotland, from where he moved briefly to Lindisfarne Island, which was at that time a well-known centre of religious endeavour. Preferring the peace and rugged solitude of the Farne Islands, he lived on Inner Farne for thirty years. News of his piety spread, however, and he was head-hunted to become Bishop of Lindisfarne, a position he accepted reluctantly. Uncomfortable in the limelight, he soon returned to Inner Farne, and when he died his remains were moved to Lindisfarne before being carted off to Durham Cathedral.

century Monks' Dormitory with its magnificent oak-beamed ceiling, where interactive displays evoke the sights, sounds and smells of life in a medieval monastery. The Collections Gallery showcases some of the most precious manuscripts from the cathedral's collections; while the spectacular Great Kitchen – one of only two surviving medieval monastic kitchens in the UK – is the setting for The Treasures of St Cuthbert, featuring beautifully preserved Anglo-Saxon artefacts.

Palace Green Library

MAP P.101

Palace Green, Durham DH1. ⊕ Durham. ⓦ dur.ac.uk/palace.green. Daily 10am–5pm; free.

Palace Green Library, between the cathedral and the castle, shows off a wonderful collection of the university's treasures, including medieval manuscripts and incunabula – early printed books. The library is divided into four separate galleries, two of which host permanent exhibitions that are free to view: the Museum of Archaeology Gallery, which showcases Durham's rich

prehistoric and Roman history; and the DLI Collection Gallery: Courage, Comrades, Community. The Durham Light Infantry (DLI) were one of the most famous county regiments in the British Army and the exhibit tells the story from their beginnings in 1181, via World War I (when it lost twelve thousand soldiers) to its last parade in 1968. Other exhibitions change but could feature anything from Japanese enamel pots to Chinese imperial textiles and ancient Egyptian relics.

Durham Castle

MAP P.101

Durham DH1. ⊕ Durham. ⓦ dur.ac.uk/durham.castle. Open for guided tours only, times vary. Book online; charge.

Durham Castle lost its medieval appearance long ago, as each successive Prince Bishop modernized the building according to the tastes of the time. The university was bequeathed the castle in the nineteenth century and subsequently renovated the old keep as a hall of residence. It's only possible to visit the castle on a guided tour, departing from outside Palace Green Library, highlights of which include the

Palace Green Library

Tram at the Beamish Museum

enormous hanging staircase and the underground Norman chapel, one of the few surviving interiors from the period. It's notable for its lively Romanesque carved capitals, including a green man, and what may be the earliest surviving depiction anywhere of a mermaid. Note that out of term time you can stay here (see page 123).

Beamish Museum

MAP P.98

Regional Resource Centre, Beamish DH9. Ⓦ beamish.org.uk. Daily April–Oct 10am–5pm, Nov–March 10am–4pm; hours can be reduced in winter; check online; charge.

The open-air Beamish Museum spreads out over three hundred acres, with buildings taken from all over the region painstakingly reassembled in six main sections linked by restored trams and buses. Complete with costumed shopkeepers, workers and householders, four of the sections show life in 1913, before the upheavals of World War I, including a colliery village complete with drift mine (regular tours throughout the day) and a large-scale recreation of the high street in a market town. Two areas

date to 1825, at the beginning of the northeast's industrial development, including a manor house, with horse yard, formal gardens, vegetable plots and orchards. You can ride on the beautifully restored steam-powered carousel, the Steam Galloper, which dates from the 1890s, and the Pockerley Waggonway, which is pulled along by a replica of George Stephenson's *Locomotion*, the first passenger-carrying steam train in the world.

Auckland Castle

MAP P.98

Market Place, Bishop Auckland DL14. Ⓣ Bishop Auckland. Ⓦ aucklandproject.org. Opening times vary; check online; charge.

Bishop Auckland, a busy little market town eleven miles southwest of Durham, grew up slowly around its showpiece building, Auckland Castle. Looking more like an opulent Gothic mansion than a traditional fortress, the castle served for 900 years as a private palace for the Prince Bishops of Durham, who stood second in power only to the King of England. The castle is one of the most important and best-preserved medieval bishops' palaces in Europe and today it's being transformed into an arts, faith and heritage destination. The Spanish Gallery is the first in the UK dedicated to the history and culture of Spain, and the Mining Gallery showcases the unique work of local mining artists, such as Norman Cornish and Tom McGuinness, who captured local life, work, and culture during County Durham's mining decades. You can get a bird's-eye view over proceedings from the adjoining Auckland Tower, a modern construction of steel tubes; or stroll through the 150 green acres of the castle's Deer Park.

Binchester Roman Fort

MAP P.98

Binchester, Bishop Auckland DL14. Ⓦ durham.gov.uk/binchester. Daily July–Oct 10am–4pm; charge.

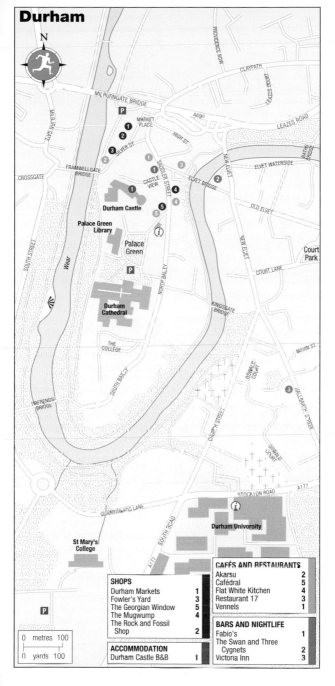

Durham

N

SHOPS

Durham Markets	1
Fowler's Yard	3
The Georgian Window	5
The Mugwump	4
The Rock and Fossil Shop	2

ACCOMMODATION

| Durham Castle B&B | 1 |

CAFÉS AND RESTAURANTS

Akarsu	2
Cafédral	5
Flat White Kitchen	4
Restaurant 17	3
Vennels	1

BARS AND NIGHTLIFE

Fabio's	1
The Swan and Three Cygnets	2
Victoria Inn	3

0 metres 100
0 yards 100

From Bishop Auckland's marketplace, it's a pleasant twenty-minute walk along the banks of the River Wear to the remains of Binchester Roman Fort. Known to the Romans as Vinovia or Vinovium, the fort is thought to have been established late in the first century AD, with the purpose of defending the Roman road between York and Hadrian's Wall where it crossed the nearby River Wear. Like the forts at Vindolanda and Housesteads, it would have followed the architectural blueprint common to Roman forts across the empire, with a rather Mediterranean look and a central commander's house surrounded by rather more spartan barracks and other soldiers' areas. While most of the stone fort and a civilian settlement (*vicus*) that occupied the area remain hidden beneath surrounding fields, the bathhouse with its sophisticated underground heating system (hypocaust) is visible. Excavations are ongoing.

Locomotion (National Railway Museum Shildon)

MAP P.98

The Bowes Museum

Dale Rd Industial Estate, Shildon DL4. Ⓦ locomotion.org.uk. Wed–Sun 10am–4pm; free.

The first passenger train in the world left from the station at Shildon in 1825 – making this the world's oldest railway town. It's a heritage explored in the magnificently realized *Locomotion* (also known as *NRM Shildon*), the regional outpost of York's National Railway Museum. It's less a museum and more an experience, spread out around a 1.5-mile-long site, with the attractions linked by free bus from the reception building. Depots, sidings, junctions and coal drops lead ultimately to the heart of the museum, Collection – a gargantuan steel hangar containing an extraordinary array of seventy locomotives, dating from the very earliest days of steam. With interactive children's exhibits, summer steam rides, rallies and shows, it makes an excellent family day out.

Barnard Castle

MAP P.103

Galgate, Barnard Castle DL12. Ⓦ www.english-heritage.org.uk/visit/places/barnard-castle. Daily April–Sept 10am–6pm; Oct 10am–5pm; Nov–March Sat & Sun 10am–4pm; charge.

Affectionately known as "Barney", the honey-coloured market town of Barnard Castle lies fifteen miles southwest of Bishop Auckland. The skeletal remains of the town's castle sit high on a rock overlooking the River Tees. It was founded in 1125 by the powerful Norman baron Bernard de Balliol – hence the town's name – and later ended up in the hands of Richard III. Richard's crest, in the shape of a boar, is still visible, carved above a window in the inner ward. The castle achieved unlikely notoriety during the coronavirus pandemic in 2020, after it emerged that the Prime Minister's chief adviser Dominic Cummings had driven to the castle with his family, in breach of lockdown regulations. He claimed, to widespread

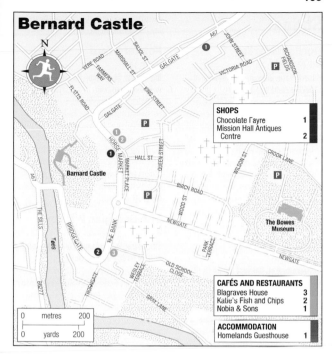

Bernard Castle

SHOPS

Chocolate Fayre	1
Mission Hall Antiques Centre	2

CAFÉS AND RESTAURANTS

Blagraves House	3
Katie's Fish and Chips	2
Nobia & Sons	1

ACCOMMODATION

Homelands Guesthouse	1

bemusement, that he made the drive in order to test his eyesight.

The Bowes Museum

MAP P.103
Newgate, Barnard Castle DL12.
ⓦ thebowesmuseum.org.uk. Daily 10am–5pm; charge.

Aside from the eponymous castle, the prime attraction in Barnard Castle is the grand French-style chateau that constitutes The Bowes Museum. Begun in 1869, the chateau was commissioned by John and Josephine Bowes, a local businessman and MP and his French actress wife, who spent much of their time in Paris collecting ostentatious treasures and antiques. Don't miss the beautiful Silver Swan, a life-size musical automaton dating from 1773 – every afternoon at 2pm it puts on an enchanting show, preening its shiny feathers while swimming along a river filled with jumping fish. Visiting exhibitions rotate every few months,

ranging from ceramics to quilting and normally showcasing the work of local artists.

Egglestone Abbey

MAP P.98
Abbey Ln, Bowes DL12. ⓦ www.english-heritage.org.uk/visit/places/egglestone-abbey. Daily 10am–6.30pm; free.

It's a fine mile-long walk from the castle, southeast (downriver) through the fields above the banks of the Tees, to the lovely shattered ruins of Egglestone Abbey, a minor foundation dating from 1195. A succession of wars and the Dissolution destroyed most of it, but you can still see the remnants of a thirteenth-century church and the remains of the monks' living quarters, including an ingenious latrine system. The monks who lived here bore the rather tongue-twisting name of the Premonstratensians, more simply known as the White Canons for the colour of their habit.

Shops

Durham Market

MAP P.101

Market Place, Durham DH1. ⓣ Durham.
ⓦ durhammarkets.co.uk.

A market has stood in Durham since Saxon times, and the current market hall is housed in a splendid building several centuries old. As is often the case with markets, this is a great place to get a feel for the pulse of life in the city, and you can pick up all sorts of things here from secondhand books to watches, cards, clothes, and traditional British sweets.

Chocolate Fayre

MAP P.103

10 Horsemarket, Barnard Castle DL12.
ⓦ chocolatefayre.co.uk.

Chocoholics rejoice: exquisite handmade chocolates are the order of the day at this lovely, teal-hued shop. You can choose the size of your box and its contents, which could include chocolate orange truffle, dark chocolate cherry and kirsch ganache, or coffee cream. They're a feast for the eyes, too,

Mission Hall Antiques Centre

Fowlers Yard

MAP P.101

Back Silver St, Durham DH1. ⓣ Durham.
ⓦ fowlersyard.com.

A series of workshops, housed in historic buildings behind the marketplace, showcasing local trades and crafts. These include fleecing, wool spinning, furniture restoration, and tapestry weaving. Drop by to watch the craftspeople at work, commission a piece, or buy off the cuff.

The Georgian Window

MAP P.101

50 Saddler St, Durham DH1. ⓣ Durham.
ⓦ thegeorgianwindow.co.uk.

A cut above your standard souvenir shop, this little Durham boutique contains some lovely items, like mugs bearing the patterns of Iberian *azulejo* tiles, billowing scarves (the largest collection in the Northeast, apparently), and some very pretty handmade postcards and greetings cards.

Mission Hall Antiques Centre

MAP P.103

51 The Bank, Barnard Castle DL12.
ⓦ missionhallantiquescentre.co.uk.

If you're on the hunt for a one-of-a-kind gift or souvenir, or a statement piece of furniture for your home, County Durham's only antiques centre is worth a look. There's no telling what kind of magic you might find here, but at the time of writing, featured pieces included an Edwardian brass bed, 1930s chandelier, and a collection of 1970s Whitefriars glass.

The Mugwump

MAP P.101

37 Saddler St, Durham DH1. ⓣ Durham.
ⓦ facebook.com/themugwumpdurham.

Beginning life back in the mid-Sixties, this quirky boutique radiates all the sunshine and

Durham Market

psychedelia of that era, with six separate rooms dedicated to a different category: women's and men's vintage fashion, homeware, ceramics, toiletries – pretty much everything you can imagine, you can find in some form here.

The Rock and Fossil Shop

MAP P.101

Market Place, Durham DH1. ⓘ Durham. ⓦ rockandfossilshop.co.uk.
Run by avuncular geologist Colin, who will talk you through his varied collection, this unusual shop in Durham Market stocks a wide range of fossils, minerals, worry stones, and rocks of all kinds. Each one is different, of course, so it's hard to find a more unique gift or souvenir of your trip.

Cafés

Bean Social

MAP P.101

53 North Rd, Durham DH1. ⓘ Durham. ⓦ facebook.com/BeanSocialDurham.
There's an atmosphere of friendliness behind all that goes on at this vegetarian and vegan café, where

the menu includes delicious and nutritious delights such as red wine and basil tomato soup with a home-made cheese scone, and Cajun tofu salad. The veggie sausage rolls, roasted with rosemary and mushrooms or infused with mango and madras, are particularly legendary. £

Broom House Farm

MAP P.98

Witton Gilbert, five miles northwest of Durham DH7. ⓦ broomhousedurham.co.uk.
More than worthy of a detour on the way north from Durham to the Beamish Museum (see page 100) is this farm shop café, famous among walkers and cyclists for its restorative English breakfasts, sausage and bacon buns, salads, ciabattas and pizzas. There's also the Forest Adventure, where kids can play on zip-lines and slides in the forest. £

Cafédral

MAP P.101

Owengate House, Durham DH1. ⓘ Durham. ⓦ facebook.com/cafedral.
In between the cathedral and the market place, this laidback café is a lovely place to spend a few hours. The cream teas are superb

Shoppers in Durham

and served on fine china, while the coffee and sandwiches are good, too; toasties, quiches, ploughman's platters and more are among the traditional lunches on offer. **£**

Clarendon's

MAP P.103

29 Market Place, Barnard Castle DL12.
Ⓦ clarendonsofbarnardcastle.co.uk.
Barnard Castle is a traditional sort of place, and this market place café fits in perfectly, with its classic decor and an atmosphere which is relaxed, yet extremely polite. The afternoon teas are always worth a visit, while the all-day menu includes classic club sandwiches, all day breakfasts, and wholesome salads with goat's cheese and pear. **££**

Cross Lanes Organic Farm

MAP P.103

Cross Lanes, Barnard Castle DL12.
Ⓦ crosslanesorganics.co.uk.
If you're visiting Egglestone Abbey, you could do much worse than popping into this charming farm shop and café, one mile to the southwest. Food is all organic and locally grown, much of it on-site – the menu highlights include

a grass-fed steak burger, home-made soup and a sandwich, and breakfasts with home-cured bacon and home-reared sausages. **£–££**

Flat White Kitchen

MAP P.101

40 Saddler St, Durham DH1. Ⓣ Durham.
Ⓦ flatwhitekitchen.com.
Durham's hippest café, housed within an elegant townhouse dating back to the 1600s and serving barista-standard coffee and hearty sandwiches served on wooden boards. The menu is small but very well done, and features some very British dishes – ham hock hash with peas, poached egg, and a mustard dressing – alongside modern brunch staples like baked eggs and avocado on toast. **££**

Nobia & Sons

MAP P.103

19 Horsemarket, Barnard Castle DL12.
Ⓦ facebook.com/NobiaAndSons.
A lovely Ghanaian-run café which sells a wide range of home-cooked treats including Scotch eggs and cakes – the Ferrero Rocher slice is particularly tempting – jerk chicken pastry pockets, hearty goat

curries, and lovely cheese scones. The selection of home-made pineapple, mango and sorrel drinks are delicious too. **£–££**

Restaurants

Akarsu

MAP P.101

32a Silver St, Durham DH1. 🚇 Durham. 🌐 akarsuturkishrestaurantdurham.co.uk.
Durham's finest Turkish restaurant serves up a lip-smacking selection of shish kebabs, meze platters, charcoal grills and *durum* wraps. There's a good vegetarian selection too, and the seafood dishes – including chargrilled seabass and mixed seafood stew – are also well worth a look. The setting's not bad, either, in a timber-framed, stone-walled Grade II-listed building. **££–£££**

Blagraves House

MAP P.103

30–32 The Bank, Barnard Castle DL12. 🌐 blagraves.com.
In the atmospheric surrounds of what is said to be the oldest house in Barnard Castle, dating back 500 years, this refined restaurant has low oak wooden beams, open log fires and plush furnishings, and specializes in traditional British cuisine. Dishes include pan-fried fillet of beef, roasted pheasant, and stone bass fillet. **£££**

Finbarrs

MAP P.101

Aykley Heads House, Durham DH1. 🚇 Durham. 🌐 finbarrsrestaurant.co.uk.
This chic restaurant, its tables adorned with crisp white tablecloths, may have an Irish name, but boasts a very cosmopolitan menu. It serves up anything from full English breakfasts and banana pancakes to dinners of Moroccan lamb with golden raisins; the sweet cherry and pistachio sundaes are delicious. The setting is lovely,

Cafédral

too, within a renovated farmhouse dating from the 1800s. **£££**

Katie's Fish and Chips

MAP P.103

15 Horsemarket, Barnard Castle DL12. 🌐 facebook.com/katiestraditionalfishandchips.
Sometimes, only fish and chips will do, and if you're looking for the perfect meal to take with you for a picnic – perhaps in Deepdale, just across the river – this chippy will do very nicely. The classics like Whitby scampi and battered cod are here, while the smoky sausage and home-made fishcakes are particularly good here too. **£**

Restaurant 17

MAP P.101

17 Elvet Bridge, Durham DH1. 🚇 Durham. 🌐 restaurant17.co.uk.
This elegant restaurant, warmed by a brick fireplace and dimly lit by chandeliers, serves a menu of considered European dishes such as slow-roasted pork belly with apple purée, slow-cooked beef with red wine jus, and sautéed chicken liver with shallots and vinegar. More exotic offerings,

such as Thai monkfish curry, are also available. £££

Vennels

MAP P.101

71 Saddler St, Durham DH1. ⊕ Durham. ⓦ vennels.com.

Named after the skinny alley or "vennel" where it stands – near the junction with Elvet Bridge – this café serves up generous sandwiches, salads, quiches and tasty cakes in its sixteenth-century courtyard-facing building. Hearty pies, quiches and lasagnes are also on offer. It's thought that this historic property may have been the birthplace of modern English mustard. ££

Bars and Nightlife

Fabio's

MAP P.101

66 Saddler St, Durham DH1. ⊕ Durham. ⓦ fabiosdurham.com.

Just above *La Spaghettata* pizzeria, *Fabio's* occupies a series of rooms filled with comfy, rug-draped sofas and chalked-up blackboards offering good-value drinks deals.

Durham at night

The atmosphere is cool and relaxed, with the music a melange of rap, r'n'b and dance – something which contributes to its appeal to students, who imbue the place with a youthful energy during term time. £–££

The Swan and Three Cygnets

MAP P.101

Elvet Bridge, Durham DH1.
⊕ Durham. ⓦ facebook.com/
TheSwanandThreeCygnets.

Sitting proudly at the end of Elvet Bridge overlooking the River Wear, this loud and cheery pub serves cheap drinks and is filled with a mixed crowd of locals and students. There are two floors of seating inside, and also a nice beer terrace with views over the River Wear. £

Three Horseshoes Inn

MAP P.98

Running Waters, Durham DH1.
ⓦ threehorseshoesleamside.co.uk.

In the countryside off the main A181 road southeast of Durham lies this lovely inn, which has a beer terrace overlooking the fields, a warm, wine-red interior, and a good selection of real ales, other beers, and wines. There's also lovely food, with a particularly good line in steaks, burgers, and roast meats. ££

Victoria Inn

MAP P.101

86 Hallgarth St, Durham DH1. ⊕ Durham.
ⓦ victoriainn-durhamcity.co.uk.

With its three open fires and rickety wooden stools, this cosy, traditional pub specializes in local ales – try the creamy Tyneside Blonde or the hoppy Centurion Bitter – and stocks more than thirty Irish whiskeys. As befits the pub's name and heritage, there is plenty of memorabilia here honouring Queen Victoria and the Victorian age, from portraits to pottery. £–££

Further afield

The island of Great Britain is narrow this far north – Bowness-on-Solway to Wallsend is little more than 100km (62 miles) as the crow flies – which means that it's easy to explore the country from coast to coast, particularly if you have your own means of transport. Within the Northeast, the often overlooked Tees Valley harbours interesting relics of industrial history; Middlesbrough is home to one or two interesting museums; and the spirit of the classic Victorian seaside resorts abides at Saltburn. Wild, dramatic natural landscapes lie to the west, in the form of the Lake District and the Yorkshire Dales, while York, Whitby, and the North York Moors are among the other highlights of the great county of Yorkshire.

Tees Valley

Admittedly not much of a tourist hotspot in comparison to Northumberland or Durham, the Tees Valley – once an industrial powerhouse and birthplace of one of the greatest developments in Britain, the public steam railway – nevertheless has some enjoyable attractions. Darlington, with its strong railway heritage, is a pleasant place to spend a day, while Middlesbrough's MIMA is also worthwhile, particularly if you have children to entertain.

Darlington

Abbreviated to "Darlo" by the locals, the busy market town of Darlington hit the big time in 1825, when George Stephenson's "Number 1 Engine", later called *Locomotion*,

The funicular railway in Saltburn that connects the lower and upper towns

hurtled from here to nearby Stockton-on-Tees at the terrifying speed of fifteen miles per hour. The town subsequently grew into a rail-engineering centre, and it didn't look back till the closure of the works in 1966. The origins of the rest of Darlington lie deep in Saxon times. The monks carrying St Cuthbert's body from Ripon to Durham stopped here, the saint lending his name to the graceful riverside church of St Cuthbert. The market square, one of England's largest, spreads beyond the church up to the restored and lively Victorian covered market.

Head of Steam

North Rd Station, Darlington DL3. ❶ North Road. ⓦ head-of-steam.co.uk. April–Sept Tues–Sun 10am–4pm, Oct–March Wed–Sun 11am–3.30pm; charge.

Darlington's railway history is celebrated at the wonderful little Head of Steam museum, which is actually the restored 1842 passenger station on the original Stockton and Darlington railway route. The highlight is Stephenson's *Locomotion No. 1*, a tiny wood-panelled steam engine, the first-ever steam train to carry fare-paying

The bucolic Yorkshire Dales

passengers. Other locomotives jostle for space alongside, including the shiny, racing-green Derwent, the oldest surviving Darlington-built steam train. These, along with a collection of station and line-side signs, uniforms, luggage, a reconstructed ticket office and carriages, successfully bring to life the most important era in Darlington's existence.

Middlesbrough Institute of Modern Art

Centre Square, Middlesborough TS1. ❶ Middlesborough. ⓦ mima.art. Tues–Sat 10am–4.30pm, Sun noon–4pm; free.

The stunning Middlesbrough Institute of Modern Art (MIMA) is one of the few tourist draws in the industrial town of Middlesbrough. Bringing together its municipal art collections, changing exhibitions concentrate on fine arts and crafts from the early twentieth century to the present day, with a heavy emphasis on ceramics and jewellery. The collection features work by David Hockney, L.S. Lowry and Tracey Emin, among others. Many of the rotating exhibitions showcase the work of local artists, often with a corresponding theme of industry – at the time of writing, one such exhibit, 'Chemical City', focused on the past and present of chemical manufacturing on Teesside.

Saltburn

South of the Tees estuary along the coast, it's not a difficult decision to bypass the kiss-me-quick tackiness of Redcar in favour of Saltburn, twelve miles east of Middlesbrough, a graceful Victorian resort in a dramatic setting overlooking extensive sands and mottled red sea-cliffs. Soon after the railway arrived in 1861 to ferry Teessiders out to the seaside on high days and holidays, Saltburn became a rather fashionable spa town boasting a hydraulic inclined tramway, which still connects upper town to the pier and promenade, and ornate

Italian Gardens that are laid out beneath the eastern side of town.

Yorkshire Dales

The Yorkshire Dales – "dales" from the Norse word *dalr* (valley) – form a varied upland area of limestone hills and pastoral valleys at the heart of the Pennines. Protected as a National Park (or, in the case of Nidderdale, as an Area of Outstanding Natural Beauty), there are more than twenty main dales covering 680 square miles, crammed with opportunities for outdoor activities. Southern dales like Wharfedale are the most visited, while neighbouring Malhamdale is also immensely popular due to the fascinating scenery squeezed into its narrow confines around Malham village. Ribblesdale is more sombre, its villages popular with hikers intent on tackling the famous Three Peaks – the mountains of Pen-y-ghent, Ingleborough and Whernside. To the northwest lies the more remote Dentdale, one of the least known but most beautiful of the valleys, and further north still Wensleydale and Swaledale, the latter of which rivals Dentdale as the most rewarding overall target. Both flow east, with Swaledale's lower stretches encompassing the appealing historic town of Richmond.

York

York is the North's most compelling city, a place whose history, said George VI, "is the history of England". This is perhaps overstating things a little, but it reflects the significance of a metropolis that stood at the heart of the country's religious and political life for centuries, and until the Industrial Revolution was second only to London in population and importance. These days a more provincial air hangs over the city, except in summer when it comes to feel like a heritage site for the benefit of tourists. That said, no

York Minster and the historic City Walls

trip to this part of the country is complete without a visit to York and its magnificent cathedral.

York Minster

Deangate, York YO1. ⊙ York.
ⓦ yorkminster.org Mon, Wed–Sat 9.30am–4.30pm, Sun 12.45–3.15pm; charge.

York Minster ranks as one of the country's most important sights. Seat of the Archbishop of York, it is Britain's largest Gothic building and home to countless treasures, not least of which is an estimated half of all the medieval stained glass in England. The first significant foundations were laid around 1080 by the first Norman archbishop, Thomas of Bayeux, and it was from the germ of this Norman church that the present structure emerged. Nothing else in the minster can match the magnificence of the stained glass in the nave and transepts. The West Window (1338) contains distinctive heart-shaped upper tracery (the "Heart of Yorkshire"), while in the nave's north aisle, the second bay window (1155) contains slivers of the oldest stained glass in the country. The greatest of the church's 128

Steps down to the harbour in Whitby

windows, however, is the majestic East Window (1405), at 78ft by 31ft the world's largest area of medieval stained glass in a single window.

The Minster's foundations, or undercroft, have been turned into a museum, featuring a new interactive gallery "Revealing York Minster". Among precious relics in the adjoining treasury is the eleventh-century Horn of Ulf, presented to the minster by a relative of the tide-turning King Canute. There's also access from the undercroft to the crypt, the spot that transmits the most powerful sense of antiquity, as it contains sections of the original eleventh-century church, including pillars with fine Romanesque capitals. Access to the undercroft, treasury and crypt is from the south transept, which is also the entrance to the central tower, which you can climb for exhilarating rooftop views over the city.

Castle Howard

15 miles north of York YO60. ⓦ castlehoward.co.uk. Late March to late Oct & late Nov to mid-Dec house daily 11am–4pm, grounds 10am–5pm; grounds also open Jan to late March & Nov to mid-Dec; charge.

Immersed in the deep countryside of the Howardian Hills less than two hours south of Newcastle, Castle Howard is the seat of one of England's leading aristocratic families and among the country's grandest stately homes. The grounds especially are worth visiting, and you could easily spend the best part of a day here. The colossal main house was designed by Sir John Vanbrugh in 1699 and was almost forty years in the making – remarkable enough, even were it not for the fact that Vanbrugh was, at the start of the commission at least, best known as a playwright and had no formal architectural training. Shrewdly, Vanbrugh recognized his limitations and called upon Nicholas Hawksmoor, who had a major part in the house's structural design – the pair later worked successfully together on Blenheim Palace. Vanbrugh also turned his attention to the estate's thousand-acre grounds, where he could indulge his playful inclinations – the formal gardens, clipped parkland, towers, obelisks and blunt sandstone follies stretch in all directions, sloping gently to two artificial lakes. The whole is a charming artifice of grand, manicured views – an example of what three centuries, skilled gardeners and pots of money can produce.

Whitby

If there's one essential stop on the North Yorkshire coast it's Whitby, with its historical associations, atmospheric ruins, fishing harbour, lively music scene and intrinsic charm. The seventh-century clifftop abbey here made Whitby one of the key foundations of the early Christian period, and a centre of great learning. Below, on the harbour banks of the River Esk, for a thousand years the local herring boats landed their catch until the great whaling boom of the eighteenth century transformed the fortunes of the town. Melville's Moby Dick makes much of Whitby whalers such as William Scoresby, and James Cook took his first seafaring steps from the town in 1746, on his way to becoming a national hero. All four of Captain Cook's ships of discovery – the Endeavour, Resolution, Adventure and Discovery – were built in this town.

Walking around Whitby is one of its great pleasures. Divided by the River Esk, the town splits into two halves joined by a swing bridge: the cobbled old town to the east, and the newer (mostly eighteenth- and nineteenth-century) town across the bridge, generally known as West Cliff. Church Street is the old town's main thoroughfare, barely changed in aspect since the eighteenth century, though now lined with tearooms and gift shops. Parallel Sandgate has more of the same, the two streets meeting at the small marketplace where souvenirs and trinkets are sold, and which hosts a farmers' market every Thursday.

Whitby Abbey

Abbey Lane, Whitby YO22. Ⓦ www.
english-heritage.org.uk/visit/places/
whitby-abbey. April–Sept daily 10am–6pm;
Oct daily 10am–5pm; Nov–March Sat & Sun
10am–4pm; charge.

The clifftop ruins of Whitby Abbey are some of the most evocative in England. Its monastery was founded in 657 by St Hilda of Hartlepool, daughter of King Oswy of Northumberland, and by 664 had become important enough to host the Synod of Whitby, an event of seminal importance in the development of English Christianity. It settled once and for all the question of determining the date of Easter, and adopted the rites and authority of the Roman rather than the Celtic Church. You'll discover all this and more in the visitor centre (same hours), which is housed in the shell of the adjacent mansion, built after the Dissolution using material from the plundered abbey.

North York Moors

Virtually the whole of the North York Moors, from the Hambleton and Cleveland hills in the west

Bram Stoker and Dracula

The story of Dracula is well known, but it's the exact attention to the geographical detail of Whitby – little changed since Bram Stoker first wrote the words – which has proved a huge attraction to visitors. Using first-hand observation of a town he knew well – he stayed at a house on the West Cliff, now marked by a plaque – Stoker built a story which mixed real locations, legend and historical fact: the grounding of Count Dracula's ship on Tate Hill Sands was based on an actual event reported in the local papers. It's hardly surprising that the town has cashed in on its Dracula Trail. The various sites – Tate Hill Sands, the abbey, church and steps, the graveyard, Stoker's house – can all be visited, while down on the harbourside the Dracula Experience attempts to pull in punters to its rather lame horror-show antics. Keen interest has also been sparked among the Goth fraternity, who now come to town en masse a couple of times a year (in late spring and around Halloween) for a vampire's ball, concerts and readings.

to the cliff-edged coastline to the east, is protected by one of the country's finest National Parks. The heather-covered, flat-topped hills are cut by deep, steep-sided valleys, and views here stretch for miles, interrupted only by giant cultivated forests. This is great walking country; footpaths include the superb Cleveland Way, one of England's premier long-distance National Trails, which embraces both wild moorland and the cliff scenery of the North Yorkshire coast. Barrows and ancient forts provide memorials of early settlers, mingling on the high moorland with the battered stone crosses of the first Christian inhabitants and the ruins of great monastic houses such as Rievaulx Abbey.

Carlisle

The county capital of Cumbria, Carlisle has been fought over for more than 2000 years, ever since the construction of Hadrian's Wall – part of which survives at nearby Birdoswald Roman Fort. The later struggle with the Scots defined the very nature of Carlisle as a border city: William Wallace was repelled

Carlisle Cathedral

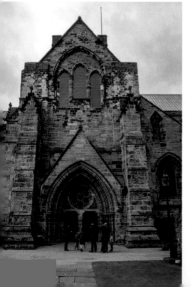

in 1297 and Robert the Bruce eighteen years later, but Bonnie Prince Charlie's troops took Carlisle in 1745 after a six-day siege, holding it for six weeks before surrendering to the Duke of Cumberland. It's not surprising, then, that the city trumpets itself as "historic Carlisle", and it's well worth a night's stop.

Carlisle Castle

Bridge St, Carlisle CA3. Ⓦ english-heritage.org.uk/visit/places/carlisle-castle. April–Sept daily 10am–6pm; Oct daily 10am–5pm; Nov–March Sat & Sun 10am–4pm; charge.

With a thousand years of military occupation of the site, Carlisle Castle is loaded with significance – not least as the place where, in 1568, Elizabeth I kept Mary Queen of Scots as her "guest". Guided tours help bring the history to life; don't leave without climbing to the battlements for a view of the Carlisle rooftops.

Carlisle Cathedral

Castle St, Carlisle CA3. Ⓦ carlislecathedral.org.uk. Mon–Sat 7.30am–6.30pm, Sun 7.30am–5pm; free.

Carlisle Cathedral was founded in 1122 but embraces a considerably older heritage. Christianity was established in sixth-century Carlisle by St Kentigern (often known as St Mungo), who became the first bishop and patron saint of Glasgow. Parliamentarian troops during the Civil War caused much destruction, but there's still plenty to admire in the ornate fifteenth-century choir stalls and the glorious East Window, which features some of the finest pieces of fourteenth-century stained glass in the country.

The Lake District

The eastern edge of the Lake District can be reached within two hours' drive of Newcastle. A vast expanse of lakes, forests and hills, it's no wonder that the landscapes in these parts were such a source of inspiration to William Wordsworth, Samuel Taylor Coleridge, and their fellow 19th-century Lake Poets. Owing to the Lakes' historic and literary associations, there is much in the way of cultural attractions here, although many come here purely for the hiking.

Windermere

Lakeland's most famous sight is Windermere, the largest lake in England. A ribbon lake that sprawls for almost 17km, its shores are surrounded by forested hills, the setting for some fantastic walking routes. Those in pursuit of a more leisurely stroll should try one of the 'miles without stiles' routes such as the 2km Bowness to Cockshott Point, or the 9km Western Shore route, which affords beautiful views north to the Troutbeck Hills on a clear day. Further from the lakeshore, the lovely Greenwood Trails amble through old-growth forests between quaint villages like Satterthwaite and Rusland. The pretty church in Rusland is the resting place of British author Arthur Ransome, whose Swallows and Amazons book series details children's adventures in the Lakes and has been credited with kickstarting the popularity of the Windermere area as a tourist destination.

Blackwell

Rydal, LA22. ⊕ Windermere. ⓦ lakelandarts.org.uk. Daily 10am–4pm; charge.

It's hard to disagree with Blackwell's claim to be the 'most beautiful house in the Lakes'. Built in 1901 as a holiday home by the wealthy Manchester brewer Sir Edward Holt, the house was designed by the famous architect Baillie Scott and is a magnificent example of the Arts and Crafts style, typified by steep roofs and a basis in earthy, vernacular styles rather than cold classicism. Today the house remains as beautiful as it ever was. Highlights include the Dining Room, notable for its blue-and-white striped fireplace and antique

Windermere from Loughrigg Fell

hessian wall hanging; the simple but charming Yellow Bedroom, which commands spectacular views over Windermere; and the Main Hall, its wooden ceiling and wall beams having a Tudor feel.

Rydal Mount House and Gardens

Rydal, LA22. ⓦ rydalmount.co.uk. April–Oct daily 9.30am–5pm, Nov–March Wed–Sun 10.30am–4pm; charge.

In between the town of Ambleside and the village of Grasmere and overlooking Lake Windermere, Rydal Mount was the family home of William Wordsworth from 1813 to 1850, the year of his death. The house, a lovely whitewashed building dating from the 16th century, is still owned by the Wordsworth family and has been appointed to look much as it would have done when the poet lived here, with its antique wooden furniture, elegantly fading wooden rugs, and airy living room. The property's nicest feature, though, is the five acres of landscaped gardens, designed by Wordsworth himself – he was known to say that it was the grounds, rather than the study within the house, that served as his office.

ACCOMMODATION

Seaham Hall

Accommodation

Newcastle boasts a great variety of places to stay, from luxurious boutiques in historic townhouses to slick business hotels housed in sleek modern monoliths. Grainger Town offers some lovely properties right in the core of the city which share the area's exquisite Georgian and Victorian architecture, while Newcastle's compact size means that you can stay in an upscale Jesmond boutique while still within walking distance of Quayside. Away from the city, Northumberland and Durham are home to some gorgeous rural B&Bs and farmhouse hotels which make the perfect base from which to explore the countryside.

Grainger Town

ALBATROSS HOSTEL MAP P.26. 51 Grainger St, Newcastle NE1. Ⓜ Central. Ⓦ albatrossnewcastle.co.uk. A modern backpacker hostel in a historic setting is what you'll find in *Albatross*, which has a fantastic communal area downstairs with pool tables and American football in the brick cellar. Rooms also maintain period features, like wooden floorboards and antique fireplaces, and sleep between two and twelve in no-frills, but comfortable, dorms. **£**

COUNTY HOTEL MAP P.26. Neville St, Newcastle NE1. Ⓜ Central. Ⓦ countyhotel. co.uk. Another good-value choice near Central train station is this historic hotel, which dates back to 1874 and boasts a lovely Victorian façade. Within, it's not quite as grand, and the rooms, though comfortable, could do with a refresh; for

more space, opt for one of the apartments, which feature kitchens and large seating areas with comfy sofas. **££**

CROWNE PLAZA MAP P.26. Hawthorn Square, Newcastle NE1. Ⓜ Central. Ⓦ ihg.com/crowneplaza/hotels/gb/ en/newcastle-upon-tyne. This stylish business hotel sits near the Centre for Life and right beside Newcastle Central, making it perfect for rail travellers – but it's a commendable choice for any visitor. Rooms have a sleek colour palette of royal purple and grey, and the dark-tiled health suite and pool are particularly atmospheric. A good-quality buffet breakfast is included, too. **££–£££**

GREY STREET HOTEL MAP P.26. 2–12 Grey St, Newcastle NE1. Ⓜ Manors. Ⓦ greystreethotel.co.uk. Newcastle locations don't come much better than Grey Street, whose splendid Georgian

Accommodation price codes

Throughout the guide, accommodation is categorised according to a price code, which roughly corresponds to the following price ranges. Price categories reflect the cost of a double room, without breakfast, in peak season.

£ under £80
££ £80–150
£££ £151–250
££££ over £250

architecture includes this boutique hotel. The historic exterior is complemented by a more modern look within, with stylishly lit rooms decked out in a modish colour scheme of subtle purples and greys, while a range of indulgent wellness treatments are on offer at the spa. **££**

MALDRON HOTEL MAP P.26. 17 Newgate St, Newcastle NE1. Ⓜ **Central.** Ⓦ **maldronhotelnewcastle.com.** There's a bright, contemporary feel to the guestrooms at this buzzy, good-value city centre hotel, which have a light, neutral colour scheme brightened up by flashes of yellow and with walls adorned with coastal Tyneside photography. Opt for an executive room for sweeping views over the city. Afternoon tea in the restaurant's outdoor courtyard is a lovely way to pass a summer's afternoon. **££**

MOTEL ONE MAP P.26. 15–25 High Bridge NE1. Ⓜ **Central, Manors.** Ⓦ **motel-one.com/en/hotels/newcastle/hotel-newcastle.** This modern 222-bed budget chain hotel has retained period features while embracing contemporary style. Rooms are small but perfectly formed, with dark wood details and splashes of electric blue in the textiles. Some rooms have great views over the cathedral and other city landmarks. It's one of the best-value spots in town, and staff go the extra mile. Breakfast extra. **££**

ROYAL STATION HOTEL MAP P.26. Neville St, Newcastle NE1. Ⓜ **Central.** Ⓦ **royalstationhotel.com.** Right next to Central station, this hotel can't be beat on location for train travellers. The extremely grand Victorian exterior is another draw, which extends to the midnight carpets and impressive staircase of the lobby, rooms don't quite compare, with blocky furniture and a bland design, but are very comfortable regardless. **£–££**

SLEEPERZ MAP P.26. 15 Westgate Rd NE1. Ⓜ **Central.** Ⓦ **sleeperz.com/Newcastle.** A great-value option in the heart of town, part of a little chain that marries functionality with good design. Despite the city-centre location, the 98 compact but comfortable rooms provide a quiet respite from Saturday-night mayhem, and there's a funky breakfast bar/café downstairs. **£–££**

YHA NEWCASTLE CENTRAL MAP P.26. 17 Carliol Square, Newcastle NE1. Ⓜ **Manors.** Ⓦ **yha.org.uk/hostel/yha-newcastle-central.** Ever popular with backpackers disembarking from Central station not too far away is the main branch of Youth Hostelling International in Newcastle. Dorms have bright yellow ceilings and colourful artworks on the walls and are clean and comfortable, while en-suite privates are also available; for even more exclusivity, opt for the premium suites, which feature lounge areas, two bathrooms, and sleep up to fourteen – perfect for trips with friends. **£**

Quayside and Gateshead

HILTON NEWCASTLE GATESHEAD MAP P.40. Bottle Bank, Gateshead NE8. Ⓜ **Central.** Ⓦ **hilton.com/en/hotels/nclhihi-hilton-newcastle-gateshead.** Something of a landmark which looms above the Gateshead side of the Tyne Bridge, this honey-hued monolith is a classic hotel in the city which can be relied upon for comfort and quality. Rooms have a neutral, almost Scandi-ish style, all pine furniture and natural light, the best ones are the deluxe rooms, which boast unbeatable panoramas over the Tyne Bridge. All are very comfortable, and the included breakfast is very good, too. **££–£££**

MALMAISON NEWCASTLE MAP P.40. 104 Quayside, Newcastle NE1. Ⓜ **Manors.** Ⓦ **malmaison.com.** The vibrant *Malmaison* chain finds its home on Tyneside in Newcastle's former Co-operative Society warehouse, converted into a buzzing modern hotel with a keen eye for style. The tiled *Chez Mal* bar is hung with hops and serves international small plates, with heartier offerings available at the restaurant; the rooms are darkly stylish with a slightly industrial feel, with some boasting views over Sage Gateshead and the river. **££–£££**

STAYBRIDGE SUITES MAP P.40. Buxton St, Newcastle NE1. Ⓜ **Manors.**

Ⓦ malmaison.com. If it's a home from home you're after during your time in Newcastle, the reliable *Staybridge Suites* might be a good choice, with each of the self-contained suites featuring a fully equipped kitchen and a comfortable sitting area. Should you feel the compulsion to venture beyond your own four walls, there's a very appealing breakfast area in a charming mid-century modern style. **££–£££**

VERMONT MAP P.40. Castle Garth, Newcastle NE1. Ⓜ Central. Ⓦ vermont-hotel.com. Exceedingly swish, yet decent-value, offering which ranks among the most stylish in the city centre (though this is not a particularly crowded field). The hotel sits in an eye-catching 1930s building and upholds the glamour of that era in the decor of its guestrooms, which have lovely carved beds and striped wallpaper. **££–£££**

Ouseburn and Jesmond

GREAT NORTH HOTEL MAP P.49. Great North Rd, Newcastle NE3. Ⓜ Regent Centre. Ⓦ greatnorthhotel.co.uk. If you're after a comfortable stay away from the hustle and bustle of the city centre, you could do much worse than this modern red-brick property, three miles north of the centre in the well-to-do suburb of Gosforth. Rooms are elegantly appointed with racing green walls and grey wood furnishings, while the New York pizzas at the on-site restaurant are top-drawer. **££**

HOTEL DU VIN MAP P.50. City Rd, Byker NE1. Ⓜ Byker. Ⓦ hotelduvin.com. Ranking among the very best hotels in Newcastle, and sitting between Ouseburn and the city centre, is this luxurious small property in an Edwardian former shipping building. Rooms retain period features like red-brick walls, fireplaces and ceiling beams, while the breakfasts at the restaurant downstairs are as good as you'll find anywhere; that quality extends to lunch and dinner, when top-drawer British cuisine is served alongside a good selection of wine. **£££**

JESMOND DENE HOUSE MAP P.49. Jesmond Dene Rd NE2. Ⓜ Ilford Rd, West Jesmond. Ⓦ jesmonddenehouse.co.uk. It's hard to find a more gorgeous historic hotel than this one, the former home of a wealthy industrialist built in the Arts and Crafts style. Rooms have lovely wooden ceilings and bay windows, some of which overlook the leafy Jesmond Dene river valley – nodding off and waking up to the sound of the gurgling water is a rare and pleasant treat. Be sure to make use of the several lovely living rooms, and enjoy the included breakfast. **£££**

Tyneside & the Coast

GRAND HOTEL TYNEMOUTH MAP P.64. 14 Grand Parade, Tynemouth NE30. Ⓦ grandhoteltynemouth.co.uk. The *grande dame* of Tynemouth hotels sits resplendent on the Grand Parade, and its guestrooms are as grand as the stately Victorian exterior. All have lovely dark wood furniture, while the sea view rooms feature beautiful four-poster beds and Jacuzzi bathtubs. Afternoon tea in the *Brasserie Restaurant* is a fitting way to spend a few hours. **£££**

WATERFORD ARMS MAP P.60. Collywell Bay Rd, Seaton Sluice NE26. Ⓦ booking.com. In the little seaside village of Seaton Sluice, a ten-minute drive north of Whitley Bay, is this charming black-and-white brick hotel. Rooms are those of a traditional B&B, with floral wallpaper, en-suite bathrooms and pine furniture, while the food and ales in the pub downstairs are great – people come from miles around for the Sunday roasts. **£–££**

The Northumberland Coast

MARSHALL MEADOWS MANOR HOUSE MAP P.72. Marshall Meadows, Berwick-upon-Tweed TD15. Ⓣ Berwick-upon-Tweed. Ⓦ marshallmeadowsmanor.co.uk. An eighteenth-century country house set in delightful grounds. The nineteen en-suite guest rooms are traditional – but without chintz – and very clean, and the whole thing is very good value considering the level of luxury you get. The oak-panelled restaurant has a menu of comforting seasonal dishes, featuring local produce such as Lindisfarne oyster. **££–£££**

OLD RECTORY HOWICK MAP P.72.

Howick, Craster NE66. ⓦoldrectoryhowick. co.uk. Just 400yds from the wind-whipped North Sea, on an unspoiled stretch of coastline south of Craster, this fantastic B&B sits in its own peaceful grounds and has extremely pretty bedrooms and comfortable sitting areas. Superb breakfasts feature plenty of cooked options, including Craster kippers. **£££**

RED LION MAP P.72. 22 Northumberland St, Alnmouth NE66. ⓦredlionalmouth. com. Choose from six spacious and modern rooms, with pine furniture, cream walls and fresh bathrooms, above a popular, traditional pub. Despite the pub's long history, the rooms are fresh, bright and airy. The beer garden is perfect for sunny days, and the menu has everything from big open sandwiches to sirloin steak. **££**

YHA ALNWICK MAP P.72. 34–38 Green Batt, Alnwick NE66. ⓔAlnwick. ⓦyha. org.uk/hostel/yha-alnwick. A handsome Victorian courthouse nicely converted into a hostel, with dorms sleeping between four and eight and some private rooms. Whatever room type you choose, you'll find a comfy, carpeted space with simple but comfortable furniture. You're a stroll away from the gardens and castle, and there's a bus stop right outside the front door. **£**

YHA BERWICK MAP P.72. Dewar's Ln, Berwick-upon-Tweed TD15. ⓣBerwick-upon-Tweed. ⓦyha.org.uk/hostel/yha-berwick. The Berwick branch of the ever-reliable Youth Hostelling International is housed in a remarkable eighteenth-century granary building which, thanks to a fire in 1815, has a lean greater than that of the Leaning Tower of Pisa. There are thirteen en-suite rooms here, some private and family, with a clean and contemporary style – even if the lime-green sheets take some getting used to – plus a bistro and gallery. **£**

VICTORIA HOTEL MAP P.72. 1 Front St, Bamburgh NE69. ⓦstrhotels.co.uk. This smart boutique hotel has elegant rooms in a variety of sizes – one with lovely castle views – in a contemporary yet cosy style with an eye-catching monochrome colour scheme. There's also a couple of relaxing

bars and a more expensive brasserie (dinner only). Pets are welcome for a small additional charge. **££–£££**

The Northumberland Interior

BATTLESTEADS MAP P.86. Wark NE48. ⓦbattlesteads.com. It's not every day you get the chance to spend the night at a hotel-restaurant-observatory, but that's exactly what's on offer at the fantastic *Battlesteads*. Sitting in the quiet village of Wark, the hotel's on-site observatory makes the most of Northumberland's dark skies for regular stargazing evenings. Rooms have a traditional style and are very comfortable, particularly in the case of the outdoor wooden lodges, and the restaurants (see page 94) is superb. **£££**

CARRAW MAP P.86. Military Rd, Humshaugh NE46 ⓦcarraw.co.uk. It's not often you can say "I've slept on Hadrian's Wall", but here you can – this beautiful B&B, run by a friendly couple, is built right next to Hadrian's masterpiece and boasts stunning views. Lovely homely touches like home-made shortbread and cake on arrival, hot-water bottles and luxurious toiletries make this place really special. Delicious breakfasts – the nutty granola is a winner. **££–£££**

CHILLINGHAM CASTLE MAP P.86. Chillingham NE66. ⓦchillingham-castle. com. The chance to spend the night at "Britain's most haunted castle" will either draw you in or make you run a mile, depending on your inclination. Paranormal happenings are often reported, but for what it's worth, when we stayed here, we experienced nothing spooky – just a lovely apartment with both period features (wood-burning stove, antique furniture) and modern comforts, including a kitchen. **£££**

COUNTY HOTEL HEXHAM MAP P.86. Priestpopple, Hexham NE46. ⓣHexham. ⓦcountyhotelhexham.co.uk. A charming pub set in a stately Georgian townhouse, with seven spacious and elegant en-suite rooms with a stylish, greyscale colour scheme. The staff are incredibly welcoming and there's great food served here, too, from the hearty included breakfasts, with cooked and Continental options, to the superb pub grub. **££–£££**

HADRIAN'S WALL CAMPSITE MAP P.86. Melkridge Tilery NE49. Ⓦ hadrianswallcampsite.co.uk. Friendly, family-run site half a mile from the Wall, and sitting around an hour's walk west of the Roman forts at Vindolanda and Housesteads. There are showers, a café, washing machine and dryer, as well as bike storage; breakfast and evening meals are also available. There's also a heated bunk room sleeping ten people. Open all year. **£**

HOLLY BUSH INN MAP P.86. Greenhaugh NE48. Ⓦ hollybushinn.net. This super little pub sits in the remote Northumberland village of Greenhaugh, well placed for exploring Kielder Forest and Water. It serves great ales and food, and has seven simple and attractive bedrooms upstairs or in the quiet cottage next door, all with a cosy farmhouse feel and with pastoral artworks decorating the walls. **££–£££**

KIELDER WATERSIDE MAP P.86. Kielder Waterside Park NE48. Ⓦ kielderwaterside. com. Scandinavian-style self-catering lodges, sleeping between four and six, and all with access to the park's pool, sauna, bar and restaurant. Some, like the Catcleugh Spa lodge, also have their own hot tubs. Bring plenty of midge repellent. Two-night minimum stay; rates vary widely. **££**

LANGLEY CASTLE MAP P.86. Langley, Hexham NE47. Ⓦ langleycastle.co.uk. There are suitably regal rooms – four-poster beds, sumptuous furnishings and beautiful bathrooms with saunas and spa baths – in this turreted medieval castle, which dates all the way back to 1350. The cheaper rooms are in the grounds, looking onto the castle. There's also an atmospheric restaurant, cocktail bar, lounge and gardens. **£££**

PHEASANT INN MAP P.86. Stannersburn NE48. Ⓦ thepheasantinn.com. A traditional country pub on the road from Bellingham, the *Pheasant Inn* has eight very comfortable

bedrooms (including one family room). The real highlight, though, is the food, served downstairs in the cosy restaurant; expect game pies, Northumbrian cheeses and plenty of fish. The breakfasts are traditional and superb, and packed lunches are available for your day's adventures. **£££**

THISTLEYHAUGH MAP P.86. Longframlington NE65. Ⓦ thistleyhaugh. co.uk. Gorgeous, ivy-smothered Georgian farmhouse in the bucolic Northumberland countryside on the banks of the River Coquet. There are five luxurious, chintzy bedrooms here – the look is beautifully considered and traditional, with subtle half four-poster beds in the bedrooms and freestanding tubs in the bathrooms. **£££**

TILLDALE HOUSE MAP P.86. 34 High St, Wooler NE71. Ⓦ tilldalehouse. co.uk. Snug seventeenth-century stone cottage in the middle of town with three en-suite bedrooms. With enormous, soft beds, deep-pile carpets, an open fire and great breakfasts, it makes a very cosy and enticing base after a long day hiking in the hills. There are several pubs and restaurants within walking distance. **££**

TOSSON TOWER MAP P.86. Great Tosson NE65. Ⓦ tossontowerfarm.co.uk. Seven lovely rooms are available on this little working farm in a quiet hamlet with spectacular views out over the Cheviot Hills. Rooms have a traditional, cosy feel, with plush green carpets, floral wallpaper, and carved pine furniture. The tiled en-suite bathrooms are very spacious. Four charming self-catering cottages are also available for longer stays. **£££**

TWICE BREWED INN MAP P.86. Military Rd, Once Brewed NE47. Ⓦ twicebrewedinn. co.uk. This friendly community pub close to the hostel, café and gallery *The Sill* (see page 95) has simple en-suite rooms that have a traditional cosy feel adorned with splashes of colour and vibrant textiles and wallpaper. On site there's a microbrewery and beer garden; breakfast is included, but must be ordered the night before. **££**

YHA THE SILL MAP P.86. Military Rd, Once Brewed NE47. Ⓦ thesill.org.uk. A quite unexpected sight rising from (yet somehow blending into) the landscape of windswept ridges and Roman ruins is *The Sill*, a 'landscape discovery centre', café, art gallery and youth hostel. A range of rooms are available from two- to four-bed dorms, all with a minimalist style and most with their own bathrooms. There's also a shop and kitchen so you can self-cater. **£**

Durham and around

DURHAM CASTLE B&B MAP P.101. Durham Castle DH1. ⊕ Durham. Ⓦ dur. ac.uk. Out of term time you can enjoy the unique experience of staying in the rarefied and historic surrounds of Durham Castle. Accommodation ranges from standard rooms with shared bathrooms to two grand "state rooms", one with a four-poster and seventeenth-century tapestries. Breakfast is served in the thirteenth-century Great Hall. **£–£££**

HOMELANDS GUESTHOUSE MAP P.103. 85 Galgate, Barnard Castle DL12. B Barnard Castle. Ⓦ homelandsguesthouse. co.uk. An assortment of pretty rooms with floral soft furnishings and comfortable beds are what you'll find at this homely guesthouse. The owners are very knowledgeable about the area and can recommend plenty of good walks. Breakfast is great, too, with delicious fruit salads and generous cooked options. **££**

SEAHAM HALL MAP P.98. Lord Byron's Walk, Seaham SR7. Ⓦ seaham-hall.co.uk. Perched on a clifftop overlooking the sea, this hip, exclusive hotel makes a great coastal base for city sightseeing – Durham is only a 20min drive away. It's known for its luxurious spa and pampering treatments and has a wonderful restaurant; spa, dinner, bed and breakfast packages are available. **££££**

ESSENTIALS

Train on the Lesbury Viaduct

Arrival

By plane
Newcastle International Airport is 9km northwest of the city centre, near the posh village of Ponteland. With more than 80 domestic and international destinations, this is the northeast's major air hub and is the second busiest in northern England behind Manchester Airport, serving more than five million passengers every year. International destinations are mainly European – Ryanair (wryanair.com) flies to Alicante, Gdansk, Ibiza, and Gran Canaria among many other destinations, while Jet2 (wjet2.com) also serves dozens of Continental destinations – but it's also possible to travel further afield, with TUI (wtui.com) flying to Egypt and Tunisia and Emirates (wemirates.com) flying direct to Dubai in 2022.

By train
The main train station serving Newcastle's city centre is Newcastle Central, which sits in historic Grainger Town; opened in 1850, it was built as part of a coast-to-coast line connecting Newcastle and Carlisle. Central connects the city with Birmingham, Manchester, Leeds, Liverpool, London King's Cross, Carlisle, and Edinburgh. Train companies running services into and out of the station include Cross Country (wcrosscountrytrains.co.uk), Northern (wnorthernrailway.co.uk), and LNER (wlner.co.uk). A fifteen-minute walk east of Central, Manors connects Newcastle with other destinations in the north, including Morpeth, Carlisle and Hexham, via Northern Railway. Both of these train stations are in the heart of the city centre, and many hotels and attractions can be reached on foot; otherwise, both are also connected to the local Metro train network, and to local bus routes.

By bus
Two major bus companies connect Newcastle to other cities in the United Kingdom: National Express (wnationalexpress.com) and Megabus (wuk.megabus.com). Destinations include London, Manchester, Birmingham, Cardiff, Glasgow, Leeds, and Leicester. Long-distance buses arrive at the Newcaslle Central bus station, just west of the main train station in the city centre.

By car
The main road connecting Newcastle with the rest of the country is the A1, which goes north to Edinburgh and south all the way to London. This in turn connects to the M1, which goes south past Sheffield, Nottingham, Northampton and Milton Keynes to London. The A69 heads west towards Carlisle and the coast, while the A68 takes you through Northumberland and up to the Scottish Borders.

Getting around

Newcastle's city centre is compact, and most of it is navigable on foot. A guided walk is a great way to get a feel for the city while learning about its history; Newcastle Tour Company (wnewcastletourcompany.com) are a fantastic operator.

For those with reduced mobility, however, or to travel further afield, there are numerous transport options available. Newcastle's traffic is relatively light compared to bigger cities like London and Manchester, and renting a car can be a good option. Sixt

(ⓦ sixt.co.uk), Europcar (ⓦ europcar. co.uk) and Enterprise (ⓦ enterprise. co.uk) have outlets at Newcastle International Airport; Europcar and Enterprise also have offices at Newcastle Central Station.

Taxis are plentiful in Newcastle. Black Hackney carriages can be flagged everywhere and are a comfortable but more expensive way to get around; alternatively, call a trusted local company like Newcastle Taxis (0191 232 3232). Uber (ⓦ uber. com) is available across Newcastle and is invariably cheaper and quicker than using a traditional taxi service.

Newcastle and the surrounding area is connected by the Tyne & Wear Metro light rail system (ⓦ nexus.org.uk), which runs on two lines (Green and Yellow), partly underground, and connects 60 stations. The Metro is a convenient way of getting between Newcastle city centre and outlying places of interest including Tynemouth, Whitley Bay, and Sunderland. Route information and status updates can be found online and on the Tyne & Wear Metro app, which you can also use to buy tickets as an alternative to the ticket machines found at every station. If you'll be making several journeys in one day, it's worth buying an Explorer ticket, which allows

for a day's unlimited travel and can be purchased online or at a station. Weekly tickets are also available. Children under five travel free on the Metro.

The most extensive local transport option is the Nexus bus network (ⓦ nexus.org.uk), which covers hundreds of bus stops across the city. The main city centre terminuses include Haymarket and Eldon Square. The one-day Explorer ticket which you can buy for the Metro also allows for unlimited bus travel on the network.

Newcastle's relatively compact size makes cycling an appealing way of getting around. Information and routes can be found at (ⓦ newcastlegateshead. com/blog/cycling-routes-in-newcastlegateshead), while more information and bikes to hire are at the Cycle Hub in Ouseburn (see page 47).

Another fun and eco-friendly way to get around (or a scourge on Newcastle and other city centres, depending on your point of view) is the Neuron e-scooter, which can be found all around Newcastle city centre and surrounding suburbs; download the Neuron app and you can pay the hourly rate for your scooter, which can be picked up or dropped off at many points around the city.

Directory A-Z

Addresses

Addresses are written in the form "8 Grainger St NE1", with NE1 being the postcode area. House and building numbers in the UK tend to jump across the street, so one side will have numbers 1, 3, 5 etc while 2, 4, 6 etc will be found opposite them.

Children

Newcastle is very child-friendly, and children are welcome in nearly all restaurants and cafés, with

many offering dedicated children's menus. The exception to Newcastle's child-friendly spaces are bars (and, obviously, nightclubs) which will generally insist on an over-18 only policy – the same is true of some pubs, although many pubs allow children who are accompanied by adults.

Cinema

Mainstream films are shown at chain cinemas and multiplexes across the city, while art house, indie and foreign-language films are also shown at venues like Side Gallery (see page 36). Film listings can be found online at odeon.co.uk. For a more deluxe film experience check out the Everyman Cinema at 75–85 Grey Street (ⓦ everymancinema.com), where a historic building houses a bar, restaurant, and plush auditorium where you sit on sofas to enjoy the film.

Crime and emergencies

Violent crime against tourists is extremely rare in the UK, but petty theft, mugging and pickpocketing are more common – you're unlikely to be affected, but it pays to be vigilant. The rules are the same as anywhere else: don't flash cash or expensive gadgets, keep hold of your bags, and make sure you're aware of items in your pockets.

Discount passes

Most of Newcastle's museums are completely free, including some of the most famous like the Great North Museum: Hancock (see page 28) and the Discovery Museum (see page 25). At the time of writing, there was no combined 'City Pass' or similar option for gaining discounted entry to the paid attractions, but most of these offer discounted rates for children, students, and senior citizens.

Electricity

Like the rest of the UK, Newcastle uses three-pin type G plugs, and the current is 230V AC. North American appliances will need a transformer and adaptor; those from Europe, South Africa, Australia and New Zealand only need an adaptor. Increasingly, modern hotels may have USB mains plug sockets, though you should not rely on this.

Embassies & consulates

Belgium, 30 Cloth Market, 0191 232 8345
France, 25 Forth Place, 0191 637 5999

Germany, c/o Newcastle Civic Centre, 07954 034 744
Italy, 7 Martindale Walk, Killingworth, 07508 408 047

Health (doctor, dentist, emergencies, 24hr pharmacy)

Pharmacists (known as chemists in England) can advise you on minor conditions but can dispense only a limited range of drugs without a doctor's prescription. Most are open roughly 9am–7pm, though some are open later; the Boots at Kingston Park shopping centre has a pharmacy open until midnight. For generic pain relief, cold remedies and the like, the local supermarket is usually the cheapest option. Visitors to Newcastle and Northumbria should check current and incoming Covid-19 restrictions at ⓦ gov.uk/coronavirus.

Internet

Most hotels and hostels in Newcastle have free wi-fi. In addition, many museums, public buildings, tourist offices and some train stations provide free wi-fi, as do numerous cafés, restaurants and bars. Increasingly less common are dedicated internet cafés, but some public libraries also offer free access. Many public wi-fi networks extend into public streets, such as the free wi-fi offered by Eldon Square shopping centre.

LGBTQ travellers

England offers one of the most diverse and accessible LGBTQ scenes anywhere in Europe. Nearly every sizeable town has some kind of organized LGBTQ life, and Newcastle is no different. Listings, news and reviews can be found at Gay Times (ⓦ gaytimes.co.uk) and Pink News (ⓦ pinknews.co.uk). The website of the campaigning organization Stonewall (ⓦ stonewall.org.uk) is also useful, with directories of local groups and advice on reporting hate crimes, which, unfortunately, continue to be a concern. The age of consent is 16.

Left luggage

Newcastle International Airport has a left luggage facility next to WH Smith in the departures terminal before security. There is no equivalent at the train station, although nearby Grainger News has a left luggage service courtesy of City Spare Space (ⓦ citysparespace.com). Most hotels will also let you leave your bags behind reception, both before you check in and after you check out.

Lost property

To report lost or found property, contact Northumbria Police by calling 101 or at northumbria.police.uk. At Newcastle International Airport, visit the Lost Property Desk (0191 214 3367, lostproperty@newcastleinternational. co.uk). Items lost on the LNER, TransPennine Express and Great Northern train networks are tracked via the MissingX service (ⓦ missing.com), which connects you to the relevant lost property office

Money (including ATMs, banks, costs, credit cards, exchange)

England's currency is the pound sterling (£), divided into 100 pence (p). Coins come in denominations of 1p, 2p, 5p, 10p, 20p, 50p, £1 and £2. Bank of England notes are in denominations of £5, £10, £20 and £50. At the time of writing, £1 was worth US$1.35, €1.20, Can$1.72, Aus$1.72 and NZ$1.99. For current exchange rates, visit ⓦ xe.com.

The easiest way to get hold of cash is to use your debit card at an ATM; there's usually a daily withdrawal limit, which varies depending on the money issuer, but starts at around £250. You'll find ATMs everywhere in Newcastle, although they are fewer and further between in suburban and rural areas; look for banks and newsagents.

Credit cards are widely accepted in hotels, shops and restaurants – MasterCard and Visa are almost universal, charge cards like American Express and Diners Club less so.

Paying by plastic involves inserting your credit or debit card into a "chip-and-pin" terminal, beside the till in shops, or brought to your table in restaurants, and then keying in your PIN to authorize the transaction. Contactless payments, where you simply hold your credit or debit card on or near a card reader without having to key in a PIN, are prevalent for transactions for up to £100. Note that the same overseas transaction fees will apply to contactless payments as to those made with a PIN. Contactless has increased the number of establishments that take card – even market stalls may do – though some smaller places, such as B&Bs and shops, may accept cash only, and occasionally smaller shops and pubs charge a minimum amount for card payments (£5 or £10 usually).

You can change currency or cheques at post offices and bureaux de change – the former charge no commission, while the latter tend to be open longer hours and are found in most city centres and at the airport and train stations.

Opening hours

Though traditional office hours are Monday to Saturday from around 9am to 5.30pm or 6pm, many businesses, shops and restaurants in Newcastle, as throughout England, will open and close at different times. The majority of shops are open daily, but some places – even the so-called "24hr supermarkets" – are closed or have restricted hours on Sunday. Banks are not open at the weekend. We have given full opening hours throughout the Guide, noting where they're especially complex or prone to change and you should check before visiting. While many local shops and businesses close on public holidays, few tourist-related businesses observe them, particularly in summer. However, nearly all museums, galleries and other attractions are closed on Christmas Day and New Year's Day, with many also closed on Boxing Day (Dec 26). England's public holidays are usually referred to as bank holidays (though it's not just the banks who have a day off).

Phones

The prefix 07 is for mobile phones/cellphones. UK landlines are prefixed with an 'area code'; most of the numbers you'll see in this Guide begin with Newcastle and Durham's area code, 0191. However you'll also see 01670 for Northumberland.

For directory enquiries, there are numerous companies offering the service, all with six-figure numbers beginning with 118, but charges are extortionate (with minimum charges of £5-plus and costs quickly escalating) and so best avoided. Numbers and addresses in the public domain can be found at ⓦ 192.com.

Most hotel rooms have telephones, but there is almost always an exorbitant surcharge for their use. Public payphones – telephone boxes – are still found, though with the ubiquity of mobile phones, they're seldom used.

To use your mobile/cellphone, check with your provider that international roaming is activated – and that your phone will work in the UK. Any EU-registered phones will be charged the same rates for calls, text messages and data as your home tariff (at the time of writing this had remained the case despite the UK's withdrawal from the European Common Market, but could change in future). Calls using non-EU phones are still unregulated and can have prohibitively expensive roaming charges. If you're staying in England for any length of time, it's often easiest to buy a local SIM card in the UK.

Post offices

The British postal service, Royal Mail, is pretty efficient. First-class stamps to anywhere in the UK currently cost 95p and post should arrive the next day; if the item is anything approaching A4 size, it will be classed as a "Large Letter" and will cost £1.29p; if you want to guarantee next-day delivery, ask for Special Delivery (from £6.85). Second-class stamps cost 68p, taking up to three days; airmail to the rest of Europe and the world costs £1.85 and should take three days within Europe, five days further afield. Stamps can be bought at post offices, but also from newsagents, many gift shops and supermarkets, although they usually only sell books of four or ten first-class UK stamps. To find out your nearest post office, see ⓦ postoffice.co.uk.

Smoking

Smoking is banned in all public buildings and offices, restaurants and pubs, and on all public transport. In addition, the vast majority of hotels and B&Bs no longer allow it. E-cigarettes are not allowed on public transport and are generally prohibited in museums and many other public buildings; for restaurants and bars it depends on the individual proprietor.

Time

Greenwich Mean Time (GMT) – equivalent to Coordinated Universal Time (UTC) – is used from the end of October to the end of March; for the rest of the year Britain switches to British Summer Time (BST), one hour ahead of GMT.

Tipping

Although there are no fixed rules for tipping, a 10 to 15 percent tip is anticipated by restaurant waiters. Tipping taxi drivers ten percent or so is optional, but most people at the very least round the fare up to the nearest pound. Some restaurants levy a "discretionary" or "optional" service charge of 10 or 12.5 percent, which must be clearly stated on the menu and on the bill. However, you are not obliged to pay it, and certainly not if the food or service wasn't what you expected. It is not normal to leave tips if you order at the bar in pubs, though more likely if there's table service in bars, when some people choose to leave a few coins. You may well also see a tip jar on the bar at cafés and pubs, although there is never any pressure to contribute. The only other occasions when you'll be expected to tip are at the hairdressers, and in upmarket hotels where porters and bell boys expect and usually get a pound or two per bag or for calling a taxi.

Toilets

In the last twenty years, the number of public toilets in the United Kingdom has dropped by a third due to public spending cuts. However, at the same time there has been a rise in the number of high street cafés, which nearly all have toilets but only for the use of paying customers. The handy Great British Public Toilet Map (🖰 toiletmap.org.uk) is a useful website aimed at helping people locate their nearest public toilet – aimed particularly at the young, elderly, and those with medical conditions.

Tourist information

Up-to-date visitor information is available online (🖰 newcastlegateshead.com) and maps and brochures are available at hotels and attractions across Newcastle and Gateshead. In Durham, you'll find helpful information via telephone courtesy of the Visitor Contact Centre (0300 026 2626), while in Northumberland there are useful centres at Craster's Quarry Car Park, Seahouses Seafield car park, Alnwick Playhouse, and Hexham Library; all are best contacted via email at visitorInfo@northumberland.gov.uk.

Travellers with disabilities

All new public buildings in the UK – including museums, galleries and cinemas – are obliged to provide wheelchair access; airports and (generally) train stations are accessible; many buses have easy-access boarding ramps; and dropped kerbs and signalled crossings are the rule in every city and town. Reviews of Newcastle's attractions and hotels through the lens of accessibility for visitors with disabilities can be found online at Euan's Guide (🖰 euansguide. com). Challenges posed by Newcastle's Victorian and Georgian architecture remain, although historic venues like the Theatre Royal are accessible by wheelchair and feature hearing aid assistance and regular performances specifically geared towards visitors with other disabilities. Newcastle Football Club's St James' Park features designated seats for visitors with impaired mobility. An increasing number of hotels are wheelchair-friendly. Discounts are available for passengers with disabilities on the UK's rail network, even if you do not hold a Disabled Persons Railcard; details can be found at 🖰 nationalrail.co.uk/stations_destinations/44965.aspx.

Useful resources for travellers with disabilities include Accessable (🖰 accessable.co.uk) and Euan's Guide (🖰 euansguide.com), both of which allow you to search for restaurants, hotels and attractions by destination.

Festivals & Events

Quadrantid Meteor Shower (early Jan) Head to Northumberland's Kielder Observatory to see in the year's first meteor shower, a spectacular display of shooting stars.

Chinese New Year (Late Jan/Early Feb) Processions, fireworks and festivities mark the Chinese New Year in Newcastle's Chinatown. A Chinese market and colourful festivities can be found on Stowell Street.

Holi (March) India's vibrant festival of colours comes to Tyneside, with events organized by Newcastle Hindu Temple and the Newcastle University Hindu and Sikh Society.

St Patrick's Day (Mar 17) Newcastle's Irish population – and virtually everyone else – celebrates St Patrick's Day with a parade through the city centre and many, many pints of Guinness.

St George's Day (Apr 23) The day that commemorates England's patron saint is celebrated across the city, but what could be more English than some fish and chips on the coast?

Newcastle Beer & Cider Festival (early April) ⓦ camra.org.uk. The city's biggest beer festival is held on the first floor of Northumbria University Students' Union, with hundreds of brews to sample.

Gateshead International Festival of Theatre (late April–early May) ⓦ giftfestival.co.uk. The world of contemporary theatre is celebrated at this three-day festival at venues across Gateshead, Quayside, and the town centre.

The Late Shows (mid-May) ⓦ thelateshows.org.uk. The artists' studios, venues and galleries of Ouseburn and the wider city open late for an after-hours cultural extravaganza.

Northumberland Plate Day (late June) ⓦ newcastle-racecourse.co.uk. Newcastle Racecourse's most exciting weekend of the year sees two days of horse racing followed by upper-crust DJ performances (Pete Tong and Judge Jules in 2022).

Mouth of the Tyne Festival (early July) ⓦ mouthofthetynefestival.com. The streets of Tynemouth host live music and street theatre performances each July, with local artists showcased, some of them big names.

Magic Weekend (early July) St James' Park hosts this yearly showpiece rugby league tournament, with six of the Super League's biggest derbies taking place over two days.

Newcastle Pride (late July) ⓦ northern-pride.com. 2022 sees Newcastle host the UK's LGBTQ pride celebrations, while subsequent years will see smaller-scale festivities.

Noughty 90s Festival (late August) ⓦ noughty90sfest.com. The city-centre Leazes Park plays host to this two-day throwback fest of the best music from the 1990s and 2000s.

Great North Run (Sept) ⓦ greatnorthrun.org. The world's largest half marathon sees tens of thousands of runners take to a scenic course through the city and surrounding area, including a famous stretch across the Tyne Bridge.

Newcastle Anime Con (early Oct) ⓦ newcastleanimecon.com. Fans of comics, cosplay, sci-fi and everything pop culture descend on Event Northumbria for talks, stalls, photo ops and cast meets.

Halloween (Oct 31) Last day of the Celtic calendar and All Hallows Eve: pumpkins, plus a lot of ghoulish dressing-up, trick-or-treating and parties, with many themed club nights across Newcastle.

Guy Fawkes Night/Bonfire Night (Nov 5) Nationwide fireworks and bonfires commemorating the foiling of the

Gunpowder Plot in 1605 – atop every bonfire is hoisted an effigy known as the "guy" after Guy Fawkes, one of the conspirators.

New Year's Eve (Dec 31) Big parties all over England; in Newcastle, there's a fireworks display on the Quayside and a laser light show at the Civic Centre.

Chronology

c. 7600BC A round dwelling enclosing a hearth is built near a cliff in what is now the village of Howick, Northumberland – Britain's first known house.

c. 7000BC The area around Tynemouth was inhabited by Mesolithic humans, as evidenced by the discovery of stone tools near the coast.

c. 4500BC The Northeast is home to a human population estimated to have been in the hundreds.

c. 2500BC Northumberland's Milfield Basin, near what is now the town of Wooler, assumes a ritual importance for Neolithic people, who build henges and standing stones here.

c. 2000–700BC Bronze Age people in the Northeast build hill forts and create artwork including gold jewellery.

c. 700BC Tribal groups develop in the area including the Brigantes, who by the time of the Roman invasion are the biggest tribe in Britain, their territory stretching from coast to coast.

122AD The invading Romans build a bridge, Pons Aelius, across the River Tyne, close to what is now central Newcastle – the eastern end of Hadrian's Wall.

150AD A stone fort is built at Pons Aelius to protect the bridge.

654AD The Anglo-Saxon kingdoms of Bernicia and Deira combine to form Northumbria.

c. 715AD Work begins on the Lindisfarne Gospels, which would become the most celebrated work of a fertile Christian culture based in the region's monasteries.

875AD Many of the monasteries of the Northeast are pillaged by invading Vikings.

1069AD Amid Northumbrian resistance to the new Norman rule of Britain, Robert de Comines, Earl of Northumbria, and 700 of his men are killed at Durham.

1080AD After the Norman bishop of Durham is killed, William the Conqueror initiates the Harrying of the North, laying waste to the region in retaliation.

1239AD Blackfriars friary is established, close to what is now Newcastle's Chinatown.

1250AD Coal begins to be exported from Newcastle, by this time a thriving trading hub.

1265AD Work begins on the town walls, built to protect Newcastle from Scots invaders, parts of which survive to this day.

1579AD The plague strikes Newcastle, killing 2,000 – around one fifth of the city's population. Three further epidemics would hit in the next twenty years.

1636AD An even more serious plague epidemic hits the town, killing 5,631 of the town's 12,000-strong population.

1641AD Scots invade Newcastle, grinding trade on the Tyne to a halt.

1642AD The English Civil War begins, placing Newcastle in the spotlight as an important trading post.

1644AD Parliament blockades the Tyne, halting trade to prevent the King receiving money from the coal trade. The Scots invade Newcastle.

1645AD Charles I surrenders to the Scots and is imprisoned in Newcastle for nine months.

1715AD Newcastle declares support for George I during the Jacobite rising – a possible origin of the nickname 'Geordie'.

1834AD The builder Richard Grainger wins a competition to design a new plan for central Newcastle.

1849AD Robert Stephenson's High Level Bridge was built over the River Tyne.

1854AD A huge fire devastates Newcastle and Gateshead, destroying most of the towns' buildings, killing 53 people and injuring hundreds more.

1876AD The Swing Bridge is built across the Tyne, allowing ships to pass beyond Newcastle upriver.

1928AD The Tyne Bridge opens, and quickly becomes an icon of the Northeast.

1939–1945AD Newcastle is relatively spared by the ravages of the World War II, emerging largely unscathed from the Blitz.

1963AD Newcastle gains its own university, the University of Newcastle upon Tyne.

c. late 20th century AD The shipping and coal industries decline, a difficult period for the Northeast.

1980AD The Metro rapid transit system opens, eventually to expand to Sunderland and greater Tyne & Wear.

1996AD Newcastle United FC's team of 'entertainers', led by manager Kevin Keegan, finish second in the Premier League.

2001AD The Gateshead Millennium Bridge, the world's first tilting bridge, opens across the Tyne between Newcastle and Gateshead.

2008AD The stylish, cutting-edge Kielder Observatory opens on Black Fell in Northumberland National Park.

2010s AD The former industrial district of Ouseburn is repurposed as a hub for the arts, with venues and studios taking residence in old warehouses and factories.

2021AD A new, if controversial, dawn breaks for Newcastle United as the club is bought by a Saudi-backed consortium, becoming one of the world's richest football clubs overnight.

2022AD At the time of writing, 75.3% of Newcastle's population have received at least one vaccination against Covid-19. 70.1% of the total population have had their second dose.

Publishing Information
First Edition 2022

Distribution
UK, Ireland and Europe
Apa Publications (UK) Ltd; sales@roughguides.com
United States and Canada
Ingram Publisher Services; ips@ingramcontent.com
Australia and New Zealand
Booktopia; retailer@booktopia.com.au
Worldwide
Apa Publications (UK) Ltd; sales@roughguides.com
Special Sales, Content Licensing and CoPublishing
Rough Guides can be purchased in bulk quantities at discounted prices. We can create special editions, personalised jackets and corporate imprints tailored to your needs. sales@roughguides.com.
roughguides.com

Printed in Spain

A catalogue record for this book is available from the British Library

The publishers and authors have done their best to ensure the accuracy and currency of all the information in **Pocket Rough Guide Newcastle and Northumbria**, however, they can accept no responsibility for any loss, injury, or inconvenience sustained by any traveller as a result of information or advice contained in the guide.

Rough Guide Credits
Editor: Zara Sekhavati
Cartography: Carte
Picture editor: Tom Smyth
Layout: Katie Bennett
Original design: Richard Czapnik
Head of DTP and Pre-Press: Katie Bennett
Head of Publishing: Kate Drynan

Acknowledgements
Daniel would like to thank everybody who helped with his research for this book and made researching and writing it so enjoyable, including Shelley Johnson, Kiran Uhri, Alex Clarke, Emma Holland, Jenni Meikle, and his editor, Zara Sekhavati.

About the author

Daniel Stables is a travel writer based in England. He has authored or contributed to more than 30 travel books on destinations across Asia, Europe, and the Americas, including more than a dozen Rough Guides titles. He also writes travel articles for international publications and has appeared as a guest on the Rough Guides podcast. In 2021, Daniel was shortlisted in the Travel Writer category at the Freelance Writing Awards. You can find more of his work on Twitter @DanStables, on Instagram @DanStabs, or at his website, danielstables.co.uk.

Help us update

We've gone to a lot of effort to ensure that this edition of the **Pocket Rough Guide Newcastle and Northumbria** is accurate and up-to-date. However, things change – places get "discovered", opening hours are notoriously fickle, restaurants and rooms raise prices or lower standards. If you feel we've got it wrong or left something out, we'd like to know, and if you can remember the address, the price, the hours, the phone number, so much the better.

Please send your comments with the subject line "**Pocket Rough Guide Newcastle and Northumbria Update**" to mail@uk.roughguides.com. We'll credit all contributions and send a copy of the next edition (or any other Rough Guide if you prefer) for the very best emails.

Photo Credits

(Key: T-top; C-centre; B-bottom; L-left; R-right)

summonedbyfells on Flickr 94
CDC 19C
Graeme Peacock/BALTIC 13C
Helmgyth on flickr 61
John LordNatioa 65
Jonny Gios on Unsplash 108
Kevin Gibson Photography/
NewcastleGateshead Initiative 51,
53, 54, 55, 56, 57, 58
Kielder Observatory 11B, 90
NewcastleGateshead Initiative 15B,
18C, 21T, 32, 45
Pride of Britain Hotels 116/117
Rich Kenworthy/
NewcastleGateshead Initiative 2BL,
5, 21B, 24, 48

Seven Stories 19T
Shutterstock 1, 2T, 2CR, 2BR, 4, 6, 10,
11T, 12T, 12BL, 12/13B, 14T, 14B, 15T,
16T, 16B, 17T, 17B, 18T, 18B, 19B, 20T,
20C, 20B, 21C, 29, 30, 31, 33, 34, 35, 36,
37, 39, 41, 42, 44, 46, 52, 59, 62, 63, 66,
67, 68, 69, 70, 71, 74, 75, 76, 77, 78, 79,
80, 82, 83, 84, 85, 88, 89, 91, 92, 93, 96,
97, 99, 100, 102, 105, 106, 109, 110,
111, 112, 114, 115, 124/125
The Biscuit Factory 47
The Potted Lobster 81
Tom Parnell 95
Visit County Durham 104, 107

Cover: Bamburgh Castle and beach **Dave Head/Shutterstock**

Road		▲	Peak
Pedestrian road		⊙	Statue
Rail line		P	Parking
Ferry		⋒	Abbey
Path		ⵣ	Lighthouse
ⓘ Tourist information		⊥	Gardens
⊠ Post office		▬	Building
♦ Place of interest		⸸	Church
🏛 Stately house		▯	Park
♝ Castle		🌲	Woodland
♣ Museum		▯	Beach

Insects: A Very Short Introduction

VERY SHORT INTRODUCTIONS are for anyone wanting a stimulating and accessible way into a new subject. They are written by experts, and have been translated into more than 45 different languages.

The series began in 1995, and now covers a wide variety of topics in every discipline. The VSI library currently contains over 700 volumes—a Very Short Introduction to everything from Psychology and Philosophy of Science to American History and Relativity—and continues to grow in every subject area.

Very Short Introductions available now:

For more information visit our website

www.oup.com/vsi/

Simon Leather

INSECTS

A Very Short Introduction

OXFORD
UNIVERSITY PRESS

Great Clarendon Street, Oxford, OX2 6DP,
United Kingdom

Oxford University Press is a department of the University of Oxford.
It furthers the University's objective of excellence in research, scholarship,
and education by publishing worldwide. Oxford is a registered trade mark of
Oxford University Press in the UK and in certain other countries

Published in the United States of America by Oxford University Press
198 Madison Avenue, New York, NY 10016, United States of America

British Library Cataloguing in Publication Data

Data available

Library of Congress Control Number: 2022930036

ISBN 978-0-19-884704-5

Printed in Great Britain by
Ashford Colour Press Ltd, Gosport, Hampshire

Contents

Insects

Foreword

This is a special book, the culmination of Simon's sixty-year passion for insects, both as a hobby and a profession. His aim was to bring the wonder of insects to a wider audience so he was delighted to have the opportunity to write this *Very Short Introduction* (VSI).

Simon spent his early life in the Tropics and fell in love with insects as a child in Jamaica; he wanted to find out how insects worked and how they behaved. He studied Agricultural Zoology at Leeds University, where he discovered a passion for aphids, then completed a PhD at the University of East Anglia (UEA), studying the ecology of the bird-cherry-oat aphid. Two short post-doctoral fellowships followed, one in Finland, developing a prediction system for the same aphid, another back at UEA.

For ten years, he worked for the Forestry Commission based in Roslin, Midlothian, researching and advising on forest pests, particularly the pine beauty moth and the large pine weevil, but he missed academia and was pleased to be appointed as a Lecturer at Imperial College London, based at the Silwood Park campus, where for twenty years he lectured and conducted research on agricultural, horticultural, and forest pests. He discovered the joy of urban ecology, researching the biodiversity of Bracknell's infamous roundabouts, which later inspired the name of his blog ('Don't Forget the Roundabouts').

In 2012, he was delighted to move with his team to Harper Adams University (HAU), where he was proud to be appointed as the first UK Professor of Entomology. He spent nine happy years at HAU, basking in the collegiality, interacting with colleagues from all disciplines, and, most particularly, with students; he just loved to share his passion, and to support and mentor the next generation of entomologists.

He realized that social media could enhance science communication by reaching a far wider audience, and joined the Twittersphere (@Entoprof), tweeting and retweeting all things entomological and ecological but also personal: his walks and footpaths that needed repair, the view from home, France (where he hoped to retire), Brexit, Covid, Sunday roasts, and much more. He built up a following of almost 10,000 people, many of whom knew him only virtually.

He also started a blog ('Don't Forget the Roundabouts'), posting at about ten-day intervals for the rest of his life, on a myriad subjects, often his beloved aphids but anything that piqued his interest: insect idioms (e.g. a gnat's whisker), tidy desks (not his own!), the dearth of entomologists, insects in children's literature, classical entomological equipment, family history, papers that influenced his thinking and books that he enjoyed, dead entomologists, 'Insectageddon', together with a regular Pick & Mix of links that he thought worth sharing. He wrote natural history haikus and illustrated some blogs with hand-drawn cartoons; indeed many of his blogs were mini papers, supported by data, graphs, figures, and references He expounded on *institutional vertebratism*, a term that he coined to describe the concentration of effort and funding towards conserving vertebrates, often furry animals, at the expense of vastly more numerous and more important invertebrates.

Had he not been an entomologist, Simon might have been a writer. He was a voracious reader, owning 10,000 books, all of which he had read, and writing generally came easily to him; he published well over 200 papers and wrote or edited a number of

books. He served as an editor or editorial board member for various ecological journals over many years, and refereed countless papers. He founded the Leather Family History Society, to foster research into his family name, writing articles and books to document what he and others discovered.

Simon was convivial; he seemed to know everyone in the world of entomology. Wherever he worked, he engaged with colleagues, enjoying coffee-room chats. He loved meetings and conferences, getting together with colleagues who became friends, sharing meals and a beer or, preferably, glass of red wine. As a fellow ecologist said, 'he was the first person to look for at conferences'. As part of his outreach, he developed a suite of entertaining talks to engage groups such as the University of the Third Age (U3A), gardening societies, and the Women's Institute (WI). He contributed to summer schools, careers fairs, and initiatives such as Skype a Scientist to enthuse young people about insects. Simon was an Honorary Fellow of the Royal Entomological Society recognising his outstanding contributions to entomology.

In retirement, Simon planned to synthesize everything that he had learnt about insects and to share this knowledge as widely as possible. Sadly this book is his swansong; he died in September 2021, not long after the manuscript was accepted for publication. In his last blog post, he described the difficulty of writing this VSI as he found that he knew both too much and not enough about insects; but while it was frustrating, it was also one of his most satisfying pieces of writing. '*I just hope that … my readers will find as much to enjoy as I have since I first came across insects just over sixty years ago.*' I hope so too.

Hugely grateful thanks to Professor Helen Roy MBE Hon. FRES, ecological entomologist at the UK Centre for Ecology & Hydrology, for stepping in to see this book through to publication.

Dr Gillian Leather

Preface

Insects are a wonderfully diverse group but they are all animals with an exoskeleton (a supporting skeleton on the outside) made of the protein chitin, a three-part body plan—head, thorax, abdomen, three pairs of jointed legs, compound eyes, and one pair of antennae. They probably comprise 75 per cent of all animal life.

They range in size from tiny parasitic wasps, *Dicopomorpha echmepterygis*, a mere 139 micrometre (μm) long, to the titan beetle (*Titanus giganteus*), which can reach 17.5 centimetres (cm). Insects are found on all continents and habitats, from the hottest deserts to the frozen Antarctic, in caves, in the soil, inside plants, in other insects and vertebrates, in watercourses and bodies of water, and in the watery interiors of pitcher plants. While no insects live beneath the waves, the intrepid sea skaters, bugs in the genus *Halobates*, skim the surface of some oceans.

Insects include predators, parasites, herbivores, detritivores, fungivores, and saproxylics, that live on decaying wood. Some are regarded as pests while others are valued as beneficial. Some live colonially in a highly complex caste system; others live solitary lives, mingling only to mate or overwinter. Some, such as the honey bee and the silk moth, have been domesticated for millennia; others are used for biological control and protect our crops. Many provide highly nutritious, healthy food sources for

humans. Some are excellent vectors of plant and animal disease; others have been used in human medicine, for instance in maggot therapy, and in the treatment of children with mental health issues and adults suffering from forms of dementia. They have inspired artists, sculptors, poets, musicians, novelists, and engineers, and provide the shock element in many horror films. Their images have appeared on postage stamps and bank notes; their preserved forms, framed under glass, adorn many a household's walls.

Their rigid exoskeleton and associated musculature endow insects with great strength relative to their size while their rapid reproductive rates and adaptability have allowed many species to evolve resistance to commonly used insecticides. Many species have an intimate and obligate relationship with symbiotic bacteria that allows them to use food sources, such as wood, phloem, and xylem sap, that other animals are unable to exploit.

Their nervous system may be simple compared with that of mammals but they exhibit parental care, respond to complex visual and olfactory signals, migrate thousands of miles, 'feel' or at least react to pain, and learn from experience.

Many are masters of disguise, mimicking more well-defended species. Others sequester toxic chemicals from their host plants to protect themselves against predators while yet others disguise themselves as living or dead plant parts or blend so well into the background that it is only when they move that they reveal their true nature.

New species are described every day and many more await discovery, even in well-studied parts of the world. Climate change and habitat degradation threaten the existence of tens of thousands of species, the consequences of which will almost certainly be detrimental to ecosystems worldwide. We know much about insects, and yet there is also much we do not know.

Although there are only approximately 5,500 species of mammals, the mammal-biased perception of the animal kingdom has led to imbalances in funding and research at the expense of other more speciose vertebrate groups, such as the reptiles—*c.*10,000 species—and fish—over 30,000 species. This is, however, dwarfed by the dearth of funding and the paucity of researchers devoted to the study of insects (entomology) and other invertebrates. More than a million insect species have been described, with probably at least another five to eight million species waiting to be named. Given the diversity, utility, and beauty of the insect world, this is a calamity. Insects are the bedrock on which human civilization rests; without them there would almost certainly be no humans.

In the words of W. C. Allee (1938) in his excellent book *The Social Life of Animals*, 'A survey such as I am attempting here should not try to be exhaustive'. I have taken his words to heart; entomology is a vast subject, and I have had to omit a great deal. I have based this book on the facts about insects that I have taught to students over the past thirty years, with the aim of telling a story that conveys the wonder and awe that insects have inspired in me. I hope that you, the reader, will share my feelings of excitement about these wondrous animals.

Acknowledgements

First, a huge thank you to my wife Dr Gillian Leather, who has put up with my entomological ramblings for more than thirty years and has played the part of the educated layperson in reading, re-reading, and stripping away the more verbose and prolix of my sentences. I am extremely grateful to Dr Christine Pearson of the Open University for her comments from the viewpoint of a botanist and communicator to students with many and varied backgrounds. I am also indebted to my former colleague Dr Patricia Reader for her very helpful entomological comments and insights. Dr Simon Segar generously provided the phylogenetic trees. I am deeply grateful to Latha Menon of OUP for her generous and incisive final edit of the completed manuscript. Finally, my heartfelt thanks to the hundreds of students I have taught over the years, who have allowed me to express my love of entomology in a relatively jargon-free manner.

List of illustrations

List of tables

Chapter 1
In the beginning

Arthropods are, with good cause, often described as the most diverse and successful group of animals in the world. As well as insects, they include spiders, millipedes, scorpions, shrimps, crabs, woodlice, and, perhaps surprisingly to many, the barnacles. The word arthropod is derived from the term arthropodization—hardened (sclerotized) appendages with rings of soft unsclerotized cuticle in between, in contrast to animals with soft cuticles. The word 'arthropod' can be translated as jointed foot. Arthropods are also characterized by tagmata, functionally and structurally distinct batches of segments; in the case of the hexapoda, there are three—head, thorax, and abdomen. The body of an arthropod is covered by a chitinous exoskeleton to which the body parts and muscles are attached internally. Arthropods shed their exoskeletons to grow, a process known as moulting. After moulting, the arthropod expands its body by swallowing or taking in air to fill the new skeleton before it hardens. Once the adult stage is reached, moulting stops and there is no further growth. Their success can be attributed to their very adaptable body plan. The evolution of many types of appendage—antennae, claws, wings, and mouthparts—has allowed arthropods to occupy nearly every niche and habitat on earth.

Animal life began in the oceans and remained there for hundreds of millions of years until, about 500 million years ago (MYA), an

arthropod left the water to live on land. This was the first of many; fossil evidence shows that arthropods invaded the land several times, and that different groups, including the ancestors of the first insects and their closest relatives, the Entognatha, made the ocean-to-land transition at different times.

Within the phylum Arthropoda sits an extremely speciose and successful group of organisms: the class Insecta. Insects are six-legged organisms, or hexapods, and are further nested within the Pancrustacea alongside the non-hexapod arthropods like crabs and shrimps, possessing as they do chitinous exoskeletons and jointed appendages. The word insect is derived from the Latin *insectum*—notched or divided body. The class Insecta is well defined; all living insects arose from a common ancestor which was a six-legged creature with a three-segmented body, jointed legs, and a single pair of antennae. These antennae helped the early land colonists to navigate around their new environment using chemical cues. The ancestors of insects were probably cave dwelling crustacea, the Remipedia, and as they diversified, several groups emerged around 479 MYA. The non-insect hexapods (the coneheads, springtails, and two-pronged bristletails) can often be found in damp habitats like soil, whereas the earliest true insects (the jumping bristletails and silverfish) were already more adventurous by the time they appeared on the scene around 440 MYA. Two pairs of wings opened up a three dimensional world as insects took to the air 406 MYA. Some of the descendants of these first winged insects (the dragonflies, damselflies, and mayflies) still return to the water for breeding, but, in the case of dragonflies and damselflies, they dominate local airspace as voracious predators. From then on there was relentless diversification and constant adaptation, as they tracked the evolution of flowering plants. Other advances, for example, transitioning from continuous development to a lifecycle involving a pupal stage, allowed insects to reorganize their cells so that the adult insect was barely recognizable when compared with the larval form. This remarkable ability was something that confused many of the early

entomologists who often mistakenly described larval and adult forms as different species. The evolution of sociality (Chapter 4) allowed some insects to develop complex societies involving a redistribution of roles within the colony. Throughout their tenure on land, insects have been masters at interacting with other organisms and are found both consuming and pollinating plants, gaining sustenance as detritivores, carnivores, or even feeding off the living tissue of their prey. Their myriad adaptations and tight integration with other life on Earth have been key determinants of their success.

Bernhard Misof from Zoologisches Forschungsmuseum, Alexander Koenig based in Bonn, and a host of colleagues from around the world, recently produced an extremely detailed classification of insects, based on genetics combined with an analysis of fossil records. The phylogenetic trees (showing the relationships between organisms based on comparison of their DNA) that they produced are far too complicated for this book, but are summarized simply in Figure 1 and the accompanying text. To reiterate, insects are six-legged arthropods which are now grouped as members of the subphylum Hexapoda, which includes the Collembola, Protura, and Diplura, now all placed within the class Entognatha, in reference to the fact that their mouthparts, unlike those of insects, are retracted within the head.

The insects, which greatly outnumber the Entognatha, are grouped in the class Insecta and are *ectognathous*: their mouthparts are exposed. Despite their superficial resemblance to arachnids such as spiders, the nearest relatives to the Hexapoda are the crustaceans, from which they diverged sometime in the middle of the Ordovician Period, some 460 MYA.

Insects have lived on Earth for almost 500 million years (Figure 1), possibly even longer, as recent discoveries suggest that they arose in the Ordovician Period and were well established by the Silurian, which began some 440 MYA. Fossil insects in amber from the Cretaceous Period (145–66 MYA) are very common, but

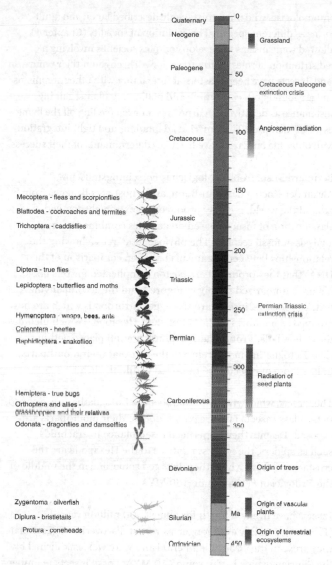

1. The appearance of insects through the ages and their evolutionary relationships.

The position of insects within the animal kingdom

Kingdom	Animalia
Phylum	Arthropoda
Clade	Pancrustacea
Subphylum	Hexapoda
Class	Insecta

Linnaeus (1758).

many insect fossils are also found in shale deposits from the mid-Triassic (around 220 MYA) as well as the Silurian.

Based on the structure and function of their respiratory system, which is based on an air-exchange system (see below), and the fossil record, it was assumed that the first insects were terrestrial. Extensive molecular genetic analysis has confirmed this, and it is now accepted that insects arose from cave dwelling crustacea derived from an earlier aquatic crustacean ancestor. Modern aquatic insects represent those that have returned to their ancestral habitat. Perhaps counterintuitively to us as relatively large mammals, the small size of insects is one of the reasons for their success. Most insects have a body size from 1 to 10 millimetres (mm), allowing them to exploit many habitats that would otherwise be inaccessible; some leaf-miners can complete their whole development within a single leaf. The evolution of flight, their diversity of feeding habits, and their flexible lifecycles allowed insects to conquer first the land and then the air.

Structure and function

The head of insects, even in the apparently soft-bodied orders, is heavily sclerotized. The thorax is divided into three segments, the

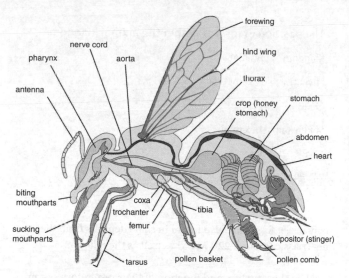

2. Basic body plan of an insect: anatomy of a worker honeybee.

pro-, meso-, and metathorax, and the abdomen can have up to twelve segments. Not all insects have wings and legs; larval stages never have wings and some, depending on where they live, also lack legs. But where present, legs and wings arise from the thorax, with one pair of legs on each segment; in the case of winged insects, the forewings arise from the metathorax and the hind wings from the mesothorax (Figure 2).

The outer skeleton, the cuticle, has two layers: the epicuticle, a thin, waxy, water-resistant outer layer covering the lower, much thicker, chitinous layer, the procuticle. This, in turn, is formed of two layers, the outer exocuticle and the inner endocuticle. The tough, but flexible endocuticle is formed of several layers of fibrous chitin and other proteins. The exocuticle, also made of chitin, is rigid and hardened (sclerotized), although in many soft-bodied insects it is much thinner, especially in the larval stages.

3. A selection of insect wings showing the wide variation in venation.

Insects are the only invertebrates that have developed the ability to fly. Wings, formed of outgrowths of the exoskeleton, are a feature of adult insects. The wings are strengthened by struts—veins—that divide them into segments—cells. Wing venation in insects ranges from the multi-celled, multi-veined complexity of the lacewings to the simplified yet extremely efficient wing of the housefly (Figure 3). Each cell and vein has a unique designation, enabling the taxonomist to distinguish among species and orders.

Ancestrally, insects have two pairs of wings but some have reduced the size of their hind or forewings, as in the Diptera (flies) and Stresiptera, to such an extent that they are no longer functional for flight but are used in a manner akin to a gyroscope. Some

insects, such as the vine weevil (*Otiorhynchus sulcatus*), have lost the ability to fly altogether; others, including aphids, only have wings at certain stages of their lifecycle.

Insects do not have lungs; their respiratory system is based on a network of tubes called tracheae, analogous to the inner structure of the vertebrate lung. The tracheal system opens to the atmosphere through a series of thoracic and abdominal pores, spiracles, often visible to the naked eye. The insect can control the aperture of the spiracles in response to environmental conditions and some can close them completely to prevent the entry of parasitic nematode worms. The tracheae branch into smaller and smaller tubes—the tracheoles—as they pervade the insect body, delivering oxygen to the various organs, in some cases almost directly to the mitochondria, the structures within cells that provide them with their energy.

Although giant insects are often featured in horror stories and films—and, in the past, some insects were indeed much larger than those that we encounter today—insects are limited in size because of the way in which they breathe. Lacking lungs, they depend on the diffusion of oxygen across the thin skin of the tracheoles. Larger insects ventilate their tracheal system by muscular pumping of the body walls but even this does not compensate for the lack of lungs. The exoskeleton also brings with it some disadvantages, in that the surface:weight ratio means that the integument—the insect's covering—becomes disproportionately heavy and susceptible to water loss. Giant arthropods are found only in water, although, somewhat perversely, the largest insects are land living.

Unlike us, insects do not have veins and arteries or a single circulatory pump. Instead, a system of muscular pumps moves the haemolymph, a watery fluid, usually colourless, but it can be yellow, green, blue, and sometimes red, through the body compartments. The main pump is, somewhat cumbersomely, called the *pulsatile dorsal vessel*, the back part of which is

sometimes referred to as the heart, and the front, the aorta. We humans do love to anthropomorphize. In a similar way, we can think of the haemolymph as a rough equivalent to the blood of vertebrates. The haemolymph bathes the organs and mediates all chemical exchanges between tissues. The haemolymph is responsible for the transmission of hormones, the distribution of nutrients, and movement of waste products to the excretory organs. Unlike human blood, the haemolymph rarely contains respiratory pigments but in some groups, for instance the Plecoptera, haemocyanin (an ancestral method for oxygen transport) is sometimes present. The haemolymph also carries the haemocytes, the blood cells, which, in a similar way to our red and white blood cells, are responsible for defence against diseases, 'blood clotting', and nutrient storage and distribution.

The structure of the insect nervous system varies among orders (Figure 4) but is, as with us, based around a central nervous system. In all insects, the nerve cells, as with other animals, are contained in structures known as ganglia and those of all the head segments are fused to form the brain. In insects, in contrast to us, where it runs along our spine (dorsally), the main nerve cord runs along the underside of the body (ventrally), connecting the thoracic and abdominal ganglia. The insect brain is divided into three parts—the protocerebrum, which is associated with the eyes and contains the optic lobes; the deutocerebrum, which controls the antennae; and the tritocerebrum, which coordinates signals arriving from the body. Insects have three types of neuron: sensory neurons, which receive stimuli from the environment and transmit them to the central nervous system; interneurons, which are responsible for between-neuron communications; and motor neurons, which receive information from the interneurons and transmit information to the muscles and the hormone-producing neuroendocrine cells.

Insect sensory organs include the eyes, the antennae, and the feet. Most insects have two compound eyes; they may also have two or

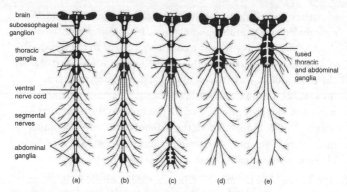

4. The central nervous systems of various insects showing the diversity of ganglia in the ventral nerve cord.

three simple eyes—ocelli. The compound eyes are composed of many single photoreceptors—ommatidia—which, although not very good for image resolution, are extremely good at detecting movement; think how difficult it is to sneak up on a housefly. The ocelli have better image resolution and have a major role in helping flying insects to keep on course when airborne. The antennae are an important part of an insect's sensory repertoire and may have more than one sensory function—able to detect touch, movement, and chemicals, including pheromones. The ability of insects to detect pheromones is amazing: some insects can detect and respond to a few hundred molecules of pheromone in a cubic centimetre of air from a distance of 30 kilometres or so. In some insects there is a trade-off between vision and smell (olfaction); insects with large eyes tend to have smaller antennae. Other insects, cave-dwellers for example, are blind, and rely entirely on their antennae and touch receptors to know where they are. Insects also have sensory organs on their feet, with which they can detect texture and 'flavour'.

Insect growth and development is known as metamorphosis, and is under the control of hormones delivered via the endocrine

system. There are three types of hormone, the ecdysteroids (ecdysone is the most common), juvenile hormones, and neurohormones (neuropeptides), which can be regarded as messengers. Most of the hormones are produced by specialist neurosecretory cells. The *corpora cardiaca*, a pair of neuroglandular organs either side of the aorta and behind the brain, store and release hormones as well as making their own. The prothoracic glands secrete ecdysteroid, and the *corpora allata* secrete juvenile hormone. These two hormones are integral to the moulting and reproductive processes of all insects. The role and source of juvenile hormone involved in moulting were determined by a series of elegant, if somewhat gruesome, experiments by the insect physiologist Sir Vincent Wigglesworth in the late 1930s. These involved the decapitation of adult and immature individuals of the kissing bug (*Rhodnius prolixus*), the bodies of which were then attached to whole individuals, resulting in changes in the moulting process. He graphically demonstrated the inhibitory effect of juvenile hormone on the moulting process by writing his initials, using juvenile hormone and applying it directly to the cuticle of pre-adult individuals with a fine paintbrush. After the next moult his initials were clearly visible as unmoulted regions on the otherwise adult insect. Juvenile hormone is present in all insect orders irrespective of their lifecycle type. Nowadays molecular techniques allow us to investigate insect hormones in a more detailed, if less dramatic manner.

The more primitive—or as taxonomists term them, less derived—insects have an ametabolous lifecycle, which does not involve metamorphosis. Once hatched, they are miniature versions of the adult, lacking only genitalia; each moult signals a change in size, without a marked change in form. Other insects, such as grasshoppers, have a hemimetabolous lifecycle, with three distinct forms—egg, larval, and adult; the later stages of the larval form gradually take on adult attributes—a process known as incomplete metamorphosis. The final type of lifecycle,

holometabolism, or complete metamorphosis, is exemplified by the Lepidoptera (butterflies and moths), in which there is a pupal stage between the larval and adult forms, during which a complete transformation of body structure occurs; this allows the insect to exploit different food sources during its lifecycle. The larger the insect, the longer it takes to moult and for the new exoskeleton to harden, thus exposing the insect to a longer period of vulnerability.

How many insects are there?

Given the recent concern about declines in insect numbers (see Chapter 9), it is important that we know how many insects there are globally. The figures given for each order in the following tables add up to just over a million described species. This is, however, only the tip of the iceberg. Insects are extremely diverse, incredibly numerous, and woefully understudied. Estimating how many species of insects there are is thus an extremely difficult task and has exercised the ingenuity of entomologists for some time. Perhaps the most controversial figure is that arrived at by the American entomologist Terry Erwin. Terry sampled trees in Panamanian forests in the early 1980s and estimated that there could be as many as thirty million insect species worldwide. Due to his many, somewhat contentious, assumptions, this figure is almost certainly an overestimate; the common consensus is five to eight million species, of which approximately 1.2 million have been named and described. Even if we accept the more cautious lower estimate, given that the rate of description is approximately 10,000 species per year, it will be at least another 400 years before all have been named and described, and of course we have to find them first.

Putting things in order

There are currently twenty-nine insect orders; there were thirty recognized orders when I started writing this book, but a detailed phylogenetic study by Eirik Tielka and colleagues at the University

of Bristol, UK, suggests that Siphonaptera (fleas) should now be placed within the Mecoptera. Over the past few decades, molecular biology has resulted in some major reclassification, with some orders being combined and others raised, so it is possible that by the time you read this the number of orders will have changed yet again.

Insects, based on their type of metamorphosis, are divided into three super-orders, the Apterygota, the Endopterygota, and the Exopterygota. The Apterygota (Table 1), which includes bristletails and silverfish, are ametabolous; the Exopterygota (Table 2), hemimetabolous; and the Endopterygota (Table 3), holometabolous.

First, a little bit of entomological jargon; broadly speaking we are talking bastardized Greek and Latin. *Pteron* is Greek for wing and is the root of the Latin *ptera*, which occurs commonly in entomology. The presence of wings is denoted by the suffix *ptera*, the absence of wings by *aptera*, which can be a little confusing and, to further complicate matters, as in pterodactyl, the p in Apterygota, Endopterygota, and Exopterygota is silent.

In entomology, when we talk about wingless insects, we use the term apterous. Most insects, the Exopterygota and the Endopterygota, are winged. The Exopterygota are insects whose wings develop outside the body and show a gradual change from immature to adult. Think of an aphid for example; when the nymph (immature hemimetabolous insect) reaches the third or

Table 1 The Apterygota

Protura	Coneheads
Diplura	Two pronged bristletails
Archaeognatha	Bristletails
Zygentoma	Silverfish

Table 2 The Exopterygota

Ephemeroptera	Mayflies (the name referring to the fact that the adults only live or are only winged for a day) are the oldest extant group with wings. They are also a bit of an oddity: unlike other Exopterygota, they have a winged subadult stage. They are a relatively small order with approximately 2,500 species worldwide. The Ephemeroptera along with the Odonata are the oldest winged insect groups, the Palaeoptera, arising about 350 MYA.
Odonata	Dragonflies and damselflies (their name is derived from the Greek for tooth, δόντι; despite their amazing flight capability, the name refers to their toothed mandibles). The wings get a mention when we get down to infra-orders: the dragonflies, Anisoptera, which are uneven; and the damselflies, Zygoptera, which are even. There are just over 6,300 species listed by the World Odonata List (https://www2.pugetsound.edu/academics/academic-resources/slater-museum/biodiversity-resources/dragonflies/world-odonata-list2/).
Dermaptera	Earwigs—leathery/skin/hide, referring to the forewings, which are also reduced in size. Despite this, the much larger, membranous hind wings are safely folded away beneath them. This is one of the smaller orders with about 2,000 described species.
Plecoptera	Stoneflies—wicker/work wings. About 4,000 species. Fossil stoneflies date back to the early Permian. Their larvae are aquatic.
Orthoptera	Grasshoppers and crickets—straight wings. As of February 2021, the Orthoptera species list puts the number of species at 28,869 https://orthoptera.speciesfile.org/HomePage/Orthoptera/HomePage.aspx
Dictyoptera (also known as the Blattodea)	Cockroaches, termites, and allies—net wings. There are around 6,800 species in this order, most of which are found in the warmer parts of the world.

Notoptera	Ice crawlers (Grylloblattodea) and gladiators (Mantophasmatodea). Despite being wingless, 'Notoptera' translates as back wings; the name was coined when only extinct, winged, members of this order were known. This is a tiny order with only sixty species known.
Mantodea	Mantids (e.g. the very familiar the praying mantis—prophet or soothsayer). There are about 2,300 species of mantids, all of which are predators, both as juveniles and adults.
Phasmotodea	Phasmids, the stick insects, and leaf insects; phasma translates as apparition or ghost and presumably relates to their ability to blend into the background. There are about 3,000 species of stick and leaf insects, most of which are found in the tropics. Many are parthenogenetic.
Psocoptera	Bark and book lice—the name translates as gnawed or biting with wings. In this case the adjective refers not to the appearance of their wings but to the fact that the insects can bite. They are also able to take up water directly from the atmosphere so that they can exploit extremely dry environments. About 5,500 species have been described so far, and most of these in the last few years.
Embioptera	Web spinners—lively wings. Each species has a characteristic way in which they spin their webs. Entomologist Janice Edgerly-Rooks at Santa Clara University, USA, collaborated with musicians assigning musical notes to each limb movement to produce a music video of embiopteran silk spinning. This is another small order with only 200 species described to date.
Zoraptera	The opposite of the Notoptera, the angel insects, Zora meaning pure in the sense of not having any wings; unfortunately for the taxonomists who named this order, winged forms have now been found. This is the smallest order, with only thirty species.

(continued)

Table 2 Continued

Thysanoptera	Thrips (both the plural and singular)—*thysan* means tassel wings, although feather might be a more appropriate description. There are just over 6,000 species of thrips, a number of which are important pollinators, but it also includes some very important pest species.
Hemiptera	True bugs—this distinction is made because many people, especially in the USA, call all insects bugs. The name Hemiptera translates as half wings. The two former official suborders (Homoptera and Heteroptera) were very useful descriptions. The Homoptera includes aphids, in which both membranous wings, fore and hind, are similar to one another. The Homoptera are now referred to as the Sternorrhyncha and Auchenorrhyncha, reflecting the position of the mouthparts, which in the former are positioned between the front legs and the chest, and in the latter arise from the back of the head in the neck region. The Heteroptera such as Lygaeids (e.g. chinch bugs, which are often mistaken for beetles) retain the existing name. Hetero (i.e. different) refers to the fact that the forewings are hardened and often brightly coloured in comparison with the membranous hindwings. About 80,000 species have been described.
Phthiraptera	Lice—wingless louse. There are just under 5,000 species in this order of highly specialized insects, three of which have evolved to exploit different sites on the human body.

Table 3 The Endopterygota

Rhapidioptera	Snakeflies—needle, in this case referring to the ovipositor (egg-laying tube), not to the wings, which are similar to those of dragonflies. They belong to the Neuropterida, three closely related orders, which includes the Megaloptera and the Neuroptera. This is one of the smaller insect orders with only 206 species.
Megaloptera	Alderflies, dobsonflies—translates as large wings. There are only about 300 known species, the immature stages of which are aquatic.
Neuroptera	Lacewings—translates as veined wings. This is the largest order within the Neropterida, with just over 6,000 described. The larvae of many species are voracious predators and some are reared commercially for use as biological control agents.
Coleoptera	Beetles—translates as sheathed wings, referring to the hardened forewings, the elytra, that cover the membranous hind wings. The complex process of unfolding and refolding their hind wings means that many beetles are 'reluctant' to fly unless they really need to. Currently this is the order with the most (approximately 300,000) species described.
Strepsiptera (sometimes referred to as Stylops)	Endoparasites of other insects. The name translates as twisted wings. Like flies, they have only two pairs of functional wings, the other pair having been modified into halteres. Unlike flies, their halteres are modified forewings. They are a very strange group of insects and their relationship to other insect orders is still unclear. They are rarely seen by entomologists which may explain why only 600 species have been described. They feature on the logo of the Royal Entomological Society.
Mecoptera	Scorpionflies, hanging flies—translates as long wings. Not all Mecoptera are winged but the winged flies do indeed have long wings in relation to their body size. There were, until they were joined by the fleas, only about 600 species worldwide.

(continued)

Table 3 Continued

Siphonaptera	Fleas—translates as tube, no wings; the tube part of the name refers to their mouthparts. Now regarded as being within the Mecoptera. Some 2,600 species of flea have been described to date and have really swelled the ranks of the Mecoptera.
Diptera	Flies—translates as two wings; the hind pair is reduced to form the halteres, which are a highly complex orientation and balancing device, sometimes compared with a gyroscope. This represents one of the largest orders with approximately 160,000 species described to date.
Trichoptera	Caddisflies, which are, evolutionarily speaking, closely related to the Lepidoptera. Instead of scales, however, they have hairy wings; at first glance, some species can be mistaken for small moths. There are about 14,500 species of Trichoptera.
Lepidoptera	Moths and butterflies—translates as scaly wings. The scales and how they interact with light are what gives many moths and butterflies their iridescent colours. There are at least 200,000 species of Lepidoptera. The Lepidoptera, Trichoptera, Mecoptera, and Diptera had a common ancestor about 300 MYA and are collectively known as the Panorpid complex.
Hymenoptera	Wasps, bees, ants—translates as membrane wings. Alternatively, and with thanks to Canadian entomologist Stephen Heard, Hymenaeus was the Greek god of marriage; Hymenoptera as 'marriage wings' makes sense because of the hamage wing coupling (fore- and hind wings coupled by a row of hooks, or hamuli, so that they beat as one wing). The Hymenoptera contain the Parasitica, wasps that have larval stages that develop within other insects; they almost certainly inspired the film *Alien*. Although 150,000 species have so far been described this is probably only the tip of the iceberg.

fourth instar (moulted stage), it seems to have shoulder pads; these are the wing buds (Figure 5). The process of going from egg to adult in this way is, as mentioned earlier, called incomplete metamorphosis.

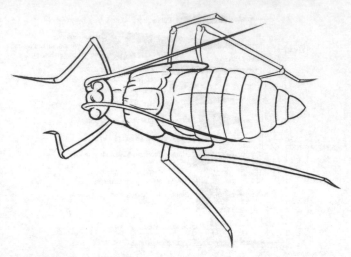

5. Fourth-instar alatiform (destined to be winged) aphid nymph, showing the distinctive wing buds.

In insects such as butterflies and moths, where the wings develop inside the body, the adult bears no resemblance to the larva and the process is described as complete metamorphosis and the lifecycle type as holometabolous.

Now on to the orders and their names (Figure 6). Remember that *aptera* means no wings and *ptera* means with wings. This can be a bit confusing as most of the orders look and sound as though they have wings. This is in part, due to our pronunciation of words; we tend to make the syllables fit our normal speech patterns, so that words are not divided into their correct component parts. Diptera and Coleoptera are two good examples—we pronounce the former as 'Dip-tera' and informally as Dips but, from a purist's point of view, it should be pronounced *di-tera*—two wings; similarly, *coleo-tera*, with a silent p.

Most of us, including entomologists, are most familiar with only seven of the insect orders, in order of species richness, the

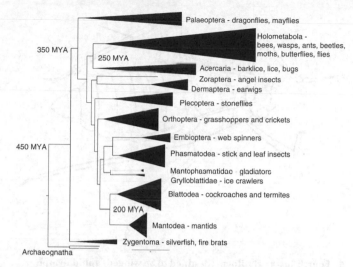

6. Simplified phylogenetic tree of the insects, focusing on the Polyneoptera, which were the first orders to evolve the ability to flex their wings over their abdomens. The width of the black triangles indicates the number of described species within each order. The approximate dates of diversification are shown as millions of years ago.

Coleoptera (beetles), the Hymenoptera (ants, bees, and wasps), the Diptera (flies), the Lepidoptera (moths and butterflies), the Hemiptera (true bugs), the Orthoptera (crickets and grasshoppers), and the Odonata (dragonflies and damselflies). Between them these orders account for about 900,000 species, so about 75 per cent of all those insects that have been described to date. Of these seven orders, the first five named actually account for just over 800,000 species. If we accept that the number of species within an order reflects their success, we might ask what it is that makes the Big Five so successful. One could argue that with the exception of the Lepidoptera, which are, with a handful of exceptions, all herbivorous, their success is because they, even the Hemiptera, range across the dietary spectrum, from scavengers through herbivores and omnivores to voracious predators, and are

20

7. Thrips wing, showing the characteristic feathery appearance.

able to exploit a wide range of ecological niches. The Orthoptera on the other hand are wholly herbivorous and the Odonata largely carnivorous. That does not mean that the other orders are not important—they all have a part to play, and some of the smaller orders, such as the Thysanoptera (thrips (Figure 7) or thunderflies), include some of the world's most important pests (Table 2). Other orders, such as the Zoraptera, are so small (sixty species) and so rare that only a handful of entomologists have ever seen them. Niche specialization does have some advantages, in that competition is reduced; the ice crawlers (Grylloblattodea), as their name suggests, live in icy caves and on frozen mountain tops, habitats where other insects are rarely, if ever, found. They are, however, extremely vulnerable to climate change and habitat loss, and are almost certainly the most endangered group of insects in the world.

There is some debate among entomologists as to which orders contain the most species. The beetles (Coleoptera), which have four wings, the forewings of which have become heavily sclerotized and cover the hind wings, to form 'casings' known as the elytra, have long been lauded as the most speciose insect order. The point was highlighted by the British evolutionary biologist and geneticist J. B. S. Haldane, who is purported to have told a group of theologians that if God existed he must have 'an inordinate fondness for beetles'. Current estimates place beetles at the top of the podium with approximately 300,000 described species. However, based on an analysis using body size, collection rates, and the ratio of beetles to other insects housed in the

Natural History Museum, London, Nigel Stork and colleagues suggest that there at least a million extant species of beetle. In second place are the Lepidoptera with 200,000, closely followed by the Hymenoptera with 150,000, and the Diptera at 120,000—although Erica McAlister, author of *The Secret Life of Flies*, puts the number at 160,000, with at least that many waiting to be discovered and named. Hymenopterists argue that as the Hymenoptera contain the Parasitica (wasps that parasitize other insects), and as all insects have parasites, the majority of which are Hymenoptera, and many of which are species specific, it is logical to suppose that the Hymenoptera must be the biggest order; we must, however, wait for the taxonomists to confirm this.

Having covered the basics of insect taxonomy and evolution, and their basic biology, we can now move on to an exploration of their behaviour and how this has enabled them to be so successful.

Chapter 2
Prolific procreators

Like other animals, the primary function of insects is to reproduce. All insects have the same basic reproductive structures (Figure 8). Females have a pair of ovaries, each of which is divided further into a series of tubes, containing rows of egg chambers, the ovarioles. The number of ovarioles varies between species, from as few as four per ovary in some aphids to more than fifteen in some species of flies. The more ovarioles, the more offspring an insect can produce. In some orders of insects, the number of ovarioles is a constant, most butterflies and moths, for example, have eight; in other groups, flies and aphids, the number of ovarioles varies both between and within species.

Male insects produce sperm, which is delivered to the female via the penis, known as the aedeagus, although in some insects, such as bed bugs, the male can inject his sperm directly into the abdomen through the cuticle of the female, very appropriately termed traumatic insemination. Female genitalia vary among orders but in general there is an external opening connecting to the ovaries, and a sperm storage/receptacle (spermatheca). The sperm is often delivered in a 'package'—the spermatophore, which, as well as holding the sperm, provides extra nutrients to the female—a type of nuptial gift (see p. 32). Most insects lay eggs, but some species, such as aphids, give birth to live young. Many insect species, such as vine weevils, some stick insects, and, most notably, aphids, are

Female Reproductive Tract

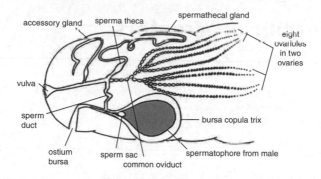

accessory gland
sperma theca
spermathecal gland
eight ovarioles in two ovaries
vulva
sperm duct
ostium bursa
sperm sac
common oviduct
bursa copula trix
spermatophore from male

Male Reproductive Tract

Insects

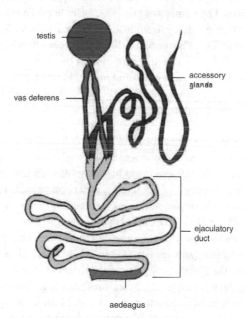

testis
accessory glands
vas deferens
ejaculatory duct
aedeagus

8. **Generalized female and male reproductive systems.**

parthenogenetic, meaning they no longer require males to fertilize their eggs. Aphids are even more special in that each adult aphid contains live young, which in turn contain strings of embryos—a living Russian doll.

The number of offspring that a female insect produces is linked closely to her size; the larger the female, the more offspring she is able to produce. The size of an insect is largely the result of the quality of the nutrition that it receives as a larva; the better the larval diet, the larger the adult insect. As a consequence, finding the best place to deposit their young is very important for female insects, especially when the larvae have limited powers of dispersal. The optimal outcome would be for insect mothers to choose those hosts on which their offspring would prosper best and to lay as many eggs as possible on those hosts and this, with few exceptions, is generally what we see in nature. Herbivorous insects and those that parasitize other insects show great prowess in host selection ('mother knows best'), choosing better quality hosts on/in which to lay (oviposit) their eggs. Predatory insects, like ladybird beetles and hoverflies, are also able to select egg-laying sites to optimize offspring survival; they lay their eggs near aphid colonies, ensuring a plentiful food supply in easy reach of their offspring when they emerge from their eggs. The offspring of herbivorous insects have been found to survive better on the host plants preferred by their mothers, and insects that are able to survive on a wide range of host plants are less 'fussy' than those with a more limited range of diets.

Fecundity, the number of offspring that an insect can produce, can be described as either potential—that which could be achieved under ideal conditions, or realized—or that which is actually achieved. An insect may have a potential fecundity of several hundred but lay only a handful of eggs, not all of which will hatch successfully. So-called capital breeders, normally those species which do not feed as adults, such as many of the Lepidoptera, use resources laid down during the larval phase, and no new eggs are

developed as adults; whereas income breeders, mosquitoes for example, continue to obtain resources to develop and mature eggs, with new eggs being developed as adults. There is no evidence to suggest that income breeders are more fecund than capital breeders, although their response to adverse conditions may be more flexible.

Insects, even those that tend to live for a long time, are very vulnerable to predation and weather events, so it is important to lay as many eggs as possible as early as possible. Most insects produce the majority of their offspring in the first few days of adult life (Figure 9). In some species, over 50 per cent of eggs are laid in the first three or four days of reproductive life. Eggs laid subsequently are a bonus and some insects, if they survive, can continue to produce offspring for several weeks, or, in very long-lived insects, even months, although the offspring that arise from later-laid eggs are not as fit as those laid earlier; they tend to be smaller and the larvae that emerge are also smaller and have a lower chance of surviving to adulthood than their siblings from the earlier-laid eggs.

Egg size can also vary according to the availability of suitable oviposition sites: the pine beauty moth (*Panolis flammea*), for

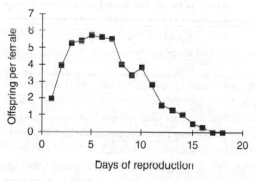

9. Typical insect reproductive pattern showing the number of offspring produced by a female insect once reproduction has begun.

example, will lay more and smaller eggs in the presence of good-quality host plants than if the available host plants are of poorer quality. On a good-quality host plant, the tiny larvae emerging from the small eggs can feed and survive with relative ease, whereas on a poorer quality host plant they need a better start in life and larger eggs are laid. Female insects will also delay oviposition if there is a lack of good-quality host plants, but given the vagaries of weather and the abundance of natural enemies, they are in a race against time to lay their eggs before they die. Stretch receptors in the abdomen tell them that they are full and eventually they will lay some eggs on a less suitable host to relieve the pressure. They then seek another host plant. If the next plant is of better quality, they will lay eggs on it; their expectations are then raised and they become choosier. However, if the next host plant is of poorer quality, they subsequently become less choosy. Of course, this pattern of oviposition depends on the overall egg-laying strategy of the species. Oviposition in insects, whether predatory, parasitic, or herbivorous, falls into three main categories—large clutches, small clutches, and singletons. There are arguments to be made in favour of all these strategies and no strategy is confined to any one order of insects. There are various reasons for the evolution of different clutch sizes among insects, ranging from reducing predation risk of the adults, and ensuring the safety of the larvae, to trade-offs between fecundity and dispersal.

Within the Lepidoptera, for example, oviposition strategies vary across families. Lepidoptera such as small ermine moths (Yponomeutidae), members of the Lasiocampidae, the eggars and lappet moths, and the Thaumetopoeidae, processionary moths, whose larvae live gregariously in silken webs or tents (hence their common names—tent caterpillars/tent moths), tend to lay their eggs in large masses, of up to 200 eggs. Other moths, such as the Lymantrinae, or tussock moths, whose females tend to be flightless or have reduced wings, also lay their eggs in large clusters, many covering their eggs with masses of spiny hairs broken off from their abdomens to protect them against predators.

It is easy to see why insects whose ability to disperse is limited would lay all their eggs at once or in a few very large batches, but what about those where the females are relatively strong flyers? One argument is that large clusters of eggs reduce overall surface area and the risk of desiccation. If your eggs are toxic or protected with irritating hairs, it may make sense to advertise your presence and toxicity more visibly. Another factor that might encourage cluster laying is if the larvae are gregarious and egg hatch is well synchronized; hatch at the same time and, if there are a lot of you, the protective webbing can be fashioned more quickly. There is also some evidence that group feeding makes it easier to overcome plant defences whether you are a defoliator feeding on leaves or a bark beetle feeding underneath tree bark. Some cluster-laying insects, for example ladybirds, lay a number of eggs that are never destined to hatch but are there to provide the first meal for their larvae to build up their strength before they have to start hunting for prey. Finally, if your food source, be it aphids if you are a predator or plants if you are a herbivore, is distributed in a non-regular, patchy way, it makes biological sense for the mother insect to deposit a sizeable proportion of her offspring at a site where a plentiful supply of food is available.

Many insects have another strategy; they lay their eggs in singletons or pairs on the basis that it is faster to lay one egg at a time than to lay dozens or hundreds of eggs in one go. Less time is spent in one place, and the chance of being predated is reduced. If you have ever watched a cabbage white butterfly laying eggs, this is very obvious; each egg-laying event takes no more than a few seconds then the mother flits to another leaf. Insects adopting this strategy also tend to lay small, well-camouflaged—cryptic—eggs placed, if a plant feeder, on the underside of the leaf. This oviposition strategy relies on not being seen. Another advantage of cryptic, non-toxic eggs is that the larvae develop faster as they do not have to incorporate (sequester) poisons from their host plants as they grow. Finally, if there are only a few individual insects scattered across a whole plant, it makes the job of predators or other natural enemies more difficult,

as they have to search harder, with fewer visual and chemical signals (in the form of leaf damage and volatile compounds) to inform them that a tasty meal is in the vicinity. Insects that lay more than one egg clutch, lay smaller clutches, containing smaller, less viable eggs, as they get older. The mortality of eggs laid by the rice stem borer, *Chilo partellus*, in the latter half of the mother's life is twice that of eggs laid at the beginning of her reproductive life. Moreover, the larvae that do hatch from these late eggs have a much lower chance of surviving to become adults than their older siblings.

By the late 1970s, it was generally accepted that the optimal egg-laying strategy in herbivorous insects would be linked, first, to the number of eggs remaining in their ovaries; and, second, to the likelihood of encountering a suitable host plant on which to lay their eggs. In general, adult Lepidoptera are able to 'remember' host suitability for oviposition sites, altering their concept of a good-quality host depending on the suitability of the previous host plants that they encountered and the number of eggs left in their reproductive tract. Their degree of 'fussiness' thus waxes and wanes according to the suitability of the last host plant encountered, but this is tempered further by how long they have been on the hunt. As the reproductive clock ticks, the probability of them accepting a less suitable host on which to lay their eggs increases.

Similarly, we know that adult Lepidoptera, such as the monarch butterfly (*Danaus plexippus*), are able to retain learned information about suitable feeding resources, for example, the flowers that are likely to give them the most nectar. This ability is not just short-term: the hummingbird hawkmoth (*Macroglossum stellatarum*) is able to remember flower preferences even after winter dormancy.

Sexual selection and mating

Unless they are parthenogenetic, which many are, insects are sexually dimorphic, with the males and females of most insects

differing in appearance. Insects have adopted a number of different strategies to locate mates, ranging from the use of sex pheromones to mass swarming and nuptial gifts, among which we can include the use of spermatophores, the casing produced inside the male containing sperm that is transferred during copulation.

In theory, female insects should choose males that will confer greatest fitness on their offspring. We would thus expect that male insects would evolve to display ever more extreme secondary sexual characteristics to satisfy the expectations of their potential mates. Although we can see some signs of this, for example the stalk-eyed flies, many insects instead show a great variation in their secondary sexual characteristics, with some male individuals investing less in display than others, yet still mating successfully.

Pheromones

Pheromones are semiochemicals, substances that elicit behavioural responses in another organism. Sex pheromones are used widely by insects: in some species females produce them to attract males, while in others males use them to attract females. Sex pheromones are usually very species specific, although in some closely related species the structure of the pheromones is identical but the concentrations at which they attract their respective recipients differ. Insects are able to detect pheromones from a considerable distance: some moths can respond to sex pheromones from as far away as 50 km. The highly specific blends of pheromones produced by insects ensures that the right mates find each other quickly and efficiently, increasing the chances of finding a mate even at low population densities. The downside for some of those insects that use pheromones to attract their mates is that chemists have been able to synthesize them and many are now used as a pest control method by attracting males into traps baited with pheromone lures.

Mating swarms, leks, displays, combative encounters

Many male insects find mates by aggregating to form swarms (referred to as leks), often of great size, that attract females and provide an opportunity for sexual competition, as the females, in theory, enter the swarm and pick the most robust and active males. This type of behaviour is termed lekking. Mayflies (Ephemeroptera) are renowned for the size and predictability of their short-lived but spectacular swarms. Ants, honeybees, some beetles, cockchafers, and many dipteran species, bibionids (march flies, known as love bugs in the USA), mosquitoes, and midges all have mating swarms. Midges tend to swarm on warm evenings, quite often at the top of a small hill or even above a human head. Within the male leks, theory has it that large insects are at an advantage over smaller members of the same species in many ways, including sexual competition. This is not always so: in the phantom midge (*Chaoborus flavicans*), while the large males form the lek, many of the smaller males rest on the vegetation and mate with females that have not yet entered the swarm. In a few species, the dance fly (*Empis borealis*) being a good example, the females form the swarm into which a single male enters, bearing a nuptial gift with which to entice a female to leave her sisters and join him in a mating flight.

Another group of flies, the stalk-eyed flies (Diopsidae), has evolved eyes that are borne on stalks, giving the appearance of a pair of antlers. This bizarre adaptation has two functions: mate attraction—females prefer males with longer eye stalks—and male competition. Males face each other and compare their relative eye spans. In some cases, they will spread their front legs apart to reinforce the message, the insect version of the power stance. If the relative eye span is similar, a fight will ensue, the winner holding the territory and gaining a suitably impressed mate.

Similar outsized modifications of body parts can be seen in male stag beetles (Lucanidae). The males have modified mandibles that resemble the antlers of stags, hence their common name. In the mating season, they use their antlers to wrestle other males, grabbing each other and using their antlers to overturn and throw each other to the ground. These fights can often be protracted and, as with stags, can result in physical injury to the loser.

Lepidoptera, in particular butterflies, adopt a strategy called 'hill topping': male swallowtails (*Papilio machaon*), for example, aggregate at the tops of hills and wait for females to fly up towards them. These hill-top sites are used year after year and are frequently visited by entomologists 'in the know'. Butterflies can also be very territorial, some being perchers, others patrollers. Perching is a 'sit-and-wait' tactic; the males guard a territory, sometimes as large as 20 square metres (m^2), in which they sit in a suitable, usually high position, from which they will emerge to investigate passing objects, either chasing away a competing male or attempting to mate with a receptive female. Patrollers, on the other hand, fly up and down a territory looking for receptive females with which to mate. Males of the North American great purple hairstreak butterfly (*Atlides halesus*) perch in the tops of trees waiting for receptive females but fly up from their perches to chase other males away from their territories, sometimes resorting to physical clashes as well as flight displays. The purple-edged copper butterfly (*Lycaena hippothoe*) is both a percher and a patroller. The aptly named speckled wood butterfly (*Pararge aegeria*) flies in partially shaded woodland with dappled sunlight. The males, which are very aggressive, usually perch in a small pool of sunlight, rising up to deter intruders; they will even attempt to chase humans away from their glades.

Nuptial gifts and spermatophores

Like some spiders, several male insects use nuptial gifts to help persuade their partners to pass their genes on. Probably the most

well-known nuptial gift is that found in a few species of the praying mantis, in which the male risks his life while impregnating his chosen mate, especially if she is hungry. Death during copulation is not the male's most favourable outcome: mating with more than one female allows a better chance of spreading his genes, although female mantids who eat their copulating partner can lay up to 30 per cent more eggs than those that allow the male to depart intact. Male scorpionflies (Panorpidae) have an array of tactics with which to attract mates. They use pheromones to attract potential mates but some species reinforce this with nuptial gifts: the male gives the female food, which she eats during copulation. The food item may be a salivary deposit from specially enlarged salivary glands or it may be a dead insect. The male waits for a female to arrive and copulates while she is busy with her meal. Some males dispense with both the gift and the pheromones and use their abdominal clamp to force the female to copulate with them; and in yet other species, the males mimic females and steal another male's gift which they then proceed to use for their own benefit.

Perhaps a more intimate nuptial gift is the spermatophore. This may have been an adaptation to life on land, as the aquatic ancestors of insects may just have released sperm into the water; once on land, the sperm needed to be prevented from desiccating on its way to the female, especially in insects where the male does not introduce the sperm directly into the female. In some Orthoptera the males produce both a spermatophore and a nuptial gift (to stop her from eating the spermatophore before the sperm have entered her).

In the monarch butterfly, the larger the spermatophore, the longer the time before they mate again, which is an advantage to the first male on the scene; although females that mate more than once lay more eggs than single-mated females. Does it cost the males anything to be so generous? In some species (e.g. *Tatochila mercedis sterodice*) their lifespan is reduced, while in others, such as the speckled wood butterfly, there is no effect on lifespan. The

33

spermatophore in Lepidoptera is an adaptation to the fact that in many insects, the last male to mate has more chance of fertilizing all the eggs. Preventing the already mated female from mating with another male by blocking her reproductive apparatus with a plug is thus a worthwhile investment. Other insect orders adopt similar tactics. In the cricket *Gryllodes supplicans*, the male attaches a large gelatinous mass (spermatophylax) to the smaller sperm package (ampulla). In this species as with other crickets, the spermatophore remains outside the body (although attached) and the female eats it. By having the attachment there is more chance of the sperm fertilizing the females, as the bigger the spermatophylax the longer it takes the female to reach the sperm parcel.

Clearly insects have a variety of means by which to pass on their genes, but to do this successfully they must also be able to move to new habitats and develop the adaptations needed to exploit them. Chapter 3 explores the ways in which insects have responded to this challenge.

Chapter 3
On the move

The insect wing is a remarkable structure. Aside from vertebrates, insects are the only animals that use flapping wings for locomotion, and winged insects make up 69 per cent of all animal species. Insects are unique among the invertebrates in that they have developed the ability to fly, although this characteristic has been lost in many species and some orders. Unlike those of other animals, insect wing muscles can contract multiple times for each single nerve impulse, allowing the wings to beat faster than would otherwise be possible. The muscles are attached longitudinally and vertically across the thorax to the exoskeletons, not directly to the bases of the wings; this is more efficient and allows more muscle connections. Dragonflies have additional small accessory flight muscles that control wing rotation while the larger muscles, which in other insects are used for both power and wing rotation, are used only for power.

The oldest winged insects, the Palaeoptera, are today only represented by the Odonata and Ephemeroptera; they differ from the other winged insects in that they are unable to fold their wings back over the abdomen. The Polyneoptera (Chapter 1, Figure 6) which arose about 350 MYA, are, like the other more recent insect groups, able to fold their wings back over their abdomens. It is thought that this modification evolved to protect their delicate wings from being damaged while moving through vegetation or

confined spaces. In many insect groups the forewings are much thicker than hind wings and act as protective covers. The most extreme forms of this are seen in the Holometabola, especially within the Coleoptera, where the forewings are highly sclerotized into protective wing cases (elytra) and are no longer used for flight. Based on their wing structure, some members of the Polyneoptera were originally placed in the super order Orthopterida. Advances in molecular biology have, however, shown that this is not a valid classification, although the grasshoppers, crickets, and stick and leaf insects are still considered to be members of the Orthopterida.

Origin of insect flight

Insects are the only flying animals that have not sacrificed a pair of legs to gain the advantage of life in the air. They were the first animals to learn how to fly, at least 300 MYA. The first 'fully fledged' winged insect fossil record dates back 318 million years, to the late Carboniferous Period. Understanding how insect wings evolved has occupied the minds of entomologists for many years, and was made more difficult by the lack of what David Alexander, the world expert on animal flight, terms 'informative fossils'. Two main theories, dating back to the latter part of the 19th century, dominated the field for more than a hundred years—the gill theory and the paranotal lobe theory.

The gill theory postulates that wings evolved from gills of aquatic larval insects. Modern aquatic insect larvae, such as mayflies, have external movable gills on the abdomen, which have air tubes arranged in branching patterns, looking very much like wings and their veins; against this theory is the fact that the gills are on the abdomen, and insect wings arise from the thorax. Proponents of the gill theory suggest that the ancestral forms also had gills on the thorax, although this does not explain why modern forms have lost them. Some modern insects use their abdominal gill plates to move, supporting the theory that the 'lost' thoracic gills were the

precursors of wings. But against this argument is the fact that the tracheal system of insect respiration evolved on land and fossils show that the earliest insects were terrestrial with a fully developed tracheal system. Moreover, freshwater insects did not appear until the Triassic, 100 million years after terrestrial insects had appeared.

The paranotal lobe theory proposes that wings are derived from flat plates that evolved from the top of the thorax, perhaps originally as a side protection, camouflage, or extra anchoring for legs. As they increased in size they became used as devices for gliding or parachuting, and eventually became flexible enough to allow them to be used as steering devices. For this to work they needed a joint, which in turn needed muscles. As the proto-wings became larger and provided more lift, what began as weak steering movements evolved to powered flight. Against this theory, which has dominated the text books, is the fact that it requires evolution from scratch rather than selection from an existing structure.

Bounded ignorance

Frustrated by the lack of fossil evidence, some entomologists decided to approach the problem from another direction. In an influential review published in 1994, Joel Kingsolver and his colleague Mimi Koehl coined the phrase 'bounded ignorance'. In essence this refers to the use of experiments and models to work out what is possible physically without knowing what the actual structure looks like. They made physical models based on reconstructions of fossil insects and came up with an alternative hypothesis: that wings arose from thoracic structures involved in maintaining core internal temperature (thermoregulation). When dislodged from their resting place on a tree, wingless ants and other arboreal non-winged insects are able to end up back on the tree more often than on the ground, despite having no specialized flight apparatus. This 'directed aerial descent', as it has been

termed, turns out to be extremely common in non-winged arthropods; spiders, bristletails, silverfish, arboreal ants, and the non-winged nymphs of several insect species all do this to a greater or lesser degree. In light of this, Robert Dudley and Steve Yanoviak have proposed the following route to the evolution of flight:

> Live on an elevated location, such as a tree → Be able to jump or fall in a controlled manner → Have the ability to flip back to front and/or land in a controlled manner → Develop the ability to parachute → Further development of directed aerial descent—body structures that are lift-based and drag-based to enable steep glide angles → Body structures enable gliding (predominantly lift-based, shallow glide angles) → Recognisable wing structures allowing sophisticated aerial manoeuvres → Flapping flight.

Until concrete fossil evidence is found, this sequence of events seems to be the most likely route to the evolution of flight in insects. A large number of species have now lost the ability to fly, which might seem strange given that the success of insects is attributed to being able to fly. Two contemporaries of Charles Darwin, Charles Lyell and Vernon Wollaston, both noticed that just over a third (36 per cent) of the beetles native to the island of Madeira were flightless. Darwin, who had been fascinated with beetles since his student days, hypothesized that on islands, natural selection would favour smaller, less flight-able beetles since larger beetles with bigger wings would have a greater chance of being blown out to sea and drowned. Their genes, unlike those of beetles living on the mainland, where being able to fly gave them an advantage over flightless individuals in locating food and mates, would then be lost to the island population. Although this is a compelling idea, it is not necessarily totally correct.

Almost a hundred years later, the American entomologist Philip Darlington, a specialist on carabid beetles, noted that many of the flightless beetles on Madeira were carabids, a family that is

well-known for having a high proportion of wingless species. Carabids, many of which are voracious predators, have evolved three different lifestyles: those that live almost exclusively on the ground (geophiles), those that frequent stream and river banks (hydrophiles), and those that live in trees (arborophiles). The geophiles, living and foraging on the ground and rarely needing to fly, have, over millions of years, evolved into long-legged, short-winged, strong-jawed killing machines. A large proportion of the beetles living on Madeira were geophilous carabids, so Darwin was only partially right in his hypothesis of how natural selection on Madeira had produced so many flightless beetles. He was, of course, entirely correct in attributing the presence of so many flightless beetles to natural selection.

Migratory urge

We often hear about the remarkable migrations of butterflies such as the monarch and painted lady, whose annual multi-generational migrations extend over thousands of kilometres, flowing north and south, with the seasons, tracking changes in their food resources that follow a predictable climate-related pattern of spring flushes and summer declines. Similarly, the plagues of locusts and armyworms that spread out across large parts of Africa to devastate crops reflect the build-up of fast-breeding populations chasing fresh food resources. Long-distance travel is, however, not just confined to the larger insects. There is a common misperception that small insects, such as aphids, are no more than aerial plankton; this is not always the case. In 1924, Charles Elton, regarded as the founder of modern animal ecology, while on an expedition to the ice-covered island of Nordaustlandet, the second largest of the Spitsbergen group, reported finding large numbers of the greater black spruce aphid (*Cinara piceae*), many of which were still alive. Elton suggested that the aphids came from the Kola Peninsula, some 1,300 km away, carried by strong south and south-east winds. He estimated that they would have made the journey in twelve to twenty-four

hours. This was regarded as an example of totally passive migration and was used as one of many examples of aerial plankton. This is probably not giving aphids credit for their ability to actively fly long distances. During the 1960s, Roy Taylor and colleagues from Rothamsted Research, UK, sampled aphids 610 m above the ground using aeroplanes, and concluded that although the aphids were using jet streams, they were flying rather than floating, and that they descended to the ground in the evening to rest for the night.

Aphids are remarkable for another facet of their migratory abilities. The ovarioles of aphids vary in number not only between but also within species. Even more remarkable is the fact that the offspring from a single clone mother—and remember, they too are clones—also vary in the number of ovarioles that they possess. In the winged forms (alate exules) produced on the secondary host plants of *Rhopalosiphum padi*, the number of ovarioles can range from four to ten. This variability of ovariole number in the dispersal morphs of aphids that spend much of their lifecycle on ephemeral host plants is quite common. So why do so many aphid species have variable numbers of ovarioles in their alate morphs?

In 1970, Michael Shaw showed that there seemed to be three types of winged black bean aphid (*Aphis fabae*)—*migrants* that flew before depositing nymphs, *flyers* that deposited a few nymphs before flying, and *non-flyers* that stayed and reproduced on their host plant. He postulated that this was an adaptation in response to host quality—the worse state the plant was in, the more likely the *migrant* morph would be produced. Many years later Keith Walters and Tony Dixon at the University of East Anglia, UK, showed that there was a very strong relationship between reproductive investment (number of ovarioles) and flight willingness and ability. The more ovarioles an aphid had, the less likely it was to take off and fly, and aphids with more ovarioles could not fly for as long or as far as those with fewer ovarioles. In other words, there was a trade-off between fecundity and

migration. Long-distance aphid migration is very costly, with less than 0.3 per cent surviving. Therefore, it makes sense to have members of your clone taking short-distance hops (trivial flights) to neighbouring plants that might be just as bad as the one left behind and within easy reach of natural enemies, but with a higher chance of survival and reproduction, compared to long-distance migratory flights, with reduced probability of finding a host plant but which might lead to a host plant high in nutrition and low in natural enemies.

Finding the right food

An integral part of an insect's life is finding the right place to live and feed. Living organisms need nitrogen to grow; animal tissue has the greatest concentration of this essential element, but not everyone can be a predator; someone or something has to be at the bottom of the food chain. Non-animal sources are more abundant so, despite their relative lack of nitrogen, insects mainly exploit these non-animal sources. It is a hard way to make a living, especially if your food source is plant sap, phloem (mainly sugars and some nitrogen in the form of amino acids), or xylem tissue (mainly water and minerals).

Most insects are herbivorous (or, to be pedantic, they are predators of plants) and, like other herbivorous animals, feed on the bottom trophic layer. As well as herbivores feeding on living plants, there are detritivores, feeding on the bits left behind from plants and other animals, and fungivores feeding on the fungi that abound in our ecosystems. Few are predators, although many are parasitic in some form.

Back in the 1960s, insect physiologists Mark Scriber and Frank Slansky devised a way of measuring nutritional quality of host plants for Lepidoptera, the *nutritional efficiency complex*, based on a number of physiological measures. Three of these measures were based on feeding and growth rate—the relative growth rate,

the relative consumption rate, and the relative metabolic rate. A further three were based on measures of how the food ingested was converted from plant to insect—approximate digestibility of the food, the efficiency of conversion of the digested food, and efficiency of conversion of consumption. Through experimentation and literature review, they calculated which type of host plant was most suitable for Lepidoptera and, by inference, other chewing insect herbivores. They concluded that woody plants, trees, and shrubs were the least suitable host plants while herbaceous plants (forbs in America) were the most suitable, and that this was related to nitrogen and leaf water content (70 per cent leaf water and 8 per cent nitrogen content being optimal) and to the toughness of leaves, those of woody plants being six times tougher than those of herbaceous plants. We would therefore expect that herbaceous plants would play host to many more insect species than would woody plants, yet this is the opposite of what we see in nature. As a general rule, trees support a greater diversity of insects than do herbaceous plants. Given the poor quality of nutrition available from trees, why should this be? The answer lies in niche availability and the concept of *apparency*. Trees are large and easy to find, and their size and complex architecture provide a wide range of niches for insects to feed on and live in.

To feed on plants requires specialist adaptations both in terms of feeding structures and metabolic pathways. Insects that feed on leaves, fruit, and other solid structures of their host plants have chewing and biting mouthparts; those that feed from the xylem and phloem vessels have piercing and sucking mouthparts. Insects equipped with biting and chewing mouthparts also have to be prepared to deal with tissue of differing hardness/toughness. Leaves are not all equally soft (Table 4). Some plant tissues such as bark and heartwood are incredibly tough, and many insects that feed on tough tissues have incorporated metal ions into their mandibles. Plant tissue is also not equally nutritious throughout the year or the lifespan of the plant. In spring, perennial plants begin to grow and move stored nitrogen from within the plant to

Table 4 The relative toughness of plants

Plant Type	Relative toughness
Herbaceous plants	1.0
Woody plants—new leaves	1.7
Temperate grasses	3.1
Tropical grasses	6.2
Woody plants—mature leaves	6.3

the growing points; annuals emerge from their seeds, soft, vulnerable, and rich in nitrogen, with a high water content. This is ideal insect fodder as many gardeners know to their sorrow. This growth phase is also extremely valuable for the plants; they need to get past this vulnerable stage as quickly as possible without losing too much of themselves to the depredations of their vertebrate and invertebrate enemies. Other insects have avoided the problems of feeding on tough leaves by emerging at the same time as their host plants burst into bud or emerge from their seeds. Many plants therefore invest in biochemical defences at this vulnerable stage of development; the young leaves of cherry trees, although tender and full of nitrogen, are also full of cyanogenic compounds. It is, however, metabolically expensive for plants to produce defensive chemicals and as the leaves grow older, tougher, and less succulent, and the plant has produced and set fruit, the need to defend the leaves chemically is reduced.

We thus see insects that have become not only host specialists but also seasonal specialists—insects that exploit the soft, highly nutritious but well-defended young plant tissues, the *flush feeders*, such as the larvae of the winter moth (*Operophtera brumata*); those that feed on the less nutritious, tougher, but less chemically defended summer foliage; and those that exploit the more nutritious but possibly more short-lived autumn foliage, the *senescence feeders*. This leads on to the concept of generalists and specialists. We can classify insect species along a gradient, ranging

from the extreme specialists, those that feed on only one species of host plant, to the extreme generalists, the polyphages, that feed on a disparate range of plant families. The peach-potato aphid (*Myzus persicae*) is often cited as being one of the most polyphagous insects on the planet, feeding on a range of plants from trees to vegetables. In between these two extremes there are the oligophagous insects, which are able to feed on a group of related plants, in either the same genus or the same family, depending on their level of oligophagy.

Although there is a school of thought that says that all insects are specialists, for the moment let us assume that specialists and generalists do exist. The first question is why? What advantages are gained from adopting each of these strategies? To be a specialist means being very well adapted to a particular host plant both in terms of season (phenology), that is, being around at the same time of year as the most nutritional part of the plant, and also being able to detoxify the host plant chemistry which the plant uses to defend itself against its predators. For example, crucifers such as cabbage are rich in sinigrin (mustard oils) that is a potent defence against many insects. Cabbage specialists, such as larvae of the diamondback moth (*Plutella xylostella*), or the cabbage white butterfly (*Pieris rapae*), have a suite of digestive enzymes that are able to detoxify these defences. Like plant defensive chemistry, a sophisticated detoxification system is metabolically expensive. If an insect has invested in one particular set of detoxification enzymes, it must sacrifice more generalist defences, so it will do superbly well when faced with a cabbage plant but will starve to death if no cabbages are available. Given that some insects are specialists on much rarer plants than cabbages, being able to find the host plant is of great importance. If, on the other hand, the insect is a generalist, it has a multi-purpose tool kit of different gut enzymes for detoxification; against some plant chemistry it works quite well, against other metabolites, less well, but in general it can cope with feeding on a range of host plants. If, however, it ends up on a cabbage plant on

which a cabbage specialist is feeding, it will lose out. This is nicely shown by studies of three species of Lepidoptera: the cabbage white butterfly; the swallowtail (*Papilio polyxenes*), which is a specialist on parsnips; and the armyworm (*Spodoptera eridania*), a generalist feeding on a wide range of host plants. When fed on a crucifer-based diet, to which sinigrin was added artificially, the cabbage white grew and developed with no ill effects, even when the levels of sinigrin were three times higher than it would normally encounter, the swallowtail died, but the armyworm survived, albeit not as well as it would have done on a non-cruciferous plant. Over time, the responses of specialist herbivorous insects and the defences of their host plants evolve, an example of what is commonly termed *the coevolutionary arms race*.

Plants can also attempt to beat their herbivores by avoiding them in space and time. If an insect is a *flush feeder*, a plant that can pass through the vulnerable tender stage before the insect has emerged or arrived is at a distinct advantage. Despite their close association, it seems that insect herbivores and their host plants do not use exactly the same environmental cues to decide when to break bud or emerge from their overwintering stage.

This can have disastrous effects, as in the case of the winter moth, which has a very particular phenological niche or window, with oak foliage (Figure 10). Hatch too early and the oak is still dormant, hatch too late and the leaves are too tough for the young caterpillars to use efficiently, with many dying before completing their development, while those that survive are smaller and less fecund as adults than in years when bud burst and winter moth egg hatch coincide.

Whether a specialist or a generalist, as an insect larva develops it becomes more tolerant and better able to fight back against the chemical and physical defences that a plant can throw at it. Bigger jaws enable older caterpillars to chew through a thicker cuticle

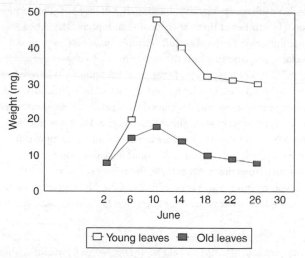

10. The 'phenological window' illustrated by the winter moth, *Operophtera brumata*. Moths that hatch too early will have insufficient food when the oak is dormant but moths that hatch too late will have to feed on tough leaves.

than newly emerged caterpillars, and their detoxification systems become more developed as they pass through successive moults. Even a specialist insect can complete its development on a 'non-host' plant if it is close to its final moult.

The interdependence of herbivorous insects and their host plants is echoed by their interactions with their siblings and conspecifics, an aspect explored in Chapter 4.

Chapter 4
Living together

The most basic form of insect association is exemplified by the aggregations that some insect species show during some parts of their lifecycle. Many ladybirds, for example, aggregate in sheltered spots over the winter, actively seeking out crevices in bark, the leeside of fence posts, the space underneath window sills, and the frames of sash windows. These are not truly social as they are often a mixture of different species that have come together because of a response to a change in behaviour, brought about by positive touch stimulus (thigmotaxis). Other insect aggregations that are not truly forms of sociality are seen in some Hemiptera, where feeding in groups emphasizes their unpalatability by magnifying their red and black warning colouration; colonial feeding by aphid clones where being part of a herd is beneficial; overwintering roosting behaviour of some butterflies, most famously seen in the monarch; feeding aggregations seen in some bark beetles, and similarly tent caterpillars that feed in large aggregations within protected silk webbing. In all these loose associations, any coordination is individual and, except perhaps in the case of aphids, not altruistic. They are thus solitary, but have, as a result of their behaviour, formed what to us appears to be a social aggregation.

Whereas most insects only come together to mate, feed, or overwinter, some insects have adopted a more social life. Ants,

bees, wasps, and termites are well known to be social insects. Most people will be aware of the complex social organization that occurs in the hives of the domesticated honey bee (*Apis mellifera*). What may be less evident is that, unlike the morphological variation seen in other highly social insect groups such as ants and termites which have distinct castes, individual bees within a colony may appear very similar (that is, they show little of the phenotypic variation evident amongst ants and termites) but have marked variation in their behaviour (polyethism). Female honey bees can be divided into five castes—the queen (reproductive caste) and four age-based subcastes among the workers: cell cleaning caste, broodnest caste, food storage caste, forager caste. Newly emerged worker bees begin life as cleaners and carers; as they grow older they move further away from the centre of the hive, eventually becoming foragers. None of the workers moves abruptly from one subcaste to another but some move earlier than others because developmental rates vary among individuals. Some roles, such as undertakers and guards, are performed by a very small proportion of the colony, perhaps due to some subtle genetic differences.

In a number of species of ants and termites, there are behavioural and very obvious morphological differences among the castes, although many ant species also show similar behavioural caste differentiation to that of honey bees. Termites and ants have three main castes—reproductive (queens and kings), worker, and soldier. The former and the latter castes have smaller and larger versions, known as secondary and primary, and minors and majors, the major soldiers having very well-developed jaws. Although termites are highly social, many producing the instantly recognizable termite hills/mounds (Figure 11), and are commonly known as white ants, sharing the same caste nomenclature as ants (Figure 12), they are not Hymenoptera, but rather—and this may come as a surprise to many—they are very closely related to cockroaches. Something of a vindication for the biologist Lemuel Roscoe Cleveland, who had suggested this in the 1930s but was largely ignored.

11. A termite mound. These remarkable structures enable their inhabitants to live in a stable and relatively cool environment.

Social organisms need to be able to communicate with each other in order to maintain colony coherence. A major difference among ants, bees, and termites is that termites are mostly blind so whereas ants and bees are able to communicate visually, the 'waggle-dance' of bees being a well-documented example, communication between individual termites is mainly by touch and chemical means. In termites, as in bees and ants, this chemical communication involves pheromones that elicit behavioural responses from the individuals, including trail chemicals that lead individual foragers from food to nest and other chemicals that allow them to recognize nest mates and, of course, locate reproductive partners. These behavioural and morphological features have enabled ants, bees, and termites to reach the apex of invertebrate sociality.

Parental care

A number of other species live together in varying degrees of togetherness, some of which may come as a surprise. Leaving

49

Caste systems in termite societies

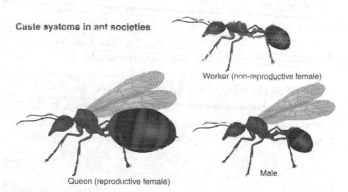

Caste systems in ant societies

Worker (non-reproductive female)

Queen (reproductive female)

Male

12. Termite and ant castes—note the subdivisions within castes: Ants are usually divided into three castes: reproductive females, reproductive males and non-reproductive females. Soldiers are also common within termite and ant caste systems. There is extreme variation in size and morphology amongst castes.

aside for the moment the vaguely social aggregations of aphids, the marvellous concept of 'spaced-out gregariousness' found in some aphid species, and the gregarious feeding habits of many lepidopteran and coleopteran larvae, parental care is found in several species not normally considered to be social.

Parental care is more common in species in which offspring face high risks due to natural enemies or environmental pressure and the mothers are longer lived than, for example, insects in which the eggs are laid in one massive clutch and the mother then dies. In the case of the flightless female of the vapourer moth (*Orgyia antiqua*), parental care, such as it is, involves the egg clutch being covered by her dead, unpalatable body.

Maternal provisioning, in which the mother leaves a prey item with each egg, is common in solitary bees and wasps. The ability of some moth and butterfly species to lay eggs with more nutritional reserves on poorer quality host plants is perhaps not what would normally be termed maternal care. More recognizable maternal care is seen, for example, in some dung beetles, where the parents feed their offspring in response to 'begging' behaviour, similar to that seen in birds. Many dung beetles share parental responsibility; females excavate brood chambers and lay eggs in the dung-ball food source while the males bring dung for the females to deploy as necessary. This type of behaviour is known as subsociality.

The silphids (carrion and sexton beetles), which feed on dead animals, also show parental care and male/female cooperation. In some circumstances they also show quasi-social behaviour. In a series of elegant trials, Stephen Trumbo and David Wilson demonstrated that in some contexts, such as when the carcass is large, the females, which are normally highly competitive, form cooperative breeding associations, leading to better survival rates of their offspring.

The earwig also provides a good example of subsocial behaviour, tending her eggs carefully, protecting them from predators, and staying with the newly hatched larvae until their second moult, when they can fend for themselves. If the mother earwig dies before her parenting role is complete, the nymphs will eat her dead body before they disperse.

True bugs, perhaps not commonly regarded as being advanced enough to exhibit parental care, do however, provide many examples of this behaviour. Female burrower bugs (*Sehirus cinctus*) show extended care for their offspring; they guard their clutch and feed the hatched nymphs up to the third larval instar. Hungry nymphs use a pheromone to solicit food from their mothers. Another hemipteran, the membracid oak tree hopper (*Platycotis vittata*), guards her eggs and, in response to vibrational signals from her offspring, chases predators, including ants, away. Similar to vertebrate mothers, they also keep their nymphs in aggregations, herding straying offspring back into the group. And the hemipteran *Parastrachia japonensis*, a species of true bug from eastern Asia, keeps watch on her eggs and moves them to new sites if they become flooded or are in danger of desiccation.

Aphids and their soldiers

Perhaps more remarkable and hardly known outside the world of aphidologists are the subsocial aphids. The phenomenon is not common, being found only in about 1 per cent of aphids. It was only discovered in the 1970s, and was viewed initially with some scepticism. Among aphids, the Pemphigine aphids are renowned for their gall-forming activities, many galls being formed along the leaf petiole. The position of the gall is very important; the closer the gall is to the base of a leaf, the better the quality of the food for the gall inhabitants. There is thus a premium to be gained by either being first to form a gall or, if in second place, to usurp the aphid mother that got there first and push her further up the leaf petiole. We thus see two strategies. Newly emerged first-instar

13. Japanese fighting aphids 'Ninja aphids'. In (a) they are fighting rear to rear, in (b) head on.

nymphs of the beet aphid (*Pemphigus betae*) fight each other for the best position on the petiole (Figure 13). These fights are serious affairs and, incredibly, can last for up to two days. And in a related species, *Epipemphigus niisimae*, where a gall has already been formed by an earlier arrival, the first-instar nymphs fight to gain possession of this premium dwelling place. These fights are even more vicious and protracted and the Japanese entomologist Shigeyuki and colleagues reported that they sometimes result in the death of the loser.

As a further development, some gall-forming aphids, *Ceratoglypnia styracicola* and *Hamamelistes cristafolaie*, have a specially adapted nymphal morph, with thicker and broader front legs, whose function is to defend gall usurpation by other aphid mothers, so-called soldier aphids. These soldiers stay outside the gall and repel possible invaders. So, it is not surprising to find that in some species, the soldiers do not just fight other aphids but actually defend their siblings against predators, even being able to kill lacewing larvae.

Ant–insect–plant associations

The relationship between ants and sap-feeding insects, such as aphids, has long been recognized. The first scientific description of this phenomenon was by the 17th-century Dutch naturalist and painter Jan Goedaert, and by the latter half of the 19th century the phenomenon was well known, appearing in many popular science books of the time, including Ernest van Bruyssel's excellent and very readable book, *The Population of an Old Pear Tree* (1870).

The ant–aphid association is usually defined as a *mutualism*, as the two species exist in a relationship in which each benefits from the activity of the other; it is also sometimes termed trophobiosis, which is a more symbiotic relationship.

We tend to think of aphids as soft, defenceless insects that are easy to squash when we find them on our house and garden plants. To predatory insects, however, they present a bit more of a challenge. Aphids have structural and behavioural defences to keep them safe in the dangerous world of bug eat bug. Alarm pheromones and the seemingly dangerous habit of simply dropping off a plant (dropping behaviour) when a predator approaches are commonly used by aphids to avoid meeting predators face to face. Aphids also have a number of physical defences: their siphunculi, or cornicles, tubules that protrude from the back of their abdomen, can produce a quickly hardening wax to gum up ladybirds' jaws. Other aphid species cover themselves with dense waxy coats that make them less palatable or accessible to natural enemies. Yet others have thick skins (heavily sclerotized) and what entomologists term saltatorial leg modification (long legs), and are able to give a ladybird or other insect predator a good kicking. These characteristics, which are all costly, are reduced or absent in aphids that are associated frequently with ants; presumably with ant bodyguards in attendance, there is no need for the aphids to invest in extra anti-predator defences.

The degree of dependence of the aphid on the ants varies by species. Some aphids, especially those that live underground on plant roots, are unable to survive without their ant attendants. The entomologist John Pontin describes seeing yellow meadow ant (*Lasius flavus*) workers licking aphid eggs, which he suggested stops them from going mouldy by removing fungal spores. He noted that eggs that were not cared for in this way did not hatch. Other aphids have a more facultative relationship, and are able to survive quite successfully without the help of their friendly neighbourhood ants.

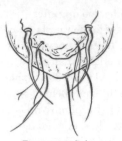
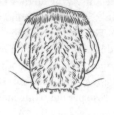

Tetraneura ulmi   *Geoica utricularia*   *Forda marginata*

14. Three aphid trophobiotic organs, some hairier than others.

Apart from reducing their defensive armoury, aphids that have obligatory ants in attendance have a specially adapted rear end, essentially a hairy bottom, known more scientifically as the trophobiotic organ (Figure 14). This organ is an enlarged anal plate surrounded by special hairs that acts as a collection and storage device, allowing the aphid to accumulate honeydew (aphid equivalent of faeces): a mixture largely composed of sugars, but also of free amino acids and amides, proteins, minerals, and B-vitamins, which is, all in all, quite a useful food source for the ants, ready for the ants to remove at their leisure. Trophobiosis is a symbiotic association between organisms in which food is obtained or provided. The provider of food in the association is referred to as a trophobiont. The name is derived from the Greek τροφή, *trophē* (nourishment) and βίωσις, *biosis* (short for symbiosis).

Non-ant-attended aphids without the trophobiotic organ deposit their honeydew directly onto the leaf surface, the ground, or, if you are unlucky enough to park under an aphid-infested tree, your car. Ants lick and collect sycamore aphid (*Drepanosiphum platanoidis*) honeydew from leaves but not directly from the aphids, although they will collect honeydew directly from the maple aphid (*Periphyllus testudinaceus*), which also lives on sycamore trees.

So what's in it for the ants? Why do they bother looking after aphids, even in some cases keeping aphid eggs in their nests through the winter? The obvious answer is: for the honeydew that the aphids produce. The amount of material that an aphid can remove from a plant is quite astounding: a large willow aphid (*Tuberolachnus salignus*) adult can imbibe the equivalent of 4 milligrams (mg) sucrose per day, equivalent to the photosynthetic product of one to two leaves per day. Admittedly, they are large aphids and not ant attended, but even an aphid half their size passes a lot of plant sap through its digestive systems. All aphids produce honeydew but not all aphids are ant attended and, as pointed out earlier, not all ants attend aphids. My research group found that 41 per cent of ant genera have trophobiotic species, but these are not distributed equally among ant families. Some ant subfamilies, such as the Formicinae, specialize in ant attendance, whereas in other ant families aphids are used only as prey and the honeydew is gathered from plant and ground surfaces. The ant species that are most likely to develop mutualistic relationships with aphids seem to be those that live in trees, have large colonies, are able to exploit disturbed habitats, and are dominant or invasive.

Ants that do tend aphids do not just protect them from predators and other natural enemies; they also seek to maximize the return for their investment. The black bean aphid, which is often tended by the black garden ant (*Lasius niger*) has its ability to produce winged forms reduced by the ants, thus making sure that the aphids are around for longer to provide food for them. The ant *Lasius fuliginosus* transports young giant oak aphids (*Stomaphis quercus*) to parts of the tree with the best honeydew production; *Lasius niger* goes one step further, moving individuals of the black willow bark aphid (*Pterocomma salicis*) to better quality willow trees. *Lasius niger* seems to have a propensity for moving bugs about; it has also been seen moving scale insects from dying clover roots to nearby living roots.

In the mid-1970s John Whittaker and Gary Skinner of Lancaster University, UK, studied the interactions between the wood ant (*Formica rufa*) and the various insect herbivores feeding on sycamore trees in Cringlebarrow Wood, Lancashire. They excluded some ants from some of the aphid-infested branches and allowed them access to other branches on the same trees; they also looked at trees that were foraged by ants and those that were not. They found that *F. rufa* was a heavy predator of the sycamore aphid, but tended the maple aphid. Ant-excluded colonies of the maple aphid decreased while those of the sycamore aphid did not; the reverse pattern was seen on branches where ants were able to access the aphids.

The presence of thriving aphid colonies in the neighbourhood of ant nests (and in some cases aphid colonies only exist near ant nests) has made some people wonder whether aphids look actively for ant partners. There is no evidence for this but the fact that wing production is reduced in the presence of tending ants means that aphid colonies can accumulate around and close to ant nests.

That does not mean that the aphids rely only on honeydew production to guarantee the presence of their ant bodyguards. The aphid *Stomaphis yanonis*, which, like other *Stomaphis* species, has giant mouthparts, needs plenty of time to remove its mouthparts safely and definitely needs ant protection when involved in the delicate operation of stylet unplugging. In this case, it turns out that the aphids smell like the ants. The skin of these aphids has cuticular hydrocarbons that resemble those of their ant protector *Lasius fuji*, which encourages the ants to treat them as their own. Earlier work on the ant-attended tree-dwelling aphids, *Lachnus tropicalis* and *Myzocallis kuricola*, in Japan showed that the ant *L. niger* preyed on aphids that had not been attended by nest mates but tended those that had previously been tended. This too would indicate the presence of some sort of chemical marker or brand.

Although aphids do not seek ant partners actively, they may compete with each other to retain the services of their ant bodyguards by producing more honeydew. Christophe Fischer and colleagues from the University of Liège, Belgium, showed that ants decide whether to predate or tend aphids by monitoring honeydew production and choose to prey on aphids in colonies that produce less honeydew. They have also shown that the honeydew of the black bean aphid (*Aphis fabae*) is often colonized by the bacterium *Staphylococcus xylosus*. Honeydew so infected produces a bouquet of volatile compounds that are attractive to the ant *L. niger*, thus increasing the chances of the aphids being ant attended. This adds yet another layer of complexity to the already complicated mutualistic lifestyle that aphids have adopted.

Finally, although the wonderful colour variations seen in some aphid species can be modified by their symbionts, it seems that ants may have a say in this too, albeit at a colony level rather than at the clonal level. The improbably named mugwort aphid (*Macrosiphoniella yomogicola*), which is obligately ant-attended by *Lasius japonicus*, is found in colonies that are typically composed of 65 per cent green aphids and 35 per cent red aphids. Saori Watanabe and his colleagues at the University of Hokkaido, Japan, questioned why ants like this colour balance. One possibility is that red and green aphids have slightly different effects on the mugwort plants where they feed. Though green aphids produce more honeydew, red aphids seem to prevent the mugwort from flowering. Given that aphid colonies on a flowering mugwort go extinct, ants looking to maintain an aphid herd for more than a year might see an advantage in keeping red aphids around to guarantee a long-term food supply from their green sisters.

Ants and plants

As well as 'farming' aphids to obtain sugar from their honeydew, ants have a similar mutualistic relationship with plants that give them a sugary reward to protect them from herbivorous insects,

except those that also provide the ants with sugar. Perhaps the most studied, familiar ant–plant mutualism is that of the swollen-thorn acacia and *Pseudomyrmex* ants, which American ecologist Dan Janzen described in the mid-1960s. In essence the swollen thorns of the acacias provide housing for the ants and an additional reward via extra-floral nectaries. In return the ants drive away insects and other herbivores. Such mutualisms are not just confined to the tropics or single plants; they can be very sophisticated, as ecologist Dave Tilman showed in the 1970s. In Michigan, the North American black cherry, *Prunus serotina*, times nectar production from its extra-floral nectaries to attract the ant *Formica obscuripes* when the larvae of its major herbivore, the eastern tent caterpillar (*Malacosoma americanum*) are at their most vulnerable. Protected trees have greatly reduced levels of herbivory. When more than one ant colony is involved, rather than single trees being protected, a group of trees can be saved from defoliation, and form a green island. The areas covered by green islands can be quite extensive: two ant colonies of the ant *Formica polyctena* were enough to protect pine trees from the nun moth (*Lymantria monacha*) in Sweden within a 45 m diameter around the colonies (0.16 hectares (ha)) and green islands of up to 3 ha have been reported. Finnish entomologists reported that one colony of the ant *Formica aquilonia* was sufficient to create green islands of subarctic mountain birch, *Betula pubescens*, of up to 0.12 ha.

Insects and their symbionts

Many insects, especially those feeding on nutrient-limited diets, like blood, wood, phloem, and xylem, need help in obtaining essential nutrients. Termites, for example, have a mutualistic relationship with protozoa and bacteria that enables them to process cellulose, and bed bugs need the help of *Wolbachia* bacteria to process their blood meals. Recent evidence has revealed that both termites and bedbugs have symbionts that confer defence against disease; this is especially relevant in female

bedbugs as many potentially harmful bacteria are introduced via the male method of traumatic insemination. To my mind, however, the most interesting and, to date, most extensively studied symbiotic/mutualistic relationships are found in aphids.

Like humans, aphids have a thriving internal ecology; they are inhabited by a number of bacteria or bacteria-like organisms. The existence of these fellow travellers and the fact that they are transmitted by the mother has been known for over a century: Thomas Henry Huxley first described them in 1858, although he had no idea what they were. The Czech entomologist Jaroslav Peklo (1881–1955) proved in 1912 that they were bacteria but their role within the body of the aphids was not entirely understood until, some years later, the Hungarian entomologist László Tóth hypothesized that because the plant sap that the aphids feed on did not contain enough proteins to meet their demands for growth, they must be obtaining the extra nitrogen that they needed from their symbionts.

To demonstrate this, entomologists treated insects with antibiotics and proved that the symbionts were, first, bacteria; and, second, that they provided benefits for their insect hosts. They concluded that there was enough evidence to suggest that the endosymbionts were involved in some way in the nutritional and possibly reproductive processes of the insects studied—mainly cockroaches. A few years later two American entomologists sprayed aphids with several different antibiotics and found that this caused increased mortality and reduced fecundity compared with untreated aphids. Further studies on other aphid species showed that the antibiotics eliminated and damaged their symbionts and that once 'cured', aphids developed more slowly, if at all, and produced fewer offspring. Yet more evidence that the symbionts were an essential part of the aphid biome. There was still much debate as to how the symbionts provided proteins to the aphids, a question that remained unanswered until the 1980s.

Rosalind Hinde and colleagues were able to show that material produced from the symbionts was passed into the body of the aphid and that the primary symbionts were able to synthesize amino acids and sterols for the benefit of their aphid hosts (partners). By the early 1980s it was accepted that aphids were unable to reproduce or survive without their primary symbionts; and, by the late 1980s, that dietary sterols were provided by the primary symbionts.

Despite the huge amount of research and the general acceptance that the endosymbionts were an integral part of the aphid's biome, their putative identity was not determined until 1991, when they were named *Buchnera aphidicola* and given their own genus; note, however, that *B. aphidicola* represents a complex of closely related bacteria rather than a single species. It was soon confirmed that they were responsible for the synthesis of essential amino acids used by the aphids, such as tryptophan, and that it was definitely an obligate relationship on both sides.

Next, attention turned to the presumably facultative secondary symbionts, first noticed in the rose aphid (*Macrosiphum rosae*) more than twenty years earlier by Rosalind Hinde. Nancy Moran and colleagues at the University of Arizona, USA, identified three species of secondary bacterial symbiont, *Serratia symbiotica*, *Hamiltonella defensa*, and *Regiella insecticola*. As these are not found in all individuals of a species, they are facultative rather than obligate. The secondary symbionts were shown to be linked to a whole swathe of aphid life-history attributes, ranging from resistance to parasitoids, resistance to heat and other abiotic stressors, and to host-plant use.

Like a number of other aphid species, the pea aphid (*Acyrthosiphon pisum*) occurs in different colour morphs ranging from a pale green to deep reddish-pink. Tsutomo Tsuchida and colleagues in Japan showed that the intensity of green colouration

depends on the presence of yet another endosymbiont, a *Rickettsiella*. They hypothesized that being green rather than pink or red may reduce predation by ladybirds, as the aphids would be less obvious on the leaves.

New secondary symbionts continue to be discovered and new hypotheses are raised and tested. There seems to be a whole ecology of secondary symbionts within the aphid biome waiting to be explored and documented.

Green islands

Some insects, such as aphids, induce early leaf senescence to improve the quality of their host plant (the nitrogen content of senescent leaves is higher than that of mature leaves). Some plants induce senescence and early leaf-fall in leaves that have been colonized by gall aphids in order to reduce their infestation load. Other insects try desperately to prevent senescence in order to prolong their feeding life on what would otherwise be a dead leaf (Figure 15).

The phenomenon of the green islands in autumn leaves associated with leaf-mining Lepidoptera has been known for some time, but, although the adaptive value of this was easy to understand, the causal mechanism remained unknown for some time.

Plant pathologists had known since the 1930s that fungi produced secretions containing plant growth substances, such as the auxin (plant hormone) indole acetic acid. They hypothesized that the levels present in the surrounding leaf tissue were associated with the resistance or lack thereof to the fungal agent. A further class of plant growth substances, initially termed kinins because of their similarity to kinetin (a cell growth promoting plant hormone) but later renamed cytokinins, were discovered in the 1960s by Folke Skoog and co-workers and linked to the production of green islands by plant pathogens.

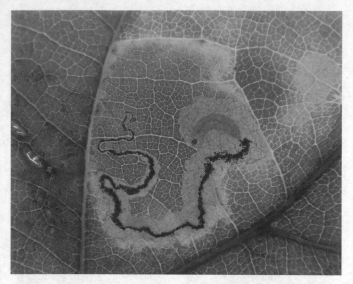

15. Green island leaf-mine of the moth *Stigmella atricapitella*.

How does this relate to leaf-mining insects? Lisabeth Engelbrecht, working on nepticulid leaf-miners on birch, *Betula pendula*, and aspen, *Populus tremula*, set up a study in the mid-1960s to test the hypotheses that the green islands were caused by insect saliva or by the larvae physically cutting the leaf veins that would otherwise have delivered the chemical signal responsible for beginning leaf senescence. She discovered that the green islands contained large concentrations of cytokinin and, with other colleagues, discovered that the labial glands of leaf-mining larvae also contained cytokinin. In the mid-2000s the French entomologist David Giron and colleagues showed that the leaf-miner *Phyllonorycter blancardella* manipulates the nutritional quality of its host leaves by increasing the levels of cytokinin in the surrounding leaf tissue.

Insects

16. Influence of *Wolbachia* on green island formation; (left) infected leaf-miners, *Phyllonorycter blancardella*, surrounded by nutritious plant tissue; (right) 'cured' by antibiotics, the leaf-miner soon runs out of food.

As we know from aphids, where insects play, bacterial symbionts are never far away, and sure enough it wasn't long before it was shown that *Wolbachia* 'infections' were helping leaf-miners to produce their 'green islands'. Wilfried Kaiser and colleagues treated leaf-miner larvae with antibiotics to remove the symbiont and found that the 'cured' larvae, although still able to feed and form leaf-mines, were unable to produce 'green islands', and the

levels of cytokinin were much lower than those found in the 'green islands' formed by untreated leaf-miners (Figure 16).

In Chapter 5 we leave the terrestrial habitat to explore the adaptations and lifestyles of insects that spend some or all of their life in or on water.

Chapter 5
Aquatic insects

Aquatic insects, adaptations, the marine environment

Although largely terrestrial, insects have not abandoned the world of water. Every inland water body, whether a river, stream seepage, or lake, supports a biological community. Insects can also be found in puddles and some, such as the pitcher plant mosquito, *Wyeomyia smithii*, are especially adapted to exploit the water-filled 'stomachs' of carnivorous plants. In larger water bodies, the most familiar inhabitants are often the vertebrates, such as fish and amphibians. At the macroscopic level, however, invertebrates provide the highest number of individuals and species, and the highest levels of biomass and production. In general, the insects dominate freshwater aquatic systems, where only nematodes can approach them in terms of species numbers, biomass, and productivity. Crustaceans may be abundant in saline (especially temporary) inland waters but are rarely diverse in species. Some representatives of nearly all the orders of insects live in water and there have been many invasions of freshwater from the land. Recent studies have even revealed a diversity of aquatic diving beetles (Dytiscidae) in aquifers (underground water bodies). Insects, however, have been almost completely unsuccessful in marine environments, with a few sporadic exceptions such as some water-striders (Hemiptera: Gerridae) and larval dipterans.

There is little doubt that insects evolved on land, albeit from an aquatic crustacean ancestor (Chapter 1). The tracheal system of respiration, based on diffusion, is very unlikely to have evolved in water; oxygen levels are much lower in water than in air, reaching only 15 parts per million (ppm) even in flowing water. It is much more plausible that the tracheal system facilitated the subsequent development of the 'gills' used by insects that are truly aquatic for part or all of their lifecycles.

Many insects have aquatic larvae, such as dragonflies, mayflies, and several species of fly, including mosquitoes. There are also some adult forms, mainly predators, that make a living in these environments, either below the surface or striding or skating across the surface. Insects that live on the surface of the water—water boatmen and pond skaters—rely on the fact that their light weight and limited contact with the water surface keeps them high and dry. Insects that feed in water but are otherwise terrestrial have special adaptations that allow them to spend prolonged periods of time underwater. Adult diving beetles store air underneath their wing cases while other semi-aquatic insects encase themselves in a bubble of air, which they refresh as needed by returning to the surface.

Insects that are truly aquatic have developed gill-like structures—fine filamentous, thin-skinned outgrowths that are able to absorb oxygen through diffusion. They depend, however, on being in a well-aerated water body or having the ability to generate a flow of fresh water over their gills, as seen in some of the 'sedentary' caddisflies that live in a 'burrow' and use their legs to produce an artificial current.

Other aquatic insects with an open spiracle system, fly larvae such as mosquitoes, and rat-tailed syrphid maggots maintain contact with the water surface with a siphon and use atmospheric oxygen. Some mosquito larvae (*Mansonia* spp.) can pierce the roots of aquatic plants and use the oxygen in the air pockets.

Insects with closed spiracle systems are unable to rely on simple cutaneous diffusion except at very early larval stages, and in these we see the development of structures based on external extrusions of the tracheal system. These are analogous to gills as they have a large surface area, are moist and vascular, and can be ventilated. In dragonflies and mayflies, they have been shown to account for up to 70 per cent of oxygen uptake.

Modes of life in water

Aquatic insects can be divided into six functional groups: *shredders, collectors, scrapers, piercers, predators,* and *parasites.*

Shredders feed on living or decomposing plant tissues, including wood, which they chew, mine, or gouge. Shredders break down large particles of plant material into smaller pieces that are transported downstream or made available to other stream consumers. This group includes stoneflies (Plecoptera), caddisflies (Trichoptera), and crane flies (Diptera).

Collectors feed on fine particulate organic matter by filtering particles from suspension or fine detritus from sediment; gatherers collect from the stream bottom; and filterers collect fine particulate matter from the water column. This group includes several subfamilies of chironomid midge. Filterers have special adaptations to capture particles directly from the water column. These include the construction of nets to filter water like those used by some Trichoptera larvae. Even though some Trichoptera catch animals in their nets and would therefore be classed as predators, functionally they are still considered collector-filterers. As well as the Trichoptera, this group (Collectors) includes mayflies, stoneflies, midges, and blackflies.

Scrapers feed on attached algae and diatoms by grazing solid surfaces. This group includes mayflies and caddisflies.

Piercers feed on cell and tissue fluids from vascular plants or larger algae, by piercing and sucking the contents. An example is Hydroptilidae, a tiny caddisfly species that pierces individual algal cells to consume cellular fluids, avoiding consumption of cellulose-rich cell walls.

Predators feed on living animal tissues by engulfing and eating the whole or parts of animals, or piercing prey and sucking body fluids. They use a diversity of strategies for capturing prey, including modified mouthparts and behaviour. Although many predators have abundant, strong teeth for prey consumption, some are highly specialized: the labium in Odonata, for example, is a highly modified, unique structure among aquatic insects. This group also includes one species of mayfly and one group of caddisflies.

Parasites, or more properly parasitoids (Chapter 8), complete their development within a number of aquatic larvae, for example the hymenopteran *Agriotypus armatus* that parasitizes caddisflies. The adult female walks down plant stems to search the stream bottom for suitable hosts. Another wasp, the egg parasitoid *Pseudoligosita longifrangiata*, lays its eggs within the eggs of the damselfly *Argia insipida*, which it finds on submerged leaves of the tropical aquatic plant *Tonina fluviatilis* (a common aquarium plant). And the tiny trichogrammid wasp *Trichogramma julianoi* parasitizes eggs of the aquatic fly *Sepedon fuscipennis*.

Although several orders of insect, including the Coleoptera, Diptera, Neuroptera, Megaloptera (alderflies), and the Hemiptera, have species that are aquatic, there are four orders in which almost all members spend their larval life underwater—the Ephemeroptera (mayflies), the Plecoptera (stoneflies), the Odonata (dragonflies, damselflies), and the holometabolic Trichoptera (the caddisflies). These orders are of particular importance to both the aquatic ecosystem through their various activities, and to humans as environmental indicators of water quality.

The Ephemeroptera

Worldwide there are estimated to be about 2,500 species of
Ephemeroptera, commonly called mayflies, or, less commonly,
dayflies. As the latter name suggests, the adults live for only a
short time, a few days at most. They do not feed, having
non-functional mouthparts, although some species will take on
water. Their guts are filled with air and many species have
vestigial legs. The sole function of the adults is to mate and for the
females to lay eggs.

The immature stages (nymphs) are aquatic, and, depending on
species, take one to three years, with up to fifty moults, to reach
adulthood (Figure 17). The nymphs are mainly herbivorous,
feeding on algae, or detritivorous, feeding on decaying material;
they provide a food source for many predators. A few species are

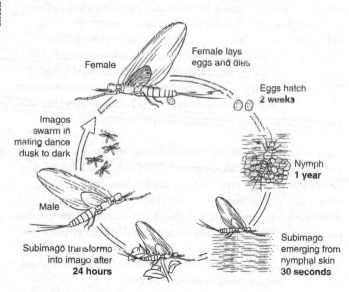

17. Generalized lifecycle of a mayfly (Ephemeroptera).

predators, with chironomid midge larvae and other small aquatic larvae as their prey. Mayflies are unique in that they have a short-lived, winged pre-adult stage, the subimago, known to anglers as the dun, which, once emerged from the water, flies to a sheltered spot where it rests for a short while before moulting yet again to become the full adult. Many species emerge synchronously, although contrary to popular belief, not all species do so in the spring, some species having autumn swarms. The mass emergences are probably an adaptation to their short lifespans, enabling mating swarms to form. The females enter the swarms, copulate in flight, and lay their eggs either directly on the water surface or on submerged vegetation. The number of eggs laid ranges among species, from a modest 400 to an astounding 3,000. Some mayfly species are also facultatively parthenogenetic, meaning that unfertilized eggs are able to produce viable larvae; this may be an adaptation to their short adult lifespan and limited dispersal ability as they are weak flyers.

The Plecoptera

The Plecoptera, or stoneflies, number approximately 4,000 species. They are found on all continents except Antarctica, mainly along stream margins or lake shores; about half the species are found in Asia and only about 150 in Europe. The common name may reflect the fact that larvae are often found under stones in streams and rivers. The adults are all terrestrial with one exception, *Capnia lacustra*, which has only been found at depths of 60–80 m in Lake Tahoe. Like the mayflies, the larvae of stoneflies, which are all aquatic, are extremely intolerant of pollution, have a very high oxygen requirement, and are most often associated with running or well-aerated water. The larvae resemble the adult forms very closely but have gills and no wings (Figure 18).

Stoneflies are temperature limited, with an upper thermal threshold of 25°C. Their very narrow habitat requirements and poor dispersal ability mean that they are probably

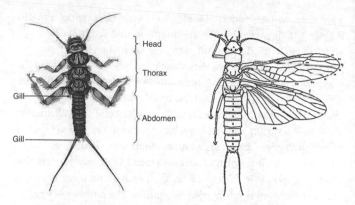

18. Larval and adult forms of the Plecoptera. Note the gills in the larval stage and absence of wings.

one of the most endangered groups of insects globally, surpassed only by the ice crawlers (Chapter 7).

The larvae have generalized biting mouthparts, and feed on dead and decaying plant material and other organic detritus. Some species are carnivorous and tend to specialize on particular prey items as they age.

The adults emerge at night, mainly in the spring or early summer, but some species emerge in the autumn. They are protandrous—the males emerge and mature before the females and die soon after copulation. Surprisingly little is known about the ecology and biology of the adults. They have functional mouthparts, and the females live for longer than the males. As they need to mature before laying eggs, they, unlike the very short-lived males, almost certainly need to feed; it is thought that they may feed on lichens. Depending on species, the eggs are either dropped onto the surface of the water or laid on submerged vegetation. In both cases, the eggs have a sticky surface that is activated on contact with water. Some species lay up to 1,000 eggs; they vary greatly in size, from 5 to 50 µm, and, ranging in colour from black to green

or yellow, they are often marked with distinctive light or dark patterns. Some species are wingless, but most are winged although they are poor flyers. Their hind wings have an expanded posterior lobe that folds longitudinally under the main wing, giving them their characteristic appearance when at rest (Figure 18).

The Odonata

Everyone is probably familiar with the Odonata, the dragonflies and damselflies. There are about 6,300 species, again found on all continents except Antarctica. They are ancient insects: fossil records of their ancestral group, the Protodonata, date back to at least as far as the Upper Carboniferous (Pennsylvanian) sediments in Europe, formed about 325 MYA. The Protodonata were fast-flying insects with spiny legs and wingspans up to 75 cm. This group went extinct in the Triassic, about the time that dinosaurs began to appear.

Odonates use their wings in a unique manner. Other four-winged insects beat them synchronously, but dragonflies can beat the fore and hind pairs independently, allowing three different modes of flight in which the pairs beat synchronously, alternately between the two sets, or synchronously but out of phase with each other. This allows odonates to display a variety of aerial aerobatics, including hovering, backward flight, and the ability to turn on a mid-air pivot. No wonder they are such good predators.

Adult and larval odonates are generalist predators: they eat whatever suitable prey is abundant and catchable. Their main diet is small insects, especially flies, but they will also take advantage of termite, ant, and mayfly swarms, sometimes hunting in groups. Adult dragonflies do not hunt in cold weather, unlike damselflies, which have a lower temperature threshold. As with many other insect species, the odonate males are territorial and patrol their areas, which can extend some distance from water sources as they are very strong flyers, unlike other aquatic insects. Except for a

few Hawaiian damselflies which have terrestrial larvae, most
return to their aquatic habitats, where they lay their eggs in or
very near water. The eggs hatch shortly afterwards and the larvae
emerge in the water or crawl into it as quickly as they can.

Once hatched they begin to feed and grow. Another difference
between dragonflies and damselflies is the length of their larval
(nymphal) period. Whereas most damselflies complete their larval
development within a year, most of a dragonfly's life is spent in the
larval stage, moulting from six to fifteen times; some complete
this within one or two years while others can take as long as six
years, varying according to altitude and latitude. The aquatic
larvae are very different from the terrestrial adults (Figure 19).
Wing buds begin to show about halfway through the
developmental period.

Like the adults, the larvae (nymphs) are voracious predators. The
early instars feed on small prey items, such as crustaceans and

19. Larval stages of a dragonfly.

protozoans. The later instars graduate to larger animals including snails, water beetles, and even small fish. Although they are ferocious predators, they too can fall victim to predators and provide a valuable food source for a range of amphibians, reptiles, and birds; they also host a range of parasites. If they survive to their final instar, the nymphs crawl out of the water and moult into the winged adult with which we are all familiar.

Despite their beauty, in folklore dragonflies are often associated with the devil. As well as helping the devil weigh and measure souls, they were also reputed to sew up the mouths of naughty children—hence the devil's darning needles—and to make people blind and deaf, with their claspers being the needles and pokers. One of the common names in Romania is St George's Horse, which, according to legend, was the devil transformed into a giant dragonfly.

The Trichoptera

Except for specialists, most people tend not to give much thought to caddisflies; if they know anything about them, it is probably limited to the fact that they are aquatic and live inside a case of bits of vegetation, particles of sand, or small pebbles, spun together with silk thread. As a child I discovered that if I very carefully removed the case from a larval caddisfly and reared it in an aquarium with a suitable food supply and a range of different substrates, such as coloured sand and pebbles, I could end up with a technicoloured caddis case. This attribute has been used by canny entrepreneurs who sell very expensive caddis jewellery.

The origin of the word 'caddis' is unclear, but it dates to at least Izaak Walton's *The Compleat Angler* (1653), in which 'cod-worms or caddis' are mentioned as being used as bait. Thomas Muffet (Moufet) used the term *cados* worm in his book *Insectorum sive Minimorum Animalium Theatrum* ('great variety of cados

worms'), which was published posthumously in 1658 (Muffet died in 1604). The term *cadyss* was used in the 15th century for silk or cotton cloth, and 'cadice-men' were itinerant vendors of such materials but a direct connection between these words and the insects has not been established.

Most people probably would not recognize an adult caddisfly; and those who do usually think that they are some sort of moth. This is actually quite a sensible guess as evolutionarily speaking the Lepidoptera and Trichoptera are closely related and are in the same super-order, the Amphiesmenoptera. Trichoptera literally translates as hairy wings, Lepidoptera as scaly wings, and many adult caddisflies look remarkably similar to micro-moths.

The majority of caddisflies have aquatic larvae although there are a few that have become completely terrestrial and spend their lives foraging in damp leaf litter and hiding in bark crevices. The adults lay their eggs in water, on aquatic vegetation, or on nearby trees. On hatching, the larvae go through several (usually five) moults before pupating. The adults emerge in spring or early summer.

Caddisflies are probably the most successful of the aquatic insects. Data from stream surveys frequently list as many species of Trichoptera as species of Ephemeroptera, Odonata, and Plecoptera combined. Their success can be put down to their use of silk and ability to exploit a range of aquatic habitats. They can live in running water, or in ponds and lakes. Some of the 'ponds' can be very temporary, such as puddles, or pools formed in plants such as bromeliads. As we noted earlier, insects that live in running water are well supplied with fresh, aerated water while those living in ponds and pools have to make their own currents by flexing their bodies and moving their legs, in order to pass 'fresh' water over their gills. Sedentary caddisfly larvae live in fixed shelters and use silk 'fishing nets' to catch their food

20. Caddisfly fishing net.

(Figure 20). Those that live in fast-flowing streams have coarse, tight nets. Insects living in slow-flowing streams use baggy, fine-grained nets.

Some caddisfly larvae are free-living foragers with portable cases. Like other insects, they use silk, leaving a thread behind them, to attach themselves to the substrate so that they are not floated downstream willy-nilly. If they live in fast-flowing streams their cases are streamlined.

As well as the very few terrestrial caddisflies, another family of caddisflies, the Chathamiidae, deserve a mention, being one of the few insects that have returned to the marine environment, although only to the tide line. These marine caddisflies are case bearers and found only in Australasia. The larvae feed on algae and live in deep rock pools with a connection to the open sea and, unlike their terrestrial and freshwater relatives, the adults do not have a synchronous emergence phase, emerging instead over a period of several months.

Marine insects

Having emerged, via a cave-dwelling crustacean ancestor, from the sea about 400 MYA, insects seem to have been reluctant to return there. Of the 1.2 million insects so far described, a mere 30,000 to 40,000 species, 3 per cent or so, are aquatic or have aquatic larval stages. Of these, about 9,000 species (mostly bugs and beetles) spend their entire lifecycle under or on water. In about 30,000 species, the flies, mosquitoes, mayflies, caddisflies, dragonflies, only the larval stage is aquatic. Although the oceans cover something like 75 per cent of the Earth's surface, insects are relatively absent from this habitat. Why, apart from a few exceptions, which I will mention later, are insects so scarce in the marine environment?

Dr Lanna Cheng, of the University of California, San Diego, suggested the following ideas. First, the marine environment is salty, and it is possible that insects are limited by this salinity. This may be true for most insects but, thanks to their highly efficient osmoregulatory system, some fly larvae are able to tolerate salinity in excess of three times that of the ocean. Second, the ocean is deep, which stops insects from completing their development. Again, this is true for many insects but there are flies, such as chironomid midge larvae, that are found at depths (2,500 m) below those that even the deepest-diving whales can reach. Third, the combination of ocean depth and salinity makes the oxygen content of such habitats too limited for insect survival, but, once again, some fly larvae can survive months without oxygen. Indeed many other aquatic insects survive, if not thrive, in polluted waters with similar or lower oxygen concentrations to those found in the ocean depths. The final, and perhaps most compelling, hypothesis concerns crustacean competition. If we argue that insects are so successful because they colonized land, then by moving away from the ocean, they exploited and adapted to a terrestrial existence, while their major competitors, the

crustaceans, stayed in the sea and continued to adapt to that environment. Now, millions of years later, insects are unable to compete successfully in the ocean and their distant crustacean cousins have similar difficulties on land. Professor Cheng is a strong advocate of this hypothesis and points out that the only insects that live in the open ocean live on its surface and never meet the crustaceans living beneath its surface. Other explanations for the paucity of truly marine insects are that the difficulty of living at depth because of their air-filled tracheal system makes them much more vulnerable to predation by fish; and, additionally, it is difficult to produce aerial dispersal stages in an ocean environment. Freshwater insects are able to use semi-submerged vegetation as platforms for their newly moulted adult stages to first break the surface tension to emerge above the water and secondly to rest upon while their wings unfold and harden prior to flight. In the open ocean such structures are extremely rare. This combination of factors goes some way to explaining the lack of underwater dwelling marine insects.

There are in fact several hundred insect genera in fourteen orders associated with marine shoreline environments but only members of the genus *Halobates*, the sea or ocean skaters, are found in the open seas. These are Hemiptera in the family Gerridae and were discovered almost 200 years ago by Johann Friedrich Gustav von Eschscholtz during his voyage on the Russian expeditionary ship *Rurik* between 1815 and 1818. Although 90 per cent of gerrids are freshwater dwellers, there are forty species within the genus *Halobates*, five of which are truly marine. They are distributed in all tropical oceans between 40 N and 40 S. Gerrids are fascinating in their own right: witness their ability to skim across the surface of ponds and streams. Gerrids also have some interesting facets to their biology and ecology. They have short- and long-winged forms, use 'ripple communication', basically causing waves to attract mates, and some species show territorial behaviour and mate guarding. *Halobates* is, however, the only genus with species that are wholly oceanic. These are remarkable insects indeed; they

have a tropical distribution yet, unlike tropical terrestrial counterparts, have nowhere to hide from the sun, storms, and predators. They live on the surface, surrounded by a 3 per cent salt solution, yet maintain their blood salts levels at a lower osmotic pressure than that of seawater (hypotonic) and manage to find mates in the vastness of the ocean. They live in what, to them, must be an unbounded two-dimensional world in which they are almost solely dependent on prey falling from above or floating up from below. Furthermore, they must survive predation from above (birds) and below (fish), while keeping in touch with others of their species in order to mate and produce young, with the still further challenge of avoiding falling prey to others of the same genus that face the same existential dilemmas. They reduce their risk of predation by forming 'flotillas' of up to one hundred individuals. Their eggs are laid in batches on any convenient floating substrate—a shed feather, floating vegetation, plastic—and even on their conspecifics. They avoid drowning by wearing what amounts to 'mackintosh and boots' in the form of very small hairs (microtrichia) on their legs and larger hairs (macrotrichia) on their bodies, which repel water and hold air. If they are submerged, they can survive for at least two hours under water and up to sixteen hours in cooler waters. They are extremely difficult to keep in captivity, so much remains to be discovered about these elusive animals.

Fascinating as they are, aquatic insects are in the minority, although that is still sizeable given the species richness compared with vertebrates, which they far outnumber. In this chapter, as well as considering the lifecycles and reproductive tactics of aquatic insects, we have seen how they avoid predation. In Chapter 6 we will see the adaptations that their terrestrial relatives have evolved in order to avoid falling victim to the depredations of insectivorous vertebrates and other invertebrates.

Chapter 6
Mimicry, crypsis, and blatant advertising

Insects are food for many animals, including other insects. Their main routes to avoiding being eaten are to hide, by camouflaging themselves so that they merge into the background or pretending to be something dangerous or poisonous; or to run or fly away. Several insects mimic inanimate objects, while others take on the appearance of a dangerous animal; eyespots on butterfly wings for example, are thought to mimic the eyes of vertebrate predators. Some flies and moths are incredible mimics; how many people have thought that the harmless hoverfly is a wasp or a bee, or that the clearwing hornet moth is a hornet?

Mimicry of 'dangerous' beasts has arisen from the practice adopted by a number of insect species that advertise their lethality by warning colours—red and black or yellow and black. Caterpillars that sequester toxins from their host plants advertise this with stripes, warning experienced bird and mammal predators that eating them will result in dire consequences. In some species the toxic effects are passed on to the adult stage, which also has warning colouration although not necessarily the same colouration as the larva. The cinnabar moth has yellow and black stripes as a caterpillar but is black and red as an adult, both colour schemes being well-known danger signs in the natural world. Presumably the change in colour from larva to adult implies that the adults have a different suite of predators to avoid.

The English naturalist Henry Bates and the German entomologist Johann Müller worked independently in Brazilian rainforests in the late 19th century, observing and collecting Heliconiid butterflies. So influential was this work that their names have been immortalized by being attached to their respective concepts. *Batesian mimicry* or signal, protective, or defensive mimicry, is formally defined as mimicry in which a harmless species has evolved to imitate the warning signals of a harmful species directed at a predator of them both (Figure 21). *Müllerian mimicry* (aposematism) or cue mimicry is defined as that in which two or more often distasteful species, which may or may not be closely related and share one or more common predators, have come to mimic each other's honest warning signals, to their mutual benefit (Figure 22).

21. A plate from Bates's original article, illustrating Batesian mimicry between *Dismorphia* species (top row and third row) and various Ithomiini (Nymphalidae) (second and bottom rows). A non-Batesian species, *Pseudopieris nehemia*, is top centre.

22. **Müllerian mimicry in butterflies, showing four forms of**
H. numata; **two forms of** *H. melpomene*; **and, in the bottom row, the**
two corresponding mimicking forms of *H. erato*.

Although Batesian and Müllerian mimicry has long been
associated with tropical butterfly species, recent work has revealed
that a mimetic complex of red and black Hemiptera, providing
defence against insectivorous birds, is present in Central Europe.

Camouflage, advertising, and shock tactics

Mimicry is not all Batesian and Müllerian; other forms of mimicry
are also recognized. Insects can masquerade as physical objects, so
for example many Lepidoptera appear to be dead leaves, twigs, or
even buds, such as the buff-tip (*Phalera bucephala*), and the very

23. Adult *Uropyia meticulodina* masquerading as a dead leaf.

familiar stick insects and leaf insects that do a remarkable job of mimicking vegetation. The moth *Uropyia meticulodina* is almost indistinguishable from the real thing when at rest and masquerading as a dead leaf (Figure 23).

An example of cue and masquerade mimicry is seen in moth larvae and adults that appear to be bird droppings on leaves, presenting an unpalatable sight to potential predators. An example of aggressive cue mimicry is that of predatory insects that prey on spiders. The Australian assassin bug, *Stenolemus bituberus*, climbs on to a spider's web and strums the threads to attract the spider towards it. Once it arrives, the bug quickly stabs the spider with its piercing mouthparts and holds it in place with its front legs while sucking out the body fluids. Conversely, an example of aggressive signal mimicry is that shown by the large blue butterfly (*Phengaris arion*, formerly *Maculinea arion*), which overwinters as a fourth-instar larva in the nests of the ant *Myrmica sabuleti*. In the first three larval (caterpillar) stages, the butterfly feeds on plants, and when it has finished feeding it falls

to the ground, mimics the sound of an ant larva, and as a finishing touch mimics the skin chemistry of the ant larva too, fooling passing adult ants into taking it into their nest, where the butterfly larva becomes carnivorous and feeds on the ant brood throughout the winter. In the spring, the fully developed larva forms a pupa (chrysalis), chrysalis, emerges a few days later as an adult, and makes its way to the surface where it inflates its wings, seeks a mate, and lays eggs in a suitable habitat.

Depending on its orientation, the eyed hawkmoth (*Smerinthus ocellata*) can be thought to be masquerading as dead leaves, a bracket fungus, or even a fox. There is even a caterpillar of a moth species found in the Ecuadorian jungle that looks like a bird feather—when it moves it appears to be blowing in the wind.

Another example of impressive mimicry is the peacock butterfly (*Aglais io*). When its wings are fully open, its body is the same shape and colour as a bird's beak. Even the 'eyes' are in the right position and with only a bit of imagination you can see a resemblance to an owl's head. When the wings are closed, the colouration of the undersides resembles a dead leaf or tree bark; when disturbed, it opens its wings and hopefully startles the predator(s) away.

Christer Wiklund and colleagues at the University of Stockholm, Sweden, carried out some fascinating research with three leaf-mimicking butterfly species, the comma (*Polygonia c-album*), the small tortoiseshell (*Aglais urticae*), and the peacock. The butterflies were put in a large cage with some blue tits. The comma, which is the most realistic leaf mimic, was the last to be discovered by the blue tits, but as this butterfly lacks the wing opening 'startle' defence almost 75 per cent of this species were eaten. The small tortoiseshell butterflies, as an intermediate between the comma and peacock in terms of behaviour and mimicry, suffered 90 per cent mortality. The peacock, on the other hand, had 100 per cent survival.

Not all insects pretend to be something else; some have adopted protective colouration. Many adult insects blend perfectly into their backgrounds: the Central and South American lichen katydid (*Markia hystrix*) is gloriously green when freshly emerged, and the marvellously named merveille du jour (*Griposia aprilina*) is almost invisible when resting on a lichen-covered tree. The peppered moth (*Biston betularia*), which has different coloured forms or types, rests during the day as an adult on the trunks of trees that are similarly coloured. When air pollution was at its height, natural selection favoured adult moths that were darker in colour; this melanic form is now not as common in the UK since the Clean Air Act (1956) reduced the amount of soot in the air. The larvae are also cryptic (hiding in plain view), mimicking twigs, and recent research has shown that they can sense the colour of the twig that they are on and adjust their body colour accordingly.

It is not just during their active stages that insects need protection from natural enemies: this is also necessary for the eggs and pupae. Insect eggs vary greatly in colour, size, shape, and sculpturing. Some of this variation is very clearly defensive in function: spicules (spines), distasteful coating, and high levels of toxic chemicals. A less metabolically costly option is camouflage or mimicry. Eggs of the Indian stick insect resemble plant seeds, even having a fake elaiosome—on real seeds, a fleshy lipid-containing structure that encourages ants to carry and disperse them. It has been suggested that eggs of the map butterfly, *Araschnia levana*, mimic the flowers of its larval host plant, nettle (*Urtica* spp.) (Figure 24).

Another butterfly, *Agathymus estelleae*, lays beige or green eggs. The former are cryptic if they fall to the ground, the latter are cryptic on the host plants, ensuring that at least some of the eggs are protected, however careless the mother might be in depositing her eggs. We may not think of ants and bees as needing to hide, but despite their stings and bites, they do have enemies. Ants are probably the largest

24. The map butterfly, the plant that is the mimic model for the eggs and the eggs of the butterfly.

group of social insects that use camouflage; those species that live on tree bark, soil, and rock tend to be uniformly black, brown, or grey coloured, matching their backgrounds. We can also see variation within species, in bumblebees, for example, with those that live in dry grasslands being paler than those of the same species that live in lusher, more shaded environments.

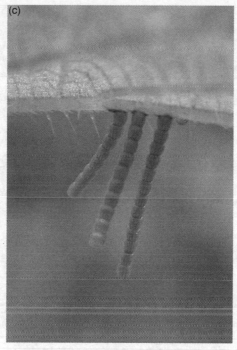

24. Continued

Distractive/disruptive marking

Distractive or disruptive marking breaks up body edges and creates false boundaries, which confuse predators in search of a juicy meal. Eggs of the lappet moth (*Gastropacha quercifolia*), the adults of which resemble a bundle of dried-up oak leaves (hence the name), have eggs that are very distinctly marked and very obvious, at least to humans, and it has been suggested that this is an example of disruptive marking (Figure 25).

25. *Gastropacha quercifolia* eggs.

Advertising

Insects that depend on chemical defence, which they gain by sequestering toxins from their host plants, such as the cinnabar moth that feeds on ragwort, *Senecio jacobaea*, make sure that they stand out from the crowd by adopting bold colouration; in the case of the cinnabar moth, as we noted earlier, the adults are red and black, and the caterpillars are striped yellow and black. The monarch butterfly (*Danaus plexippus*), which feeds on milkweed, a plant rich in cardiac glycosides, has very bright larvae, striped yellow and black, and the adults are a very distinctive orange and black. As with the cinnabar moth, this suggests that the predators attacking the different life stages are not the same. Once a predator, usually a vertebrate, has learned that these are distasteful, the rest of the population is safe from that individual.

In some predator populations the response to danger signals appears to be innate, and, for now, prey and predator have reached an evolutionary truce.

Although most species that have evolved the use of red and yellow warning colours show these characteristics across their populations, with all individuals being the same colour, some species, such as the wood tiger moth (*Arctia plantaginis*), display colour polymorphism. The hind wings of the females range from yellow to red, while those of the males can be white, yellow, red, or black. Adults of the wood tiger have two forms of chemical defence: one is the release of a toxic fluid from the thorax, produced when attacked by birds, the other is the production of a similar, but subtly different, toxic cocktail that deters invertebrate predators—mainly ants. The fluid produced by white-winged males is nastier and smellier than that produced by the other colour morphs, which would make us think that the white forms would be the most common, if not the only colour morph. Although some populations are indeed monomorphic, in Scotland, all wood tiger moths have yellow hind wings; in other places, other colour forms dominate. It turns out that the frequency of the different colour forms is a result of the learning behaviour of the most common bird predators: in Scotland tits are the main predators, in Southern Finland, where the white morph dominates, dunnocks are the main predators. What about the red-winged forms? How is it that they survive in nature? It turns out that although they are not as distasteful as the white forms, they are visually more repugnant to birds, possibly because of an innate expectation, based on their experience of similarly coloured insects, that red signals danger. On the other hand, it could be that their anti-ant defences are more effective than in the other colour forms and that this allows them to persist in the population. A great example of natural selection in action, although one could wonder what would happen to the Scottish populations if the bird community were to suddenly change.

Although yellow, red, and black are colours that many insect predators recognize innately as danger signals, the insect warning palette is not limited to those colours alone. Some insects use other warning colours: the monkshood aphid (*Delphiniobium junackianum*) is a vivid blue, and feeds in a dispersed, but obvious, crowd, on the leaves of its very poisonous host plant, monkshood. The blue pigment is derived from the aconite that the aphid sequesters from its host plant, making it a less than tasty mouthful for any predator that chooses to ignore its warning signals.

Although adult Lepidoptera have a number of predator avoidance mechanisms—mimicry, aposematism, unpalatability, or innate behaviours—there are no peer-reviewed published references to them being able to 'remember' being attacked and to avoid an area for some time afterwards. On the other hand, there are many examples of predators learning to avoid distasteful lepidopteran prey. Remembering to avoid predator-rich areas would seem to be a 'sensible' trait to evolve, so it is surprising that the existence of this phenomenon has not yet been tested, especially as other insect groups, aphids and thrips being notable examples, have been shown to avoid plants that ladybirds and predatory bugs have previously investigated.

Having seen how good insects are at avoiding death from the actions of other animals, Chapter 7 examines how insects cope with the dangers facing them from the equally taxing effects of weather and climate.

Chapter 7
Against the odds

In addition to the risk of being eaten, insects face several environmental challenges, weather and climate being the two most obvious. Imagine having to spend winters naked on the snow-covered prairies of North America or the summers naked roaming the deserts of North Africa. This is the situation in which many insects find themselves. The problems are particularly marked in insects that live in seasonal environments, or those where there are very marked differences between night and day temperatures. Insects that live in temperate or subarctic environments need to find some means to survive the winter, be that a safe overwintering site, a change in behaviour, a physiological change, or, in many cases, all three. The main challenge is to avoid dying from the cold. The solution to this is to overwinter as a cold-hardy stage, which in insects can be any part of their lifecycle—egg, larva, pupa, adult—even in the case of organisms as seemingly fragile as moths and butterflies.

The secret lies in the anti-freeze that insects produce as winter approaches. Insects that overwinter use a mixture of alcohols and proteins to prevent freezing, in some cases (aphid eggs, for example) allowing them to survive prolonged exposure to temperatures as low as −40°C, a much-needed level of protection in a Scandinavian winter. Just because an insect can be found frozen within soil or water does not mean that it is, unlike us,

freeze-tolerant (able to survive the formation of ice crystals in its body tissues); it may or may not be. If the latter, it has avoided freezing by the process known as supercooling, the ability to remain unfrozen below its melting point. The supercooling point is the temperature at which spontaneous freezing occurs in a supercooled liquid. You may have put a glass of water into your freezer and removed it some hours later to find it still liquid, but on poking a finger into it find that it suddenly solidifies, as crystallization begins when even a small speck of dust is introduced: an excellent and very satisfying example of supercooling. Purified water does not contain the impurities on which ice crystals can form. The more anti-freeze present, the lower the temperature at which an insect can supercool. Producing anti-freeze is metabolically expensive so it is in the interest of the insect to produce it only when it is needed—not all year around, but only as winter approaches. In the early days, research on insect overwintering was done largely by insect physiologists, who concentrated on the remarkable supercooling ability of insects, often as low as –20°C in some adult insects and –40°C in some eggs. Even soft-bodied insects such as aphids were shown to have supercooling points well below –10°C. This was, however, at odds with what could be seen in nature. For example, work with the grain aphid (*Sitobion avenae*) showed clearly that populations in the north of England, although initially increasing during early winter, died out before spring, despite the temperature not falling below –8°C. The answer lay in the method by which supercooling points were determined. The tested aphids were placed in small chambers, the temperature was lowered by fractions of degrees, stopped, and raised back to ambient levels to check whether the aphids were still alive. The temperature at which they died was recorded as the lethal limit. The researchers did not, however, check whether normal function was restored after the treatment. As it transpired, the aphids suffered cryo-injury at temperatures as high as 5°C if exposed to it for a prolonged period of time: they may well have been alive at this temperature when observed in experimental

conditions, but in the field their reproduction and survival were impaired, leading to population collapse.

Overwintering strategies are not all based on internal chemistry. Another way to survive winter is to change behaviour. Many insects that normally avoid each other, except when they want to mate, become much more tolerant of each other and form large aggregations in protected sites: under the bark of trees or, as often reported by the media, in people's houses. We have already noted earlier that in insects like ladybirds, such behavioural change is mediated by aggregation pheromones and a positive response to touch, thigmotaxis. In insects that would normally spend the winter in caves or tree hollows, there may also be a negative response to light.

How do insects know that winter is approaching? There are two cues for this: change in day length—days become shorter and nights longer once the summer solstice has passed—and mean temperatures begin to decrease. The latter is not as reliable a cue as the former so most insects depend mainly on the length of the day (photophase) or night (scotophase), as these are entirely predictable and do not vary from year to year. Each insect species has a critical phase. In the vetch aphid (*Megoura vicia*), the threshold is reached when night-time exceeds ten hours, whereas in the parasitic wasp Cotesia (*Apanteles rubecula*), the stimulus to begin diapause (a condition in which development and metabolism is greatly reduced) is when day length falls below sixteen hours. The next 'decision' that an insect must make is where to overwinter.

As 'naked' organisms, insects need somewhere sheltered and preferably well insulated to pass the winter. Soil is a remarkably good insulator; the surface temperature might be −12°C but the temperature at 160 cm depth can be as high as 6°C. This would seem to be the ideal situation, especially if there is deep snow cover, which acts as a further insulating layer. In Canada, for

example, where deep snow is common in winter, the cabbage root fly (*Delia radicum*) is able to survive at a lower air temperature than those in the UK, where snow is much rarer. Overwintering at depth in the soil may be fine for a hard-bodied adult beetle but imagine a soft-bodied larva first digging its way down to that depth, then emerging as a delicate winged adult in the spring and having to scramble to the surface; they would suffer irreparable damage on the way. Another problem would be knowing when spring has come. In practice, most insects that overwinter in soil tend to be no further down than $c.15$ cm. Some insects, such as the weevil *Strophosoma melanogrammum*, which overwinters as an active adult stage, move between the soil and the surface, depending on the temperature, feeding on evergreen plants during warmer spells and retreating to the relatively warm subsoil environment when temperatures dip below 0°C. This brings us neatly on to the problem of which lifecycle stage to pass the winter in. Insects exist as eggs, larvae, and adults, and, if they are holometabolic, they also have pre-pupal and pupal stages. Taking butterflies and moths as an example of holometabolic insects, in a region where winters are noted for their harshness, for instance Finland, where winter air temperatures are commonly below –20°C, most species would be expected to overwinter as immobile cold-hardy stages—egg or pupa. In fact, all stages of the lepidopteran lifecycle can occur during the winter, albeit that egg and pupa are the preferred overwintering stages. It may be risky to overwinter as a fragile larva or adult but there are also advantages, not least that of being ahead of your competitors. If the overwintering stage is a pupa, insects have to emerge, mate, and lay eggs; if they are already adult, they are ready to lay eggs and exploit the newly flushing tissue before their rivals have emerged from their overwintering pupa. If they are larvae that have survived the winter, they are already in a position to begin feeding. A substantial proportion of species overwinter at more than one stage to 'hedge their bets'.

Of course, it is important to know when spring has arrived. Insects use increasing temperatures and increasing day lengths to

know when to emerge from diapause, although some species, such as the pine beauty moth (*Panolis flammea*) and the cabbage root fly, also have to have been subjected to a period of subdevelopmental temperatures before they will respond to the spring cues, somewhat similar to the vernalization process in plants.

At the other end of the scale is extreme heat and drought. In this case, anti-freeze is not an option although tropical insects still have the ability to produce cryoprotectants. There are two aspects to this part of the insect story: insects that are desert dwellers and must cope with extreme conditions throughout their lives, and insects that only experience extreme heat and drought occasionally; the former are well adapted to the conditions, the latter less so.

Behavioural and physiological responses are the key to desert survival. Insects that are desert-adapted have special modifications compared with their temperate and tropical relatives; there are morphological, physiological, anatomical, and behavioural adaptations. Desert insects tend to be quite large, reducing relative surface area and preventing undue water loss. Unlike insects that live in dry non-desert conditions, the legs of desert insects are usually long to avoid contact with the hot desert surface, and they often have a sub-elytral cavity, again to reduce water loss. Physiologically, desert insects have three main forms of defence. They can tolerate low water content of their haemolymph: essentially, they have thick blood. Like other animals that live in dry conditions, they retain as much water as possible in their secretory processes. Insect frass (droppings) is generally dry but in desert insects it is exceptionally so; every molecule of water is precious. They exhibit discontinuous ventilation (cyclical breathing), which can be thought of as the insect holding its breath. The spiracles (Chapter 1) are kept closed for most of the time but as oxygen is used and carbon dioxide (CO_2) accumulates in the haemolymph, it is held in solution mainly in the form of bicarbonate. As CO_2 levels build up, the spiracles open slightly, allowing some oxygen to enter and a little

of the CO_2 to escape. Finally, as the level of CO_2 reaches a critical threshold, the spiracles open completely and the carbon dioxide is released in one big burst.

Other desert insects take advantage of the occasional mists or fogs and drink water from where it accumulates on bits of detritus. Some tenebrionid beetles construct troughs and mini sand dunes to collect their own water. Other tenebrionid beetles have anatomical adaptations to do the same job. The darkling beetle (*Stenocara gracilipes*), and related species, intrepid inhabitants of the Namib Desert, represent probably the most well-known examples of extreme desert adaptation. Their long legs reduce contact with the hot sand, and their cuticle, composed of hydrophilic and hydrophobic grooves and bumps, channels water harvested from the morning sea fogs to their waiting mouths (Figure 26). Other desert-dwelling insects are largely nocturnal, spending the day beneath the soil surface or under convenient stones or similar sites.

Drought, which may, if current predictions for climate change are correct, become an ever more frequent event worldwide, is likely to cause insects in temperate regions many more problems than those faced by the desert dwellers. Drought in temperate and tropical regions is usually paired with high temperatures. In tropical regions this is not such a big problem because tropical insects have higher thermal limits than temperate insects. Although, in general, higher temperatures allow insects to complete their lifecycles more quickly, there are thermal tolerances to be considered. The temperate species known as the alfalfa aphid (*Acyrthosiphon kondoi*) has an optimum temperature limit of *c*.15°C while the tropical aphid *Aphis gossypii* does best at about 25°C, a temperature that the former species finds hard to tolerate for any length of time. Drought can affect all stages of the insect lifecycle—egg hatch, larval feeding and development, adult and larval behaviour, fecundity, and oviposition.

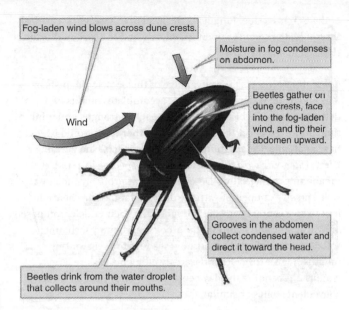

Fog-laden wind blows across dune crests.

Moisture in fog condenses on abdomon.

Beetles gather on dune crests, face into the fog-laden wind, and tip their abdomen upward.

Wind

Grooves in the abdomen collect condensed water and direct it toward the head.

Beetles drink from the water droplet that collects around their mouths.

26. The darkling beetle, *Stenocara gracilipes*.

The eggs of many beetle species need to absorb water before they can hatch; those of the Western corn rootworm (*Diabrotica virgifera*) desiccate at low humidity, while in other species, egg hatch and survival are much reduced under drought conditions. Insects with soil dwelling larvae are particularly susceptible to drought—young leather jackets (larval craneflies) are very dependent on moist soil for survival, as are larvae of the weevil *Sitona hispidulus*. The depth at which larvae of the click beetle (*Agriotes lineatus*) feed and their abundance are affected greatly by rainfall; low soil moisture results in reduced abundance. Oviposition of the southern mole cricket, *Scapteriscus borellii*, is greatly delayed once soil moisture falls below 10 per cent.

Drought in areas where it is not a regular occurrence can have marked effects on insect populations, either directly or, in the case

of herbivorous insects, through the impacts on their host plants. In the UK and USA, for example, highly mobile butterfly and moth species with southern distributions tend to increase in abundance after drought periods whereas less-mobile species with northern distributions show population decreases. Herbivorous insects are not the only insects that are affected by drought. Carabid beetles, many of which are predatory, were also affected by the UK droughts of the mid-1990s; species that were adapted to damp and moist habitats and low temperatures showed significant decreases in abundance. Insects and plants have a complex relationship when it comes to drought stress.

In 1969, an Australian entomologist, Tom White, came up with an alluring hypothesis to explain insect outbreaks, one which dominated the field for at least twenty years and is still being tested. This was the famous, perhaps infamous, plant-stress hypothesis. White noticed that outbreaks of the psyllid, *Cardiaspina densitexta*, or as the Australians call it, the Eucalyptus lerp, were associated with drought or waterlogging. He hypothesized that trees were undergoing stress, which made the soluble nitrogen content of the foliage more accessible to the insects, enabling them to develop into larger, more fecund adults, ultimately leading to the outbreaks. A few years later, an American entomologist, Doug Rhoades, supported this hypothesis but added that the defences of the stressed trees were also impaired so that, as well as having a more nutritious food source, the insects had more resource available for reproduction as fewer were being diverted to overcoming the plant defences. This hypothesis resonated with entomologists and ecologists who, understandably, saw it in human terms of susceptibility to illness when stressed.

While field observations seemed to support the hypothesis, experimental evidence was and remains harder to come by. Herbivorous insects do not all feed on plants in the same way; some have much more intimate relationships with the plants than others. Sap-feeders exploit the phloem or xylem; defoliators strip

the leaves; then there are shoot or stem borers, leaf-miners that live within the leaves feeding on the internal tissues, and gallers that manipulate plant tissue by the 'injection' of salivary compounds. It would seem obvious that insects with different feeding modes may not respond to stressed plants in the same way. A couple of influential reviews in the 1990s suggested, however, that experimental studies gave very different results from field observations. When researchers looked at outbreaks in the field they were apparently more likely to see the effects of plant stress than under experimental conditions, probably due to the fact that the conditions that supposedly induced plant stress, i.e. hot weather, also enable insects to grow quickly, develop faster, and be more fecund. Experiments under controlled conditions were much more ambiguous and related to the feeding mode of the insect. A meta-analysis in 2004, by Susan Huberty and Bob Denno, showed that phloem-feeders such as aphids performed worse on drought-stressed plants, while leaf chewers seemed unaffected.

The way in which the plants are stressed may influence the outcomes for the insects. Joanna Staley conducted an interesting set of experiments at Wytham Woods, near Oxford, UK. She subjected experimental plots to two treatments, a complete summer drought and a wet summer, with 120 per cent of normal rainfall, and studied lepidopteran and dipteran leaf-miners on different host plants. She found that some responded positively to stress while others did not, so there was no consistent response to plant stress within that feeding guild. Similarly, experiments with aphids showed differing responses depending on species and stress type—responses that were not in direct proportion to increasing drought. In nature however, drought or waterlogging is not always continuous; dry spells can be interrupted by wet spells. This leads to the pulsed stress hypothesis. To test this, we did experiments using spruce aphids on conifers subjected to a variety of treatments ranging from continuous drought, waterlogging, and intermittent rain and drought. We found that intermittent,

pulsed drought stress benefited the aphids, whereas long spells of drought and waterlogging had detrimental effects on them. Ladybird predators, on the other hand, increased their aphid consumption rates when drought was prolonged but ate fewer when drought conditions were intermittent. Aphid parasitoids also show similar interactions. These experiments reveal how complex the interactions between plants, their stress effects, and insect herbivores can be, especially when natural enemies are factored in.

In summary, whereas insects are well adapted to predictable occurrences of cold and extreme heat, the direct effects of drought can cause changes in the timing of insect development, their survival, and abundance. All stages of the lifecycle can be affected. Indirect effects, those brought about by the host plant, may be non-linear, and are inconsistent across feeding guilds and orders. Much more work needs to be done if we are to understand the effects of climate change on insect populations.

Chapter 8
The good, the bad, and the ugly

Most people think of insects as good or bad, honeybees and other pollinators versus mosquitoes and crop pests, like the ubiquitous greenfly, and that, in a nutshell, is the problem. Insects are not just pests and pollinators. Most insects do not harm humans; a very small percentage of the known one million plus species have shaped our viewpoint of these fascinating and useful animals.

Leaving aside the cultural influences, human existence depends on insects. Pollinators are important, but these are not just honeybees; flies, beetles, moths, butterflies, wild bees, and other Hymenoptera play their part in making sure that our food crops are fruitful. There are also the largely unseen, overlooked insects busy helping with the recycling processes, improving soil quality, and acting to reduce the numbers of insects that would, unchecked, threaten our very existence. It is indisputable that without modern crop protection, we would lose maybe half of our crops during growth and storage, but to a certain extent that is our fault for providing such tempting delicacies for the less than 5 per cent of insect species that share our tastes.

As well as insects that provide us directly with food and other products, honey, wax, food colourings, and protein, we have harnessed the specialist killing behaviour of many insect predators and parasites and used them to provide us with residue-free food

and hopefully sustainable agricultural systems. We still have much to learn in this area.

Insects as pests

As mentioned previously (Chapter 3), most insects are herbivorous. Insects that make a living from the same plants that feed our livestock and ourselves are thus in direct competition with us and regarded as pests. Modern agriculture and the overuse of synthetic pesticides are often cited as the cause of all our pest problems; that is far too simplistic. We only need to read the Bible to hear of plagues of locusts, or look closely at the Bayeux Tapestry to see a bird scarer in action, or read accounts of popes and bishops in medieval Europe excommunicating crop pests, to realize that pests and diseases have existed since humans stopped being hunter-gatherers and became farmers. Modern agriculture has not caused pest problems, although it has undoubtedly exacerbated the situation; the problems date back to those first humans who selected the seeds of the tastier, higher yielding plants that they first cultivated. The characteristics that they selected for—sweeter, more succulent, larger grains/ fruit—meant that the plants were less well defended against their herbivores, including us, and thus more susceptible to attack by both specialist and generalist insect species. The things that are unpalatable to us are unpalatable to the insects that feed on those plants; by making plants more human friendly, we have also made them more attractive to the insects that prey upon them.

A long-held premise for why insects can be pests is that pest outbreaks tend to be associated with pure monocultures of crops. The hypothesis is that natural enemies were more abundant and effective in vegetationally diverse areas than in monocultures, the so-called 'enemies hypothesis'. This idea has been around a surprisingly long time; in 1947 the South African entomologist George Ullyett remarked, 'where weeds occur around headlands and in hedges, they should be left for the purpose of supporting

parasites and predators important in the natural control of the diamond-back moth (*Plutella maculipennis* Curt)'. A decade later, Charles Elton referred to this statement, explaining that 'these hedgerows form a reservoir for enemies and parasites of insects and mite pests of crops'.

Richard Root, an American ecologist, explained the premise of the 'enemies hypothesis' as follows. Predators and parasites are more effective at controlling herbivore populations in diverse habitats or plant communities because diverse plant communities support a variety of herbivores appearing in different seasons, providing a steady supply of prey for the predators. In addition, complex environments provide refuges for prey, thus allowing the prey not to be completely eradicated. Diverse plant communities also provide a broad range of additional resources, such as pollen and nectar, for adult natural enemies.

Root ran his experiment for three years and did indeed find a significant difference in herbivore load between the pure plots and the weedy rows, the former having a greater abundance of pests (mainly aphids and flea beetles) than the latter (Figure 27).

He did not, however, find any difference in the numbers of natural enemies between the two treatments. He thus had to come up with another idea to explain his results. His ingenious explanation is encapsulated in what he called the *resource concentration hypothesis*, which states that herbivores are more likely to find and stay on hosts growing in dense or simple stands or monocultures, and that the most specialized species often reach higher relative densities in simple environments.

Root hypothesized that specialist herbivores were 'trapped' on the crop and accumulated while more generalist herbivores were able and likely to move away from the crops to other host plants. He added that the 'trapping effect' of host patches depends on several factors, including stand size and simplicity. His colleague Jarmo

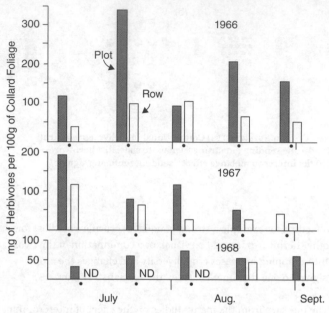

27. Difference in herbivore load between the simple plots and the weedy rows.

Tahvanainen developed two new hypotheses to explain why more diverse cropping systems have fewer pest problems than monocultures, one of which he termed *associational resistance*. He proposed that plants growing in a complex, mixed community offer an 'associational resistance' to herbivores beyond that of the individual plant species, which is lost in monoculture cultivation, allowing specialist herbivores to proliferate.

In the *Chemical Interference Hypothesis*, he postulated that reduced herbivory in diverse communities is due to chemical stimuli produced by non-host plants interfering with host finding or feeding behaviour of specialist herbivores. In simple terms, a monoculture sends out a very strong signal, which could be

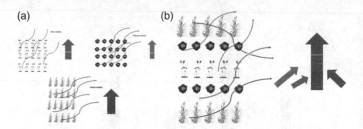

28. Cropping systems: (a) Conventional intensive agricultural landscape sending out strong 'signals' to specialist herbivores; (b) the intercrop melange effect—sending confusing signals.

olfactory, for example a strong bouquet of crucifer volatiles; for other herbivores it could be visual, or a combination of the two. Intercropping increases crop diversity and changes the crop 'signal' to one that now 'confuses' the specialists (Figure 28).

The message from the many studies on the effect of intercropping crop diversification on pest abundance is that, in general, polyculture is beneficial in terms of promoting biological control, and that incorporating legumes into the system gives the best yield outcomes.

Another form of intercropping that overcomes the potential problems of harvesting different crops from the same field is the concept of planting different genetic variants (genotypes) of the same species. Resistant plants tend to have fewer generalists present, although their individual yield may be reduced. By planting a mixture of susceptible and resistant genotypes, it is possible to have your cake and eat it, especially if it is not essential to have a single genotype crop. This approach has been used to good effect in the production of short-rotation willow coppice, where planting diverse genotypes of the same species reduces both pest and disease levels.

Insects as vectors of disease

As well as the damage that insect herbivores cause directly to crops, they can also be very efficient vectors of disease to crops, livestock, and people. Insects with piercing and sucking mouthparts feeding on plant sap or vertebrate blood need to inject an anti-coagulatory agent, which they do via their salivary glands. A number of viruses and other micro-organisms have taken advantage of this and are transmitted from their insect host to their plant or vertebrate host where they multiply and cause harm to the host. Aphids, for example, carry and spread a number of deadly plant viruses, some in a passive way, akin to disease transmission via a contaminated hypodermic needle. In other interactions, the virus multiplies in the body of the insect host. Mosquitoes and other stinging and biting flies transmit viruses and protozoan diseases to vertebrates including humans. The virus that causes blue tongue disease in domestic livestock is transmitted by biting midges; the protozoan disease malaria is transmitted by mosquitoes; Leishmaniasis, another protozoan disease, is transmitted by sandflies. These and the plant viruses are the result of coevolution between the disease-causing organisms and their intermediate hosts, many of which have resulted in behavioural modifications which improve disease transmission. Other diseases, such as those caused by bacterial infections, although no less harmful, are a result of the feeding habits of insects such as houseflies and ants, and are accidental rather than deliberate.

Biological control

Although most insects are herbivorous, 25 per cent make a living at the top of the insect food chain—the predators and parasitoids. Most people are aware of the almost ubiquitous spotted red and black ladybird beetles and their voracious appetite for aphids; some are discomfited when they encounter a spider going about

its business; few realize that there are many more hunters and killers roaming their gardens and hedge bottoms. Although predators such as these are important in keeping pest insect populations low, they are, arguably, not as efficient as the parasitic insects that carry out their activities largely unseen by humans.

Predators, parasites, and parasitoids

As with herbivorous insects (Chapter 3), insect predators have to locate their prey. Some insects such as dragonflies, carabid beetles, and ladybirds are predators as larvae and adults; others like hoverflies, only as larvae. Many larval predators, especially those that feed on herbivorous insects, are already in the vicinity of their prey, having been deposited there as eggs, so they do not have far to travel. How do the adults, either as predators themselves or as mothers needing to find a suitable home for their offspring, know where their prey are? Generalist predators, such as carabid and rove beetles, are mainly ground-dwelling and roam the soil surface, feasting on foliage-feeding insects that have fallen from above (about 15 per cent of cereal aphids find themselves on the ground) or hunting down the soil and subsurface organisms, Collembola, slugs, snails, etc. Insects with more specialist needs, such as ladybirds and hoverflies, that feed mainly on aphids, use chemical and visual cues to locate their prey; they look for plants, signs of aphid feeding, sticky honeydew, and respond to the 'scent' of their prey. Adult ladybirds and hoverflies seem to be able to judge whether an aphid infestation is growing and will lay their eggs near flourishing colonies rather than near declining colonies. This may be due to the fact that foraging aphid-eating predators leave behind oviposition-deterring and foraging pheromones. Interestingly, some aphid species also seem to be able to detect these volatile signals and avoid landing on those host plants.

Plants themselves also help natural enemies to detect their prey. When attacked by herbivores, plants produce the equivalent of an immune response. Distasteful chemicals move rapidly to the site

of the injury, encouraging the herbivore to move elsewhere to feed. They therefore cause the insects to make more holes, effectively advertising their presence to potential predators. Simultaneously, the plant sends out chemical signals telling insect predators and parasites that there is a meal or host available. Parasitoids, which live at the expense of their host organism, causing it to die, are particularly adept at recognizing plant volatiles. Some parasitoid species use the smell of the host plant of their favourite prey as the initial signal, then search the plant for their insect host. This close association between parasitoid-searching behaviour and host plant can have unexpected consequences. In the UK in the 1970s the native pine beauty moth *Panolis flammea* became a serious pest of lodgepole pine, *Pinus contorta*, which, although not as nutritious a host for the moth as the native Scots pine, *Pinus sylvestris*, was an enemy-free space in plantations. It transpired that the parasitoid wasps that kept the moth under control in Scots pine plantations were 'hard-wired' to the volatiles produced by Scots pine and did not recognize those produced by lodgepole pine. It was twenty years or more before the biotypes of parasitoids able to recognize lodgepole pine appeared in the population and the pine beauty moth problem subsided.

Before the advent of modern pesticides, farmers depended on cultural control methods like crop rotation, and direct protection against pests—scarecrows, humans with sticks and rattles, and, later, netting and other shelters. None of these methods was particularly effective and some crops were destroyed completely, resulting in famine and widespread starvation. There were many ingenious attempts to prevent crop loss from pests but it was the middle of the 19th century before a more effective method became available: this was the concept of biological control. The idea was not entirely without precedent. Charles Darwin's grandfather, Erasmus Darwin, noticed that the cabbages in his garden, although being attacked by larvae of the cabbage white butterfly, were being protected to a certain extent by parasitic wasps. He noted that this might be of use to gardeners. We know that before

and up to the late 19th century, Chinese citrus growers introduced ant nests to their orchards and tied bamboo poles between trees to encourage the ants to forage more widely and reduce the number of pests feeding in their trees. Bedouins were also known to transport ant nests to oases in the desert where date palms were grown.

It was not until the 1870s that Charles Riley, a British entomologist employed by the United States Department of Agriculture, and regarded by many as the father of biological control, began to adopt a scientific approach to the biological control of pests. The first attempt was against the plum weevil, which was causing devastation to orchards in Missouri. Riley introduced natural enemies from other parts of the United States to the affected orchards. Although some control was achieved, it was insufficient to promote widespread adoption of the technique. In the 1880s the Australian native cottony cushion scale (*Icerya purchasi*) arrived in the newly established, highly profitable Californian citrus industry. The scale rampaged through the orchards and, despite the best efforts of the growers, who even resorted to using hydrogen cyanide gas, was unstoppable and threatened the very existence of the industry. Many growers burnt their trees, sold their land at greatly reduced prices, and left the state.

In 1888, Charles Riley sent Albert Koebele to Australia to look for natural enemies of the scale. Koebele returned with a ladybird beetle, the Vedalia beetle (*Novius* (*Rodolia*) *cardinalis*), which was then reared under controlled conditions and released into the orchards. Together with a parasitic fly, this approach eradicated the scale almost completely within a few years and allowed the citrus industry to develop successfully. This was the birth of what is now known as classical biological control and heralded a huge number of introductions, some of which were very successful, others much less so. Riley also recognized that parasites and parasitoids were likely to be much better biological control agents

than predators. Unfortunately, with the arrival of efficient, modern synthetic organochlorine pesticides in the late 1920s, biological control was put on the back burner for a number of years.

Despite its relatively long history, the term 'biological control' was not coined until the 1960s, by Paul DeBach, an eminent proponent of the approach (Figure 29).

Biological control has been used in glasshouse crops for more than sixty years, and in organic agriculture. More recently, because of public concerns about the environment and the overuse of pesticides, coupled with the rise in the number of pest insects showing insecticide resistance, biological control and integrated pest management have moved up the agenda again. Biological control is a complicated process, and now encompasses a variety of approaches, some of which bring with them ethical issues, especially when introducing non-native agents.

The possible non-target effects have to be studied carefully, which can take several years of trials. If these are overlooked, unintended

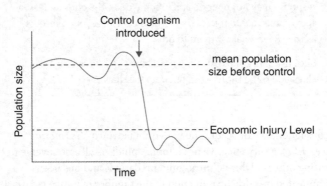

29. Biological control in theory. The introduction of the natural enemy reduces the damage caused by the pest to below the economic injury level.

Parasitoids

Parasitoids prey on other insects. They differ from parasites in that they kill their hosts, and from predators in that their victims are not killed immediately. Parasitoids lay their eggs in or on their hosts. Most parasitoids are Hymenoptera but examples are found among the Diptera, Coleoptera, and Strepsiptera.

They are divided into two types.

The *Idiobionts*, typically living on the host's body (they are ectoparasites), prey on adult or late-instar insects. They immobilize their hosts, so that no further development occurs, and then kill them. They have a broad host range and their hosts are found in concealed locations. Idiobionts do not have to adapt to the host's immune system but lay eggs in inaccessible places on the host and also prevent haemolymph clotting to make it easier for the larvae to feed.

The *Koinobionts* are typically endoparasites that do not kill their hosts after oviposition, allowing further development. They forage in exposed situations, and are specialist, sometimes genus specific. They lay their eggs in areas where immune response may not operate and in some cases the eggs and larvae show molecular mimicry. Koinobionts parasitize young insects, as they need to allow them to grow.

Both use similar host location mechanisms, volatiles, and visual clues and some Diptera use phonotactic clues.

consequences can occur. The harlequin ladybird (*Harmonia axyridis*), a very effective predator of aphids, is also not averse to eating other ladybirds (intra-guild predation) and has been implicated in a drastic reduction in the number of native ladybird species in mainland Europe and in the UK, to which it was unintentionally introduced. Although predators were, and still

are, the first choice of many biological control programmes, parasitoids are an increasingly common option, the degree of host specificity and ability to reproduce parthenogenetically being huge advantages when compared with predators.

Such issues aside, there are a number of advantages of using biological control instead of conventional pesticides. A biological control agent is extremely selective; it only attacks the target organism, and is itself able to find the target rather than having to be delivered via a spray machine. Once established successfully, biological control organisms can propagate themselves, giving lasting control, and, unlike conventional pesticides, it is highly unlikely that the pest will be able to develop a resistance to them.

There are, of course, some disadvantages, the speed of kill being one that farmers notice particularly when comparing the knock-down effects of conventional insecticides with the much slower kill rates of a biological control agent. Once they get used to seeing the pest species still in their crops but at the same time increasing their profits from reduced pesticide input, and seeing the environmental benefits that accrue, a significant minority of farmers are being converted.

Insects as ecosystem engineers

Insects fulfil many important roles within ecosystems: pollinators, saproxylics, carrion, and dung feeders.

Pollinators. Insect herbivores are able to feed on all parts of plants—leaves, stems, roots, even flowers. Flower feeders range from specialized pollen feeders, such as the aptly named rape pollen beetle (*Brassicogethes* (*Meligethes*) *aeneus*) to chrysomelid beetles in the genus *Phyllotreta* that eat petals, to the sap-feeding aphids, like those found on roses, feeding preferentially on the newly expanding flower buds. All these are loosely termed

anthophilous—flower loving. Not all anthophilous animals are insects; some bats and birds are anthophilous too.

These examples of flower feeding by insects are what we might consider exploitative, and cause direct and indirect harm to the plants; pollen removal decreases fecundity while petal removal and damage reduce the chances of pollination by altering the signals sent to pollinators. On the other hand, pollinators have evolved a mutually beneficial relationship with plants. In exchange for a quick energy boost and some amino acids—nectar—mobile pollinating insects help their sedentary plant partners to spread their genes far and wide in a much more efficient way than plants dependent on the wind.

Although important pollinators, honeybees are domesticated animals and play a minor part in the pollination of flowering plants as a whole. In fact, there is growing evidence that the recent upsurge in domestic beekeeping is posing a threat to native wild pollinators by competing for resources and spreading diseases. Flies, beetles, moths, butterflies, wild bees, and the other Hymenoptera are major pollinators that are largely overlooked. Without midges pollinating cacao plants, we would not have chocolate. There are also some vertebrate pollinators but here we will only consider insects.

Unsurprisingly, pollinators and their plant partners are physiologically co-adapted to exploit their respective needs. One obvious such adaptation is the length of the mouthpart, which decides which nectar feeders pollinate which plants. The deeper the nectar is concealed within the flower, the longer the mouthpart required to reach the sugary reward, so, for example, there are both short-tongued and long-tongued bumblebees. The common garden bumblebee, *Bombus hortorum*, has a tongue long enough to feed from lavender flowers, a nectar source inaccessible to honeybees and short-tongued bumblebees, like *Bombus terrestris*. In 1862, Darwin, to the scorn of many, predicted that the Malagasy orchid, *Angraecum sesquipedale*, whose nectar is

produced at the bottom of a 30 cm long tube, would be pollinated by a moth with a tongue long enough to reach the nectar. It was not until 1903, when Morgan's sphinx moth (*Xanthopan morganii praedicta*) was discovered, that Darwin was proved right.

Blue, purple, and mauve flowers, such as those of clovers (*Trifolium*) and louseworts (*Pedicularis*), are visited more often by bees than by other insects, and are also structurally adapted to pollination by them. Some butterflies are also attracted to purple flowers like *Phlox*, and these are adapted to butterfly mouthparts. Night-blooming flowers tend to be heavily scented and white or pale in colour, the scent acting as the long-distance come-hither to the night-flying moths, which are their main pollinators, the contrasting white colour against the dark foliage helping them navigate into the mouth of the flower. White and yellow day-blooming flowers have exposed nectar and are visited by a multitude of short-tongued insects: hoverflies and parasitic Hymenoptera, for example.

Scent plays a large part in the pollinating process. Although insects are visually capable, albeit seeing different wavelengths from humans, their powers of odour detection are diverse and acute. Scent is a way in which some plant species can enhance their chances of finding a mate. By producing an odour that is very specific to a particular group of insects, they can ensure that their pollen is deposited in the correct place. So some plants have flowers that smell of rotting meat or dung, others have musky scents attractive to biting flies, and others, like the pipevine, *Aristolochia macrophylla*, mimic the smell of fungus to attract fungus-feeding flies such as phorids.

Pollen feeders pollinate yet another subset of plants, those that reward pollinators only with pollen, no nectar provided, or, as in the case of many orchids, deceptive sexual activity. That said, orchids are generally honest brokers, most providing nectar as a resource for their pollinators. About a quarter of orchid species

are, however, frauds or cheats, pretending to be either a food source or a receptive female insect. The bee orchid, *Ophrys apifera*, for example, is pollinated by a solitary mining bee, *Eucera longicornis*, belonging to a group commonly known as long-horned bees. If you look at the female bee, which is what we suppose the flower is mimicking, you can just about convince yourself that there is a slight resemblance between the two (Figure 30). Of course, bear in mind that insects do not see things in the same way as humans do, so what we think is almost certainly irrelevant. That said, it doesn't actually have to be a particularly good visual mimic for the insects either, as it is the smell that really matters, or as long as the flower is the right shape to enable the deceived male to copulate in such a way that it picks up the flower's pollen.

The fly orchid, *Ophrys insectifera*, is also sexually deceptive but, despite its common name, is pollinated by digger wasps and bees. Some orchids are even more cunning: the scarce marsh helleborine, *Epipactis veratrifolia*, releases aphid alarm pheromone in order to attract its pollinators, adult hoverflies, the larvae of which feed on aphids.

Saprooxylics. Wood—hard, tough, fibrous, nutritionally poor, and very well defended—is not a habitat to be exploited by the run-of-the-mill insect herbivore. Wood is composed principally of cellulose, hemi-cellulose, and lignin, with hefty doses of tannins and terpenes. Lignin, tannins, and terpenes are its major defensive components, acting as digestive enzyme blockers, poisons, and deterrents. The carbon:nitrogen ratio of wood is very high, up to 1,250:1 compared with the 4.1 to 10:1 found in other material consumed by insects. Dead wood was a much-threatened habitat until fairly recently; modern forestry practice saw dead wood as an eyesore, wasteful, dangerous to humans, a fire risk, and a possible route for disease. This opinion is still held by many managers of public parkland and green spaces, although it is no longer universal.

30. The bee orchid, *Ophrys apifera*, with pollinator, *Eucera longicornis*.

But a much-overlooked part of the insect community is the insects that live in or on dead and decaying wood. This is somewhat understandable as they spend most of their lives hidden from sight under the bark or in the heart of their woody substrates. Saproxylic insects are those that live on dead or dying wood, or on the fungi and other insects found upon it. The term saproxylic is relatively modern,

coined by the French entomologist Roger Dajoz in 1966; over 50 per cent of forest beetle species are recognized as being saproxylic.

As organic matter decays it experiences and imposes changes in physical, chemical, and ecological conditions, including sequential changes in species composition, known in ecology as succession. Although often grouped under the general term 'succession', a distinction should be drawn between successions that occur on substrates that degrade and substrates that do not degrade and that culminate in *relatively* stable endpoints. A defining characteristic of wood colonization is that the decay process itself imposes a finite, relatively short-term time limit within which communities can develop. Wood decay ultimately comes to an end because the substrate is metabolized and mineralized in its entirety; the resource decomposes completely and returns to the soil. This form of succession—degradative succession—is very distinct from landscape-level successions that take place as bare ground is replaced by plant communities of increasing complexity over a period of decades. Degradative succession by contrast occurs over a shorter timescale ranging from months to years, and encompasses any element of dead organic matter experiencing sequential species invasions.

As wood decomposes, it is colonized by a succession of fungi and fauna. The fruiting bodies of wood-decaying fungi can themselves be colonized by successive complements of species throughout the course of their lifetime. The routes to mineralization are complex and varied, depending on tree species and, very importantly, on which fungal species is the first colonizer.

The evolution of woody tissue, like the development of flowering plants, provides a unique resource for insects. Wood is dense, providing a highly protective environment, especially for the vulnerable larval stages. On the downside, it is tough, nutrient poor, and many adaptations are needed to exploit it effectively. The insect group that has exploited it the most effectively is the

beetles, most notably a number of families including the buprestids, the anobids (deathwatch beetles, woodworm), the cerambycids (longhorns), the scolytids (bark beetles), and the curculionids (weevils). In some, the adults are streamlined with bullet-shaped heads, making it easier to move through the tunnels that they chew. Insects that feed as larvae are often legless or have reduced legs. To compensate for this they are wider at the thorax than elsewhere, allowing them to anchor themselves in place as they chew through the wood. The mouthparts of the wood-feeding larvae and adults are often toothed and reinforced with metal ions, most commonly zinc. They also have to be able to digest wood. The ability to digest cellulose directly is not common; instead it is accomplished by enzymes, obtained by a symbiotic relationship with protozoans, bacteria, or fungi.

The next most common inhabitants of dead wood are the wasps. These are mainly present not as part of the decay process but as natural enemies of the wood feeders. The female wasps, like the beetle wood feeders, have specially adapted ovipositors. Wood feeders like the wood wasp, *Sirex noctilio*, are equipped with a metal-tipped serrated ovipositor, which, although harmless, inspires fear in many humans, who assume it to be a particularly deadly sting. Parasitoid wasps that prey on the larvae of bark and wood beetles also come equipped with long, complex ovipositors. The sabre wasp (*Rhyssa persuasoria*) lays its eggs in the larvae of wood wasps and longhorn beetles living inside fallen trees. The female searches likely trees, drumming with her antenna on the trunk surface, and making exploratory probes with her ovipositor, until she is satisfied that there is a host below. She then drills into the wood using her extremely long (up to 40 mm), zinc-toughened ovipositor to locate the larva and lay her egg within it.

The process of degradative succession, by which a fallen tree or bough returns to the soil, is a complex interaction between the fungi colonizing dead wood and the insects. Although the decay process can succeed without the insects, they aid and, in some

cases, abet the process. The general trend is that the insects exploiting fallen trees are initially specialist with a narrow host range, seeking out particular tree species. As decomposition progresses, it is the stage of decay that becomes important, not the tree species.

Fungi and insects have enjoyed an extensive co-existence, resulting in the evolution of a diverse range of interactions. Specialization can occur at different levels: beetles, for example, that feed on bracket fungi (tree-fungus beetles or ciids) and beetles that seek out specific genera of trees. Mutually beneficial or at any rate harmless associations between insects and fungi (mutualisms and commensalisms) enable, among other things, the transportation, dispersal, and vectoring of fungal propagules. Such relationships resolve the problem of spatial discontinuity between resources. They ensure fungal transmission to new resources, inoculate fungi into otherwise inaccessible areas, and can enable cross-fertilization. The presence of insects also serves to modify the decaying wood habitat. Feeding, burrowing, and excretion can favour fungal growth by increasing the surface area available for attack, by reducing the resistance to gaseous diffusion, and by increasing the water-retaining ability of the substrate.

Bark and ambrosia beetles transport (via guts, exoskeleton, or specialized organs called mycangia) and inoculate fungi and other microbes into the wood that they colonize. Bark beetles usually colonize the inner tree bark (living and dead phloem tissues) whereas the majority of ambrosia beetles colonize the xylem (sapwood and/or heartwood) of dying or newly dead trees. Many bark and ambrosia beetles are pests capable of eliciting enormous outbreaks having severe effects on forest structure or, as in the case of Dutch elm disease, changing a whole landscape. The relationships between these two groups have various functions and differ considerably in their specificity, evolutionary history, and consistency of association. Some fungi are used as a food

source—by concentrating nitrogen or by acting as a source of sterols, they become very attractive to specialist beetles like the tree-fungus beetles. Others, such as the ambrosia beetles, feed almost exclusively on the fungal symbionts that they cultivate in galleries bored into sapwood. The beetles maintain highly specific relationships with particular fungal species; their reproduction and survival often depend entirely on the fungal symbiont. Fungal associates may also augment beetle colonization, for example by attacking and/or conditioning the wood, by helping to neutralize tree defences, or by providing protection against antagonistic fungi. Fungal symbionts may also play a role in beetle chemical ecology by contributing to pheromone synthesis and/or acting as signals themselves.

Despite the rapid growth of interest in this topic over the last few decades, the study of saproxylic insects is in its infancy; much remains to be discovered.

Carrion and dung feeders (necrophagy and coprophagy). While the sight of a fallen tree returning slowly to the soil may inspire the poet and provide a mossy bench, the stench and sight of a rotting corpse or pile of dung has the opposite effect. Happily for us, there are insects that specialize in such, to us distasteful, protein sources too: the necrophages. Most necrophagous species are flies, the most obvious being the blowflies (Calliphoridae) and flesh flies (Sarcophagidae) beloved of forensic scientists; other flies are also involved, for example the so called 'horrid phorids', an extremely versatile group, have several species that feed on vertebrate flesh. The main beetles associated with carcasses are the silphids, of which there are two subfamilies, the burying beetles (Nicrophorinae), which, as the name suggests, bury the carcasses on which their larvae feed and develop, and the sexton beetles (Silphinae). The burying beetles colonize recently dead corpses in order to avoid competition with the fly larvae while sexton beetles colonize the carcasses later in the decomposition process, the adults feeding on the maggot masses, the larvae on

the decaying remains. Both groups show parental care and cooperative behaviour (Chapter 4).

Dung beetles and dung flies (scatophagids) play a vital role in reducing animal waste products, hence the concerns regarding the use of persistent anthelmintics, drugs such as ivermectin that eliminate parasites, in farming. Not only do they kill the parasites of livestock but they remain active after passing through the animals and kill the flies and beetles that would normally remove the dung pats within weeks or, in the tropics, days, resulting in a build-up of dung in the fields.

Dung is usually an ephemeral resource and insects that rear their young on it live in a highly competitive world. Once they locate a dung pile, dung beetles roll up a ball of dung and remove it to a location away from possible 'theft' by other dung beetles before the female lays her eggs in it. They thus need to move in a straight line away from the dung pile, which they do by navigating by the moon or stars.

Dung beetles are surprisingly selective about what type of dung they use, as the farmers who introduced sheep and cattle to Australia discovered. Native dung beetles prefer marsupial dung, so, in order to combat the build-up of cattle and sheep dung, European dung beetles had to be introduced, yet another unintended consequence of not understanding the vital role that insects play in the world.

In the final chapter (Chapter 9), we will consider the consequences of ignoring the role of insects in ecosystem and global health, and what we can do to mitigate the damage already done to their existence.

Chapter 9
Ecological Armageddon— insects in decline?

I began by describing the diversity and ubiquity of insects. I discussed their origins and marvelled at the ways in which insects have adapted to a wide range of environments and the roles that they play in maintaining ecosystem health. It is thus fitting to end by discussing the harm that we are doing to insects and the planet that we, and they, inhabit, and ways in which we might act to halt or reverse our course, if it is not already too late. Eighty years ago, in his novel *The Jacob Street Mystery*, R. Austin Freeman remarked:

> To him that countryside, largely unspoiled in his early days, was an inexhaustible source of delight and a subject of endless study and meditation...And as the years passed and the countryside faded away under the withering touch of mechanical transport, that knowledge grew more and more precious. Now, the dwindling remnants had to be sought and found with considered judgement and their scanty material eked out with detail from the stores of the remembered past.

In his book *The Romance of Natural History* (1861), Philip Henry Gosse mentions a phenomenon known as blood rain:

> At various times and in various places popular superstition has been excited by the occurrence of what have been called showers of blood.

The destruction of cities and of kingdoms has been, according to historians, preceded by this awful omen. Yet this has been explained by a very natural and accountable phenomenon. In the year 1553, the hedges and trees, the stones of the pathway, and the clothes of many persons, were sprinkled copiously with drops of red fluid, which was supposed to be blood, till some observant person noticed the coincident appearance of unusual swarms of butterflies, and marked that the coloured drops proceeded from them.

The red drops were meconium, a waste substance produced by Lepidoptera shortly after they moult to adulthood. It indicates that there have been very large numbers of butterflies at certain times of the year. Many insects seem to be less abundant than they were forty years ago, almost certainly as a result of anthropogenic factors—intensive agriculture, urbanization, and, to a lesser extent, climate change and biological invasions. The last twenty years or so have seen scientific papers reporting declines in the numbers of ground beetles, dragonflies, moths, butterflies, and even caddisflies and some hemipterans. This is not a localized phenomenon but a global one, and not just from well-documented parts of Europe but also from more species-rich tropics, e.g. Costa Rica.

An increasing number of stories have appeared in the media in recent years, predicting insect apocalypse and ecological Armageddon. What does the research reveal? In 2017, Caspar Hallmann and colleagues reported a 75 per cent reduction in the biomass of flying insects in Germany over forty years, although the same sites were not sampled every year. And two years later, Sebastian Siebold and colleagues, again using data from Germany, showed similarly disturbingly high losses in biomass and abundance. Note that both of these studies were done in Germany, which is a heavily developed part of the planet.

There may be limitations in the data, but the take-home message that cannot be ignored is that many insect species, especially those associated with freshwater, are in steep decline. Even the most

scathing of commentators do not dispute the fact that insects, in general, are in decline, and that the warnings should not be taken lightly. What all the research reporting insect declines and the burgeoning number of academic papers offering solutions have in common is that they reveal that the available data are very patchy in terms of insect orders covered and geographical locations.

There are reliable and robust long-term data sets showing the declines of butterflies and moths over the last half-century or so—although, again, the geographic coverage is largely confined to the UK, some parts of mainland Europe, and North America—and stories about this worrying trend attract a lot of media attention. Other charismatic groups, such as dragonflies and damselflies, are also in decline, as are the ubiquitous and equally charismatic ground beetles (carabids). But are other insects also in decline? Julie Ewald and colleagues from the Game and Wildlife Conservancy Trust, UK, analysed a remarkable forty-two-year data set on invertebrates in cereal fields in southern England and found that of the twenty-six invertebrate taxa studied less than half showed a decrease in abundance—spiders, braconid parasitic wasps, carabid beetles, *Tachyporus* beetles, *Enicmus* (scavenger beetles), cryptophagid fungus beetles, leaf-mining flies (agromyzids), fruit flies (*Drosophila*), Lonchopteridae (pointed-wing flies), and, surprisingly (or perhaps not), aphids. The other taxa showed no consistent pattern although bugs, excluding aphids, increased over the study period. More original recent work on British moths shows that, despite the overall picture of moths being in decline, some moth species, especially habitat generalists and some woodland specialists, have increased in abundance since 1968. Cereal fields are not, of course, a natural habitat and are intensely managed, with various pesticides being applied, so are perhaps not likely to be the most biodiverse or representative habitats to be found in the UK.

So what scientific evidence do we have for a decline in these less charismatic insects? Almost a hundred years ago, bibionid flies

were regarded as a major pest, and forty years ago it was possible to catch almost 70,000 adults in traps in a four-week period from one field in southern England, suggesting that bibionids used to be very common. Only three of the Rothamsted Insect Survey traps showed downward trends in insect biomass over the thirty years (1973–2002) analysed, of which only the Hereford trap showed a significant decline. So, we are none the wiser. Two long-term studies that focus on a wider range of insect groups do not give a clear indication of insect decline, and both studies are limited in their geographic coverage so we do not know whether the results are representative of the whole country.

With the lack of funding for entomology, it is extremely difficult to get more robust data. Over a million insect species have been described to date and thousands more are described every year. Each species has a unique way of making a living: they eat different foods, live in different places, have different climatic requirements, reproduce at different rates, and have their own suite of natural enemies. Hardly any of them are monitored; those that are monitored are mainly pests. Globally only a few thousand people are collecting relevant data; considering that there are probably at least eight million insect species, the research barely scratches the surface, despite the magnificent efforts of the people involved in gathering this information. The *Insectageddon* stories are derived from a few local studies. Most are fine but there are not enough and they are too idiosyncratic for solid general conclusions. They are, however, believable, because in general they tell the same story—drastic declines over the last few decades—and they reflect what the older generation of entomologists have been reporting informally over the years.

Unlike some commentators who point their fingers directly at the use of pesticides as the major cause of decline, I am more inclined towards the idea of habitat degradation, fragmentation, and loss. It is long past time for governments around the world to invest

much more into research in this area. We desperately need more properly replicated, well-designed, long-term studies to monitor the undeniable changes that are occurring.

Whether or not we believe that an ecological catastrophe is approaching, it is obvious that humans are having a marked effect on the biodiversity that keeps our planet in good working order, and not just through the need to feed an ever-increasing population. Recent studies have shown that our fixation with car ownership is killing billions of insects every year, and that our fear of the dark, and widespread use of artificial light, is putting insects and the animals that feed on them at risk.

For humans, with relatively short lifespans, shifting baselines can also be a problem. People accept what they have known in their childhoods as the natural state but it can work the other way: I remember in the early 1990s, when a particular butterfly species was at very low numbers compared with those that I and similar-aged colleagues remembered as children, the late British naturalist Miriam Rothschild telling me how as a girl, in the 1920s, she had conversely remembered their numbers as being very low. Her message was to consider also the 'populations cycle'. It is because of this propensity, which is nicely illustrated by some of my own twenty-year data sets, all from the same fifty-two sycamore trees Silwood Park, Berkshire, UK, that we need access to long-term funding to monitor insect populations. Chop my data sets into three-year periods, the length of a typical PhD study or research grant, and you see some very different pictures of the populations of three common insect species (Figure 31).

Given these fluctuations in populations, the fact that most of the evidence for insect declines is based largely on studies from Europe, primarily the UK, and that the evidence from tropical locations has been subject to alternative interpretations, there is an urgent need for action.

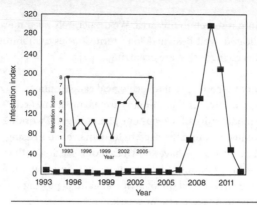

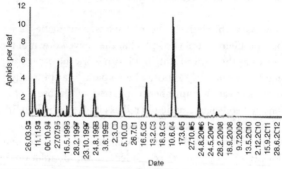

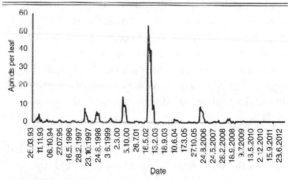

31. Changes in abundance of three common insect species over a twenty-year period: winter moth, *Operophtera brumata* (top); the sycamore aphid, *Drepanosiphum platanoidis* (middle); the maple aphid, *Periphyllus testudinaceus* (bottom). The populations can be seen to fluctuate over twenty years.

First, we need to build on the work that has been done in Germany by scientists like Caspar Hallmann, and in the UK via the Rothamsted Insect Survey and the Biological Records Centre (UK Centre for Ecology & Hydrology), and establish active insect monitoring networks using repeatable sampling methods but on a global scale. New monitoring programmes will not help to establish past baselines but they can help us to determine trends from this point forward. We can make this truly global by engaging the public through community (citizen) science. Programmes will need to use standardized, commonly and easily used methods, such as Malaise traps, pitfall traps, light traps, and effort-based counts, with species diversity, abundance, and biomass being primary measures. Although biomass is an imperfect estimator because it can be sensitive to changes in abundance of large species, it is a valuable metric from the ecosystem perspective. Determining biomass trends does not require fine-scale taxonomic knowledge, which is often lacking in community science initiatives. Even if it were possible, it would be incredibly expensive to try to monitor all insect species from any community with appreciable diversity. A much better option, and one that will certainly appeal to a wide range of community scientists, would be to monitor taxa like butterflies, macro-moths, dragonflies, bees, and some beetle groups. All these can serve as indicator species for other insect groups and, tongue in cheek, many can be observed using binoculars, thus encouraging ornithologists and mammalogists to join in.

There are already a few long-term national monitoring schemes. For example, the Environmental Change Network collects biotic and abiotic data, including many insect groups, from fifty-seven sites across the UK using identical protocols. Multiple Long-Term Ecological Research (LTER) projects track different facets of ecosystems in different ways. In fact, if expanded to a global scale, the LTER network could be the natural framework to make a global network proposal feasible, possibly through targeted funding. Unfortunately, all the active long-term monitoring

schemes are younger than modern agricultural intensification. We need to use museum collections and pre-1940s entomological journals to construct data sets. Some long-term historical datasets are already accessible, such as the 150-year record of pine beauty moth infestations in Germany dating from 1810.

Whatever we do, it will need long-term funding that is stable, substantial, and sustained. Entomological survey and monitoring work may appear mundane but is essential given the importance of insects to the health of ecosystems. Funding should reflect the diversity and abundance of taxa, not their perceived charisma. The focus of major donors needs to shift from insect eradication to insect conservation.

We also need to act quickly; there is no Planet B. I am, however, not hopeful. Despite the many 'Insectageddon' stories, the majority of young researchers tend to focus on vertebrates, many in exotic locations, continuing a pattern noted many years ago.

An underappreciation of the importance of insects is widespread, so much so that it might be time to coin some new words to describe it: *entomyopia*, entomological short-sightedness, and *entoalexia*, insect blindness. A better general understanding of the natural world and the role of insects is essential if we are to prevent any further inroads into their existence. As this book has shown, insects are not just pests and pollinators; they are part of the very fabric of our existence.

References

Chapter 1: In the beginning

Erwin, T. L. (1982) Tropical forests: Their richness in Coleoptera and other arthropod species. *The Coleopterists Bulletin*, 36, 74–5.

Forbes, A. A., Bagley, R. K., and Beer, M. A. et al. (2018) Quantifying the unquantifiable: Why Hymenoptera, not Coleoptera, is the most speciose animal order. *BMC Ecology*, 18, 21.

Giribet, G., and Edgecombe, G. D. (2019) The phylogeny and evolutionary history of arthropods. *Current Biology*, 29, RS592–602.

Hamilton, A. J., Novotny, V., Waters, K. E., Basset, Y., Benke, K. K., Grimbacher, P. S., Miller, S. E., Samuelson, G. A., Weiblen, G. D., Yen, J. D. L., and Stork, N. E. (2013) Estimating global arthropod species richness; refining probabalistic models using probability bound analysis. *Oecologia*, 171, 357–65.

Mishof, B., and Liu, S. et al. (2014) Phylogenomics resolves the timing and pattern of insect evolution. *Science*, 346, 763–7.

Mora, C., Tittensor, D. P., Adl, S., Simpson, A. G. B., and Worm, B. (2011) How many species are there on earth and in the ocean? *PloS Biology*, 9(8), e1001127. doi:10.1371/journal.pbio.1001127.

Stork, N. E. (1993) How many species are there? *Biodiversity & Conservation*, 2, 215–32.

Stork, N. E., McBroom, J., Gely, C., and Hamilton, A. J. (2015) New approaches to narrow global species estimates for beetles, insects, and terrestrial arthropods. *Proceedings of the National Academy of Sciences*, 112(24), 7519–23.

Wigglesworth, V. B. (1940) The determination of characters at metamorphosis in *Rhodnius prolixus* (Hemiptera). *Journal of Experimental Biology*, 17, 201–23.

Chapter 2: Prolific procreators

Awmack, C. S., and Leather, S. R. (2002) Host plant quality and fecundity in herbivorous insects. *Annual Review of Entomology*, 47, 817–44.

Burpee, D. M., and Sakaluk, S. K. (1993) Repeated matings offset costs of reproduction in female crickets. *Evolutionary Ecology*, 7, 240–50.

Byers, G. W., and Thornhill, R. (1983) Biology of the Mecoptera. *Annual Review of Entomology*, 28, 203–28.

Gripenberg, S., Mayhew, P. J., Parnell, M., and Roslin, T. (2010) A meta-analysis of preference-performance relationships in phytophagous insects. *Ecology Letters*, 13, 383–93.

Jaenike, J. (1978). On optimal oviposition behaviour by phytophagous insects. *Theoretical Population Biology*, 14, 350–6.

Leather, S. R., Watt, A. D., and Barbour, D. A. (1985) The effect of host plant and delayed mating on the fecundity and lifespan of the pine beauty moth, *Panolis flammea* (Denis & Schiffermuller) (Lepidoptera: Noctuidae): Their influence on population dynamics and relevance to pest management. *Bulletin of Entomological Research*, 75, 641–51.

Lin, X., Shih, C., Li, S., and Ren, D. (2019). Mecoptera: Scorpionflies and Hangingflies. *Rhythms of Insect Evolution*, 555–95.

Oberhauser, K. S. (1989) Effects of spermatophores on male and female monarch butterfly reproductive success. *Behavioural Ecology & Sociobiology*, 25, 237–46.

Stamp, N. E. (1980) Egg deposition patterns in butterflies: Why do some species cluster their eggs rather than deposit them singly? *American Naturalist*, 115, 367–80.

Svard, L. (1985) Paternal investment in a monandrous butterfly, *Pararge aegeria*. *Oikos*, 45, 66–70.

Ward, K. E., and Landolt, P. J. (1995) Influence of multiple matings on fecundity and longevity of female cabbage looper moths (Lepidoptera: Noctuidae). *Annals of the Entomological Society of America*, 88, 768–72.

Chapter 3: On the move

Alexander, D. E. (2018) A century and a half of research on the evolution of insect flight. *Arthropod Structure & Development*, 47, 322–7.

Darlington, P. J. (1943) Carabidae of mountains and islands: Data on the evolution of isolated faunas and on atrophy of wings. *Ecological Monographs*, 13, 37–61.

Englebrecht, L., Orban, U., and Heese, W. (1969) Leaf-miner caterpillars and cytokinins in the 'green islands' of autumn leaves. *Nature*, 223, 319–21.

Feeny, P. (1970). Seasonal changes in oak leaf tannins and nutrients as a cause of spring feeding by winter moth caterpillars. *Ecology*, 51, 565–81.

Kaiser, W., Huguet, E., Casas, J., Commin, C., and Giron, D. (2010) Plant green-island phenotype induced by leaf-miners is mediated by bacterial symbionts. *Proceedings of the Royal Society B*, 277, 2311–19.

Kingsolver, J. G., and Koehl, M. A. R. (1994) Selective factors in the evolution of insect wings. *Annual Review of Entomology*, 39, 425–51.

Leather, S. R., Wellings, P. W., and Walters, K. F. A. (1988) Variation in ovariole number within the Aphidoidea. *Journal of Natural History*, 22, 381–93.

Loxdale, H. D., Lushai, G., and Harvey, J. A. (2011) The evolutionary improbability of 'generalism' in nature, with special reference to insects. *Biological Journal of the Linnean Society*, 103, 1–18.

Mathur, V., Ganta, S., Raaijmakers, C. E., Reddy, A. S., Vet, L. E. M., and Van Dam, N. M. (2011) Temporal dynamics of herbivore-induced responses in *Brassica juncea* and their effect on generalist and specialist herbivores. *Entomologia Experimentalis et Applicata*, 139, 215–25.

Scriber, J. M., and Slansky, F. (1981) The nutritional ecology of immature insects. *Annual Review of Entomology*, 26, 183–211.

Shaw, M. J. P. (1970) Effects of population density on the alienicolae of *Aphis fabae* Scop.II: The effects of crowding on the expression of migratory urge among alatae in the laboratory. *Annals of Applied Biology*, 65, 197–203.

Vanbergen, A. J., Raymond, B., Pearce, I. S. K., Watt, A. D., Hails, R. S., and Hartley, S. E. (2003) Host shifting by *Operophtera brumata* into novel environments leads to population differentiation in life-history traits. *Ecological Entomology*, 28, 604–12.

Walters, K. F. A., and Dixon, A. F. G. (1983) Migratory urge and reproductive investment in aphids: Variation within clones. *Oecologia*, 58, 70–5.

Chapter 4: Living together

Aoki, S., and Makino, S. (1982). Gall usurpation and lethal fighting among fundatrices of the aphid *Epipemphigus niisimae*. *Kontyu*, 50, 365–76.

Bignell, D. E. (2016) The role of symbionts in the evolution of termites and their rise to ecological dominance in the tropics. In C. Hurst (ed.), *The Mechanistic Benefits of Microbial Symbionts: Advances in Environmental Microbiology*, vol 2, pp. 121–72. Springer, Cham.

Carroll, C. R., and Janzen, D. H. (1973) Ecology of foraging by ants. *Annual Review of Ecology & Systematics*, 4, 231–57.

Cleveland, L. R., Hall, S. R., Sanders, E. P., and Collier, Jane (1934) The wood-feeding roach *Cryptocercus*, its protozoa, and the symbiosis between protozoa and roach. *Memoirs of the American Academy of Arts & Sciences*, 17, 185–342.

Endo, S., and Itino, T. (2013) Myrmecophilus aphids produce cuticular hydrocarbons that resemble those of their tending ants. *Population Ecology*, 55, 27–34.

Fischer, C. Y., Vanderplanck, M., Lognay, G. C., Detrain, C., and Verheggen, F. J. (2015) Do aphids actively search for ant partners? *Insect Science*, 22, 283–8.

Hinde, R. (1971) The control of the mycetome symbiotes of the aphids *Brevicoryne brassicae*, *Myzus persicae*, and *Macrosiphum rosae*. *Journal of Insect Physiology*, 17, 1791–800.

Kölliker, M., Chuckalovcak, J. P., and Brodie III, E. D. (2005) Offspring chemical cues affect maternal food provisioning in burrower bugs, *Sehirus cinctus*. *Animal Behaviour*, 69, 959–66.

Laine, K. J., and Niemela, P. (1980) The influence of ants on the survival of mountain birch during an *Oporinia autumnata* (Lep., Geometridae) outbreak. *Oecologia*, 47, 39–42.

Moran, N. A., Russell, J. A., Koga, R., and Fukatsu, T. (2005) Evolutionary relationships of three new species of *Enterobacteriaceae* living as symbionts of aphids and other insects. *Applied and Environmental Microbiology*, 71, 3302–10.

Ocko, S. A., King, H., Andreen, D., Bardunias, P., Turner, J. S., Soar, R., and Mahadevan, L. (2017). Solar-powered ventilation of African termite mounds. *Journal of Experimental Biology*, 220, 3260–9.

Oliver, T. H., Leather, S. R., and Cook, J. M. (2008) Macroevolutionary patterns in the origin of mutualisms, *Journal of Evolutionary Biology*, 21, 1597–608.

Otti, O., Deines, P., Hammerschmidt, K., and Reinhardt, K. (2017) Regular wounding in a natural system: Bacteria associated with reproductive organs of bedbugs and their quorum sensing abilities. *Frontiers in Immunology*, 8, 1855. doi: 10.3389/fimmu.2017.01855

Peterson, B. F., and Scharf, M. E. (2016) Metatranscriptome analysis reveals bacterial symbiont contributions to lower termite physiology and potential immune functions. *BMC Genomics*, 17, 772.

Seeley, T. D. (1982). Adaptive significance of the age polyethism schedule in honeybee colonies. *Behavioral Ecology and Sociobiology*, 11, 287–93.

Skinner, G. J., and Whittaker, J. B. (1981) An experimental investigation of inter-relationships between the wood-ant (*Formica rufa*) and some tree-canopy herbivores. *Journal of Applied Ecology*, 50, 313–26.

Tilman, D. (1978) Cherries, ants and tent caterpillars: Timing of nectar production in relation to susceptibility of caterpillars to ant predation. *Ecology*, 59, 686–92.

Trible, W., and Kronauer, D. J. C. (2017) Caste development and evolution in ants: It's all about size. *Journal of Experimental Biology*, 220, 53–62.

Trumbo, S. T., and Wilson, D. S. (1993). Brood discrimination, nest mate discrimination, and determinants of social behavior in facultatively quasisocial beetles (*Nicrophorus* spp.). *Behavioral Ecology*, 4, 332–9.

Watanabe, S., Murakami, T., Yoshimura, J., and Hasegawa, E. (2016) Color polymorphism in an aphid is maintained by attending ants. *Science Advances*, 2, e1600606.

Whitham, T. G. (1979). Territorial behaviour of *Pemphigus* gall aphids. *Nature*, 279, 324–5.

Whittaker, J. B., and Warrington, S. (1985) An experimental field study of different levels of insect herbivory induced by *Formica rufa*. *Journal of Applied Ecology*, 22, 797–811.

Chapter 5: Aquatic insects

Cheng, L. (1985) Biology of *Halobates* (Heteroptera: Gerridae). *Annual Review of Entomology*, 30, 111–35.

Fochetti, R., and Tierno de Figueroa, J. M. (2008) Global diversity of stoneflies (Plecoptera: Insecta) in freshwater. *Hydrobiologia*, 595, 365–77.

Ikawa, T., Okabe, H., and Cheng, L. (2012) Skaters of the seas: Comparative ecology of nearshore and pelagic *Halobates* species (Hemiptera: Gerridae), with special reference to Japanese species. *Marine Biology Research*, 8, 915–36.

Mackay, R. J., and Wiggins, G. B. (1979) Ecological diversity in Trichoptera. *Annual Review of Entomology*, 24, 185–208.

Chapter 6: Mimicry, crypsis, and blatant advertising

Bates, H. W. (1861) Contributions to an insect fauna of the Amazon valley. Lepidoptera: Heliconidae. *Transactions of the Linnean Society*, 23, 495–566.

Eacock, A., Rowland, H. M., and van't Hof, A. E., et al. (2019) Adaptive colour change and background choice behaviour in peppered moth caterpillars is mediated by extraocular photoreception. *Communication Biology*, 2, 286. https://doi.org/10.1038/s42003-019-0502-7

Jamie, G. A. (2017) Signals, cues and the nature of mimicry. *Proceedings of the Royal Society B*, 284, 20162080. http://dx.doi.org/10.1098/rspb.2016.2080

Vallin, A., Jakobsson, S., Lind, J., and Wiklund, C. (2006) Crypsis versus intimidation—anti-predation defence in three closely related butterflies. *Behavioural Ecology & Sociobiology*, 59, 455–9. https://doi.org/10.1007/s00265-005-0069-9

Chapter 7: Against the odds

Collier, R. H., and Finch, S. (1985) Accumulated temperatures for predicting the time of emergence in the spring of the cabbage root fly. *Bulletin of Entomological Research*, 75, 395–404.

Knight, J. D., Bale, J. S., Franks, F., Mathias, S. F., and Baust, J. G. (1986) Insect cold hardiness: Supercooling points and pre-freeze mortality. *Cryo Letters*, 7, 194–203.

Leather, S. R. (1984) Factors affecting pupal survival and eclosion in the pine beauty moth, *Panolis flammea* (D&S). *Oecologia*, 63, 75–9.

White, T. C. R. (1969) An index to measure weather-induced stress of trees associated with outbreaks of psyllids in Australia. *Ecology*, 50, 905–9.

Insects

Chapter 8: The good, the bad, and the ugly

Dafni, A. (1984) Mimicry and deception in pollination. *Annual Review of Ecology & Systematics*, 15, 259–78.

Grove, S. J. (2002) Saproxylic insect ecology and sustainable management of forests. *Annual Review of Ecology, Evolution & Systematics*, 33, 1–23.

Huberty, A. F., and Denno, R. F. (2004) Plant water stress and its consequences for herbivorous insects: A new synthesis. *Ecology*, 85, 1383–98.

Ollerton, J. (2017) Pollinator diversity: Distribution, ecological function and conservation. *Annual Review of Ecology, Evolution & Systematics*, 48, 353–76.

Root, R. B. (1973) Organization of a plant-arthropod association in simple and diverse habitats: The fauna of collards. *Ecological Monographs*, 43, 95–124.

Tahvanainen, J., and Root, R. B. (1972) The influence of vegetational diversity on the population ecology of a specialized herbivore *Phyllotreta cruciferae* (Coleoptera: Chrysomelidae). *Oecologia*, 10, 321–46.

Ullyett, G. C. (1947) Mortality factors in populations of *Plutella maculipennis* Curtis (Tineidae: Lep.) and their relation to the problem of control. *Union of South Africa, Department of Agriculture and Forestry Entomology Memoirs*, 2, 77–202.

Chapter 9: Ecological Armageddon—insects in decline?

Dirzo, R., Young, H. S., Galetti, M., Ceballos, G., Isaac, N. J. B., and Collen, B. (2014) Defaunation in the Anthropocene. *Science*, 345, 401–6.

Ewald, J., Wheatley, C. J., Aebsicher, N. J., Moreby, S. J., Duffield, S. J., Crick, H. Q. P., and Morecroft, M. B. (2015) Influences of extreme weather, climate and pesticide use on invertebrates in cereal fields over 42 years. *Global Change Biology*, 21, 3931–50.

Fox, R. (2013) The decline of moths in Great Britain: A review of possible causes. *Insect Conservation & Diversity*, 6, 5–19.

Hallmann, C. A., Sorg, M., Jongejans, E., Siepel, H., Hoflan, N., Schwan, H., Stenmans, W., Muller, A., Sumser, H., Horren, T., Goulson, D., and De Kroon, H. (2017) More than 75 percent decline over 27 years in total flying insect biomass in protected areas. *PLoSONE*, 12(10), e0185809.

Møller, A. P. (2019) Parallel declines in abundance of insects and insectivorous birds in Denmark over 22 years. *Ecology & Evolution*, 9, 6581–7.

Montgomery, G. A., Dunn, R. R., Fox, R., Jongejans, E., Leather, S. R., Saunders, M., Shortall, C. R., Tingley, M. W., and Wagner, D. L. (2020) Is the insect apocalypse upon us? How to find out. *Biological Conservation*.

Reemer, M., van Helsdingen, P. J., and Kleukers, R. M. J. C. (2003) Changes in ranges: Invertebrates on the move. *Proceedings of the 13th International Colloquium of the European Invertebrate Survey, Leiden, 2–5 September 2001*, European Invertebrate Survey, The Netherlands.

Sánchez-Bayo, F., and Wyckhuys, K. A. G. (2019) Worldwide decline of the entomofauna: A review of its drivers. *Biological Conservation*, 232, 8–27.

Shortall, C. R., Moore, A., Smith, E., Hall, M. J., Woiwod, I. P., and Harrington, R. (2009) Long-term changes in the abundance of flying insects. *Insect Conservation & Diversity*, 2, 251–60.

Wepprich, T., Adrion, J. R., Ries, L., Wiedmann, J., and Haddad, N. M. (2019) Butterfly abundance declines over 20 years of systematic monitoring in Ohio, USA. *PLoS ONE*, 14(7), e0216270.

Further reading

General

Chapman, R. F., Simpson, S., and Douglas, A. E. (2013) *The Insects: Structure and Function*, Fifth Edition, Cambridge University Press, Cambridge.

Gillott, C. (2005) *Entomology*, Springer, Dordrecht.

Gullan, P. J., and Cranston, P. S. (2014) *The Insects: An Outline of Entomology*, Fifth Edition, Wiley-Blackwell, Oxford.

Chapter 1: In the beginning

Footit, R. G., and Adler, P. H. (2017) *Insect Biodiversity: Science and Society*, Volume 1, Wiley-Blackwell, Oxford.

Grimaldi. D., and Engel, M. S. (2005) *Evolution of Insects*, Cambridge University Press, New York.

McAlister, A. (2017) *The Secret Life of Flies*, Natural History Museum, London.

Chapter 2: Prolific procreators

Leather, S. R. (1995) *Insect Reproduction*, CRC Press, Boca Raton, FL.

Chapter 3: On the move

Alexander, D. E. (2015) *On the Wing*, Oxford University Press, Oxford.

Bernays, E. A., and Chapman, R. F. (1994) *Host Plant Selection by Phytophagous Insects*, Chapman & Hall, New York.

Chapter 4: Living together

Wilson, E. O. (1975) *Sociobiology: The New Synthesis*, Harvard University Press, Cambridge, MA.

Chapter 5: Aquatic insects

Corbet, P. S., and Brooks, S. J. (2008) *Dragonflies*, Collins, London.
Del Claro, K., and Guillermo, R. (2019) *Aquatic Insects: Behavior and Ecology*, Springer, Dordrecht.

Chapter 6: Mimicry, crypsis, and blatant advertising

Clifton, J., and Wheeler, J. R. (2011) *Bird-dropping Tortrix Moths of the British Isles: A Field Guide to the Bird-dropping Mimics*.
Quicke, D. L. J (2016) *Mimicry, Crypsis, Masquerade and other Adaptive Resemblances*, Wiley-Blackwell, Oxford.

Chapter 7: Against the odds

Alcock, J. (1997) *In a Desert Garden: Love and Death Among the Insects*, W.W. Norton & Co, New York.
Leather, S. R., Bale, J. S., and Walters, K. F. A. (1993) *The Ecology of Insect Overwintering*, Cambridge University Press, Cambridge.

Chapter 8: The good, the bad, and the ugly

Abrol, D. P. (Ed.), (2013) *Integrated Pest Management: Current Concepts and Ecological Perspective*, Elsevier, Amsterdam.
Godfray, H. C. J. (1995) *Parasitoids: Behavioral and Evolutionary Ecology*, Princeton University Press, Princeton, NJ.
Heimpel, G. E., and Mills, N. J. (2017) *Biological Control: Ecology and Applications*, Cambridge University Press, Cambridge.
McAlister, E. (2016) *The Secret Life of Flies*, Natural History Museum, London.
Ulyshen, M. D. (Ed.) (2018) *Saproxylic Insects: Diversity, Ecology and Conservation*, Springer, Dordrecht.

Chapter 9: Ecological Armageddon—insects in decline?

New, T. R. (2016) *Alien Species and Insect Conservation*, Springer-Verlag, Dordrecht.

Samways, M. J. (2020) *Insect Conservation: A Global Synthesis*, CABI, Wallingford.

Index

For the benefit of digital users, indexed terms that span two pages (e.g., 52–53) may, on occasion, appear on only one of those pages.

Insects

Insects

Insects

Index

Insects

THE HISTORY OF LIFE
A Very Short Introduction
Michael J. Benton

There are few stories more remarkable than the evolution of life on earth. This *Very Short Introduction* presents a succinct guide to the key episodes in that story - from the very origins of life four million years ago to the extraordinary diversity of species around the globe today. Beginning with an explanation of the controversies surrounding the birth of life itself, each following chapter tells of a major breakthrough that made new forms of life possible: including sex and multicellularity, hard skeletons, and the move to land. Along the way, we witness the greatest mass extinction, the first forests, the rise of modern ecosystems, and, most recently, conscious humans.

www.oup.com/vsi

GAME THEORY
A Very Short Introduction
Ken Binmore

Games are played everywhere: from economics to evolutionary biology, and from social interactions to online auctions. Game theory is about how to play such games in a rational way, and how to maximize their outcomes. Game theory has seen spectacular successes in evolutionary biology and economics, and is beginning to revolutionize other disciplines from psychology to political science. This *Very Short Introduction* shows how game theory can be understood without mathematical equations, and reveals that everything from how to play poker optimally to the sex ratio among bees can be understood by anyone willing to think seriously about the problem.

www.oup.com/vsi